# THE RAGING GRANNIES

## Wild Hats, Cheeky Songs, and Witty Actions for a Better World

### Carole Roy

BLACK ROSE BOOKS

Montréal/New York/London

Black Rose Books No. HH327

National Library of Canada Cataloguing in Publication Data

Roy, Carole, 1954-

The Raging Grannies : wild hats, cheeky songs, and witty actions for a better world / Carole Roy.

Includes bibliographical references and index.

Hardcover ISBN: 1-55164-241-7 (bound)  Paperback ISBN: 1-55164-240-9 (pbk.)

1. Raging Grannies.  2. Aged women--Political activity.  3. Protest movements.  I. Title.

HQ1236.R59 2004      361.2'3'0846      C2003-905801-8

*Cover design: Associés libres.*

*Cover Photo: Victoria Raging Grannies in 1987. Hilda Marczak Collection.*

*Cover and Title Page Raging Granny Logo © Art Simons. By permission of Art Simons.*

Although every effort has been made to secure permission for materials reproduced herein, in some cases, we have been unable to locate a copyright holder. Page 228 constitutes an extension of this copyright page.

**BLACK ROSE BOOKS**

| | | |
|---|---|---|
| C.P. 1258 | 2250 Military Road | 99 Wallis Road |
| Succ. Place du Parc | Tonawanda, NY | London, E9 5LN |
| Montréal, H2X 4A7 | 14150 | England |
| Canada | USA | UK |

To order books:

In Canada: (phone) 1-800-565-9523 (fax) 1-800-221-9985
email: utpbooks@utpress.utoronto.ca

In United States: (phone) 1-800-283-3572  (fax)  1-651-917-6406

In the UK & Europe: (phone) London 44 (0)20 8986-4854 (fax) 44 (0)20 8533-5821
email: order@centralbooks.com

Our Web Site address: http://www.web.net/blackrosebooks

A publication of the Institute of Policy Alternatives of Montréal (IPAM)

Printed in Canada

The Canada Council | Le Conseil des Arts
for the Arts | du Canada

*dédié à mes parents*
*Yvette et Jacques*
*et à la mémoire de mes grands-mères*
*Blanche Lavertu et Alice Roy*
*qui valorisaient l'éducation, l'espoir, l'humour, et la force de caractère*
*chacune à sa façon*


*dedicated to my parents*
*Yvette and Jacques*
*and to the memory of my grandmothers*
*Blanche Lavertu and Alice Roy*
*who valued education, hope, humour, and strength*
*each in her own way*

# Contents

Among the most subversive and powerful activities women can engage in are activities of constructing women's visible and forceful traditions, of making real our positive existence, of celebrating our lives and of resisting disappearance in the process.    —Dale Spender (1982/1983: 696)

*Grandmother*

Out of her own body she pushed
silver thread, light, air
and carried it carefully on the dark, flying
where nothing moved.

Out of her body she extruded
shining wire, life, and wove the light
on the void.

From beyond time
beyond oak trees and bright clear water flow,
she was given the work of weaving the strands
of her body, her pain, her vision
Into creation, and the gift of having created,
to disappear.

After her,
the women and the men weave blankets into tales of life,
memories of light and ladders,
infinity-eyes, and rain.
After her I sit on my laddered rain-bearing rug
and mend the tear with string.                    —Paula Gunn Allen (1997: 69)


*You don't have anything*
*if you don't have the stories.*
*Their evil is mighty*
*but it can't stand up to our stories.*
*So they try to destroy our stories*
*let the stories be confused or forgotten.*
*They would like that*
*They would be happy*
*Because we would be defenceless then.*
                    —Leslie Marmon Silko (1977:2)


I don't want to trickle out.
I want to pour til the pail is empty, the last bit going out in a gush, not in drops.    —Emily Carr

# Acknowledgments

For the reader, this is the beginning. For the writer, this is the end of a process and a moment of gratitude for those who enriched my life in unique ways along this journey. I thank everyone who so generously gave permission for use of photographs, graphics, cartoons, and poems.

Many provided daily sustenance of friendship, support, stimulation, and reflection. I want to thank: My parents, Yvette and Jacques, for their love, generosity, integrity, and faithfulness. Estelle and Lise Roy for their generosity. My siblings, Gilles, Sylvie, Martine, and Dr. Réal Roy, their partners and families, for support, especially during illness.

Dyane Brown for her generous and sustaining friendship, an anchor in my life, and for her inspiring commitment to social justice. Kathy McGeean for her grace, generosity, and making me laugh through the small and great crisis of life. Eva and Jim Manly for purposeful and engaging conversations, and a sense of belonging. Marjorie and Al Stewart for their reliability, dedication, and the kindness they extended my way. Dr. Josephine Fong for her strength and warm friendship that helped me look beyond obstacles to my dreams. Sharry Aiken for her compassionate intelligence and capacity for solidarity. Moira Walker for so generously sharing her brilliance and her home. Kate Mortimer for her sincerity and hospitality. Doran Doyle for sharing her creativity, intuition, and wisdom. Anne Kinsella for her poetic being and empathy that broke isolation. Anne Cubitt for enlightening conversations. Uli Rasehorn, Jacynthe Alarie, Richard Charbonneau, Deirdre Gotto, Allan Gallupe, Andrea Clarke, Marie-Josée Gautrais, and Tina Walker for friendships that span many decades. Marcel Séguin, who would have loved to read this book. Tabish Surani for her unshakeable commitment to justice. Karin Brothers for so often providing warm hospitality, wonderful conversations, and an example of unflagging commitment. Linda Green for thoughtful and insightful support. Dr. Gerta Moray for offering home and friendship when I needed it. Roula Hawa for spirited exchanges and unconditional encouragement. Jean Fraser for kindness and wild stories. Caroline Doll and Barry Hall for soulful talks, escapades, and music. Betty Ann Flogen for daring to be herself. Darlene Clover for her on-going encouragement. Professor Kathryn Barnwell and Dr. Marni Stanley, for being examples of insightful intellectuals who do not abdicate their compassion and humanity. Professor Ian Johnston, a great teacher who paid attention to each student and encouraged all to strive for excellence. Dr. Deborah Barndt, for her example of solidarity and creative scholarship. Dr. Gary Knowles who knew years ago that this was a book. Dr. Jane Couchman for welcoming creativity and my interest in the Raging Grannies. Dr. Solveiga Miezitis for her intuition, generosity of spirit, respect for creativity, and making a significant difference to my life. Dr. Budd Hall for his daring, poetic, compassionate solidarity with the world, and openness of spirit towards others. Dr. Ardra Cole for her remarkable respect for process, wholeness, and authenticity. Linda Barton, the supportive editor, for her outstanding patience, kindness, and excellent suggestions. Dimitrios Roussopoulos, for sharing the desire to offer recognition to these wonderful activists and believing in this book.

Last, but not least, the Raging Grannies. To the Grannies I did not have the opportunity to meet yet, I salute your spirit and your inspiring example of creative and caring resistance. To the Grannies I had the privilege of meeting, it has been exciting and enlightening to meet each unique and remarkable woman. I want to acknowledge the gifts of each as well as the collective wisdom you provide to our society. Time spent with each of you had a passionate and vibrant quality. As you so gracefully sat through long interviews to share your thoughts, feelings, and experiences with me—often a stranger—I felt moved to tears and laughter. In the last two years I doubt if anyone has been closer to me: you literally lived in my mind! I shared your rage at greed, injustice, ecological destruction, and the unnecessary pain inflicted on so many, yet also found myself laughing at your incredible wit and humour. Your undaunted spirit inspires hope and daring. Writing this has been many things, but thanks to you, it has also been fun, a lot of fun!

*Carole Roy*
*April 2004*

# INTRODUCTION

As the crowd loudly cheered, "Go Grannies Go," a group of older women stepped into the British Columbia Legislature Building and onto the public scene: the briefs they wanted to present at the hearing on uranium mining were contained in a laundry basket, a clothesline of female underwear. This humorous action at the end of February 1987 marks the entry on the BC political scene of a unique grassroots phenomenon. The Raging Grannies have since become a Canadian institution of protest. They challenge stereotypes and authorities with disarming smiles, an arsenal of witty satirical songs, and a dynamic imagination for theatrical actions that put their concerns front and centre. The creation of a new cultural figure across a country as vast and diverse as Canada and the claiming of public space by older women in a society that accords little value to women or age, are among their achievements. Feminist theoreticians and historians Adrienne Rich, Gerda Lerner, Joan Scott, and Sheila Rowbotham, among others, have demonstrated the usefulness of 'woman' as an analytical category of investigation yet also warned us against the crippling effect of seeing women only as victims. Although feminists have started reclaiming women's accomplishments from the past, including collective resistance in different places and times, Dale Spender cautions us:

> While we are prepared to put much energy into reclaiming women from the distant past, our record is not so good when it comes to preserving our more recent heritage. In fact, we have sometimes been careless about the way we have discarded that very heritage.[1]

While there is a plethora of articles about the Raging Grannies, since their colourful, humorous and, at times, daring actions attract media attention, no comprehensive work, recording their vibrant activism, exists. This book is an attempt to preserve the recent heritage of this group of creative and daring protesters. The Raging Grannies and their creation of a new, resistant, and seemingly enduring popular figure for the purpose of political education deserve attention.

## Women's Courage, Invisibility, and Resistance

Women's courage is ancient: women fought against slavery and offered shelter to hunted runaways, demanded economic justice for the starving or working poor (McAllister 1991), raised their voices when rights were trampled, raised their fists when their children were murdered. Women's collective acts of resistance have played, and continue to play, a vital but often unacknowledged role in humanising social, political, and economic policies. To death, danger, and oppression, women have frequently responded in life-affirming ways, contributions concealed in invisibility and silence for too long. Invisibility and the absence of women as a force to be reckoned with are conditions necessary for the preservation of patriarchy (Spender). There is a subtly denigrating myth that women have done little worthy of inclusion in the historical record (Anderson and Zinsser). "Lying is done with words, and also with silence," wrote Adrienne Rich (1979); kings and popes populate history books but of women, little is said. "Not having a history truly matters," says Gerda Lerner: without stories of resistance and opposition we internalise patriarchy's ideology and pass its rules to the following generation.[2]

The semblance of superiority of patriarchal thought comes not from any superiority in content, form or achievement over all other thought but is "built on the systematic silencing of other voices."[3] Those silenced voices have been women's voices and in this silence the "unnatural nature of patriarchy and the challenges against it are lost as are the topics of a woman-centered history."[4] The silence extends to adult education as Shauna Butterwick points out:

> Marginalization and invisibility of women—their contributions and experiences as organisers, leaders, educators and learners/participants—has unfortunately been evident in the foundational literature of adult education.[5]

Other adult educators also suggest that women's contributions are overlooked or undervalued.

Yet, in the "dangerous nooks and crannies of women's lives" we find a creativity that seeks all possible crevices for its expression (Davis in Cameron 11). In spite of women's various experiences of oppression, feminism celebrates women's strengths and resistance strategies. In fact:

> Feminist scholarship has uncovered the repetitive quality of women's resistance down through the years. We are beginning to recognise that rejection of knowledge about the lives of the preceding generation of women is part of the problem.[6]

Focussing on stories of women's resistance and agency dispels notions of passivity and quiet acceptance. These stories are what Sharon Welch calls dangerous memories, powerful because made of suffering, defiance, and hope. Stories empower us, stimulate our imaginations, lift us out of isolation, and incite us to action (McAllister 1988). Reclaiming women's stories of courageous and creative protest offers recognition for their efforts, but also serves to inspire others with practical examples. This heritage of courage and creativity is a necessary inheritance in a world desperate for notions of political action that require both defiance of oppression and respect for life. Resistance is a blend of confrontation and caring, fiercely opposing oppression while intensely working for social and political justice. Sheila Rowbotham asserts that there is no beginning to women's defiance, that women resisted all along but their resistance took different shapes, which have been ignored in the historical record.

A contemporary face of this resistance is the activism of some older women who, sadly, have been invisible not only to society in general but until recently to feminists as well. Phyllis Cunningham reports bell hooks' challenge to feminism to "widen its analysis to explicate the diversity and complexity of the female experience" (1996: 143). A look at wise meddlesome Crones who make the world their business and confront abuse of power, greed, and thoughtlessness is part of that broadening project:

The Crone does not participate in the politics of reform…She is distinguished by her ability to dream dreams and conjure up visions for the survival of the Web, weaving into the fabric a lively wit that refuses to take seriously the small mind, loaded with the self-righteous hyperbole, or conversely, the professional academic drowning in self-analysis. Her instinct for survival is at gut level, she has solved the problems of want by wanting little, possessions have little value to the true Crone. She lives to live, to speculate and to risk, she will not be found in the nest of privileged security or at the table of greed or envy, she has pared her life down to the minimum. She will speak for peace but not expect it, speak for love, but not bet on it, speak for harmony among women knowing how far off is the reality, but she will speak, for she is a spinner of possibilities, a teller of truths too long avoided.[7]

### Hey, Look Us Over

Hey, look us over,
Grannies proud and strong
Time to hear our voices,
Time to hear our song
Silent for too long,
Speaking up at last
Cause now the earth
Is crying out,
…
Hear the Grannies voices sing!

*Tune: Hey, Look Them Over. Toronto Raging Grannies. Adapted by Edmonton Raging Grannies.*

## Raging Grannies: Canadian Crones in Action

A Canadian example of Crones is the Raging Grannies. Warren Magnusson, professor of political science at the University of Victoria, called the Raging Grannies a "brilliant example of a group acting out their protests" and using their credibility as grandmothers to "undercut the legitimacy of military violence, corporate greed, and governmental insensitivity" (1996: 93-94). Consistently using wit and humour, they created a new cultural figure that challenges various authorities as well as stereotypes of older women, and engages in the education of authorities and the public on various issues. The voice of wisdom wants to be heard. The Grannies' distinctive approach is surprisingly popular and effective: in sixteen years, more than fifty groups of Raging Grannies exist across Canada, in the United States, and as far away as Australia and Greece, where Greek Grannies appropriately call themselves the Furies. Their popularity reveals the desire of older women, and of the younger women who join them, to claim their space on the political scene, a noteworthy achievement given the invisibility elder women face in our society. While the Raging Granny figure does play on the idea of older women and while many Raging Grannies are elderly and deserve recognition for their example of enduring activism, some Raging Grannies are young women who find the Granny an attractive and powerful symbol to identify with.

This is an occasion to record the active participation and vibrant engagement of the Raging Grannies with the issues of their time. It is also an opportunity to strengthen the documentation of an existing knowledge creating process which, according to Budd Hall (2001), provides a context of continuity for women, for activists, and for adult educators; our transformative struggles deserve more attention. This, then, is an attempt to offer recognition to the Raging Grannies for the inspiration they provide and allow future generations to know that at a time when environmental destruction and war threatened, when the growing chasm between poor and rich endangered justice, these women stood up with wit, humour, daring, courageous irreverence, and songs to denounce government lies, corporate greed and short-sightedness, and sought to inspire hope, compassion, solidarity, and action. There are many threads in the tale of the Raging Grannies: their beginning and growth, the creation of their identity, the educational and daring potential of their activism, the values expressed in their actions and songs, and their impact on issues, stereotypes, media and people.

## A Note on the Making of this Book

I interviewed thirty-six women from twelve groups in five regions of Canada, namely Maritimes, Quebec, Ontario, Prairies, British Columbia. Ten women were interviewed twice. While most of the interviews were done with single individuals, I also interviewed eleven women in five small groups of two or three (their choice). Interviews with six original Grannies were done in 1998 while interviews with thirty others were done between August 2001 and November 2003. All but three (whose interviews were not tape-recorded) received the transcript of their interview and had the opportunity to make corrections. All Grannies interviewed will be introduced individually at some point in the following pages. It has been such a pleasure!

> The telling of, listening to, affirmation of, reflecting on, and analysis of personal stories and experiences 'from the ground up' are potentially empowering action research strategies drawn from women's organising.
> —Patricia Maguire

## Notes

1. Cited in Reinharz, *Feminist Methods in Social Research*, New York: Oxford University Press, 1992: 215.
2. Gerda Lerner, *Why History Matters: Life and Thought,* New York: Oxford University Press, 1997: 207, 208.
3. Gerda Lerner, *The Creation of Feminist Consciousness: From Middle-Ages to Eighteen-Seventy,* New York: Oxford University Press, 1993: 281.
4. Joyce Stalker, "Women and Adult Education: Rethinking Androcentric Research." *Adult Education Quarterly: A Journal of Research and Theory in Adult Education,* 46(2) 1996: 103, 104.
5. Shawna Butterwick, "Lest we forget: Uncovering women's leadership in adult education," in Sue M. Scott, Bruce Spencer and Allan M. Thomas, eds. *The Foundations of Adult Education in Canada: Second Edition* (103-116). Toronto: Thompson Educational Publishing, 1998: 104, 105.
6. Baba Copper, *Over the Hill: Reflections on Ageism Between Women,* Freedom, California: The Crossing Press, 1988: 55.
7. Gert Beadle, "The nature of Crones," in Marilyn J. Bell, ed. *Women as Elders: The Feminist Politics of Aging,* New York: Harrington Park Press, 1986: xiii.

# Chapter One

# FIRST GRANNY GAGGLE AND ITS LEGACY
## A Trail of Passionate Granny Power

 Gaggle of Grannies

We're just a gaggle of Grannies
Urging you off of your fannies
We're telling you boys
We're sick of your toys
…
We know that it's hard for you
merchants
But this is a matter of urgency
To stop the supply
Of bombs to the sky
…
It's outright collusion
It's no longer a jest
You're counting on confusion
But you know Granny knows best!
**NO MORE WAR!**

*Tune: Side By Side. Toronto Raging Grannies.*

## Victoria, 1987

Beginnings are hard to find and Doran Doyle, one of the original Raging Grannies, agreed: "Let's say there were many beginnings." The first action by a group called Raging Grannies took place on February 14, 1987 in Victoria, BC, when they presented an Un-Valentine to Pat Crofton, the local MP—Chairman of the Defence Committee at the time—for his lack of action and commitment on nuclear issues.

Initially, they dressed as old-fashioned, conservative proper little old ladies. As far as they were concerned, this was a one-time event and no one ever imagined that sixteen years later Raging Grannies would have mushroomed across the country and abroad, or would embrace the diversity of issues they now do. Already they demonstrated their ability to generate symbols to communicate their position on an issue, in this case a broken heart to suit the current celebration.

*Figure 1. Victoria Raging Grannies in 1987. Source: Hilda Marczak.*

*Figure 2. The Victoria Raging Grannies with the Un-Valentine. Source: Doran Doyle Collection.*

*Figure 3. Victoria Grannies under the nuclear umbrella. Source: Hilda Marczak Collection.*

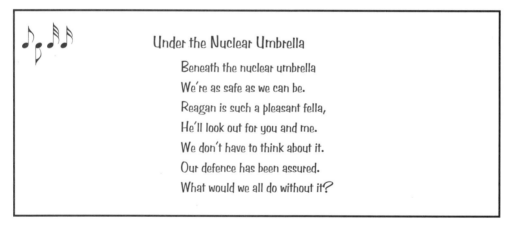

**Under the Nuclear Umbrella**

Beneath the nuclear umbrella
We're as safe as we can be.
Reagan is such a pleasant fella,
He'll look out for you and me.
We don't have to think about it.
Our defence has been assured.
What would we all do without it?

*Tune: What A Friend We Have In Jesus. Victoria Raging Grannies.*

A second action two weeks later, that of presenting "briefs" to the hearing on uranium mining, was another beginning, a public debut that allowed them to sense the potential of their new "Granny" persona. To their surprise, they were a roaring success with the crowd at the anti-uranium demonstration at the BC Parliament Building. Betty Brightwell, also a Raging Granny, wrote of the crowd's response as galvanising. Their enduring presence and expansion are beyond their wildest imagination. Like the Greenham Common women who received encouragement from all over Great Britain, the Raging Grannies were also born of a favourable public response.

*Figure 4. To the hearings on uranium mining at the BC Legislature,
the Grannies brought a laundry basket of "briefs." Source: Doran Doyle Collection.*

## Beginnings: The Nuclear Threat

Joseph F. Zygmunt suggests that "social movements originate within concrete historical contexts" (1774: 45).[1] In the 1980s, the peace movement and feminism were part of that historical context. On the local level, the visits of U.S. warships and submarines, containing nuclear weapons and/or powered by nuclear reactors, at the Canadian military base in Esquimalt, a municipality of Greater Victoria, were concrete threats to environment and health. This threat was a focus of action for the local peace group. Betty Brightwell, wife of a retired military officer and a future Raging Granny, was shocked to see a submarine out of her window and to realise they may be containing nuclear weapons: she had been under the impression that there were no such weapons in Canada. The contrasting beauty of Victoria and its prevailing appearance of serenity made the realisation even more surprising and led to Betty's involvement with the nuclear disarmament group and the Raging Grannies. But that was not the end of her surprise: as she began to research the more technical aspects, she looked for emergency programs for the civilian population in case of a nuclear accident at the base:

> It's outrageous!…I phoned around the city to the various emergency programs (municipal, provincial and federal) and found that not one of them had been informed of the nuclear submarine visit [USS Gurnard, SSN 662, a Sturgeon class nuclear powered attack submarine in early February 1989]. But more outrageous still is the fact that although the Department of National Defence has an on-base nuclear emergency response, there is no civilian counterpart should there be an accident to a visiting nuclear armed and nuclear powered submarine. This is unacceptable and I think it is about time all levels of government addressed the problem and that we civilians had explained to us what we should do if there were a nuclear accident in Esquimalt.[2]

The Grannies' fears were not unfounded: James Bush, a retired U.S. Navy nuclear submarine Captain, spoke out in Ketchikan, Alaska, and gave weight to their fears about the dangers of these ships. In a speech he made at the protest in which the Grannies took part, he advised people to ask authorities for emergency plans in case of accidents, and told them that the U.S. Navy had a policy of dumping possibly radioactive waste in the open sea. He warned that even though an accident is unlikely, it still can happen.[3]

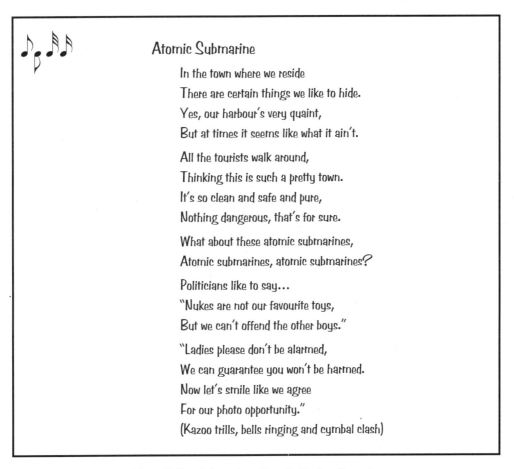

**Atomic Submarine**

In the town where we reside
There are certain things we like to hide.
Yes, our harbour's very quaint,
But at times it seems like what it ain't.

All the tourists walk around,
Thinking this is such a pretty town.
It's so clean and safe and pure,
Nothing dangerous, that's for sure.

What about these atomic submarines,
Atomic submarines, atomic submarines?

Politicians like to say...
"Nukes are not our favourite toys,
But we can't offend the other boys."

"Ladies please don't be alarmed,
We can guarantee you won't be harmed.
Now let's smile like we agree
For our photo opportunity."
(Kazoo trills, bells ringing and cymbal clash)

*Tune: Yellow Submarine. Victoria Raging Grannies.*

The future Grannies were working as volunteers at the peace office and knew where they stood politically so they "didn't have to be converted to anything," as Mary Rose put it. Many were members of Extenuating Circumstances, a subgroup of the peace group which held silent vigils at the base when U.S. nuclear-powered and/or nuclear weapons-capable—and nuclear-leaks-capable!—ships or submarines were visiting. Doran Doyle suggests these protests were also inspired by Latin American women's protests in their use of symbols of "women's work" and banged spoons on empty pots to alert the population on Thanksgiving, or brought brooms and brushes to clean up the base on International Women's Day. Hilda Marczak, Doran Doyle, and Joyce Stewart decided to take to the streets to reach the unconverted. Dressed as E.T.s (Extra Terrestrials) they leafleted and sang to movie line-ups, perfect captive audiences. It quickly expanded as others joined them.

## Taking to the Streets to Escape Sexism and Ageism

Aside from the sense of threat, sexism and ageism in the local peace group provided the motivation to look for alternative avenues of protest. "We found we were becoming the fetchers and gatherers and we said 'No more of that!' "[4] said Betty Brightwell. Doran Doyle echoes this:

> Guys in the peace movement, they wanted us still to be bringing the coffee saying, 'Oh! That's a great idea,' and not hearing us when we came up with things, but treated us as a bunch of older women…because it's the younger, more glamorous ones who would be heard more and that sort of thing. It's all those different perceptions coming through that helped us to form as a group…O.K., they are not listening to us so we'll try it this way.

Their experience of sexism in the peace movement was not unique: Shelley Romalis (1987) wrote that the Greenham Common women left the largest British peace organisation, Campaign for Nuclear Disarmament, because it was male dominated and hierarchical. The American group Women Strike for Peace (WSP) who protested against nuclear weapons and war, portrayed themselves as housewives and mothers, and stood up to the House Un-American Activities Committee with wit and humour—the last group to appear in front of the notorious committee that made everyone, except WSP, tremble—also were disillusioned by conventional organisations:

> Tired of the 'democratic centralism' of the old Left and the top-down leadership of liberal peace groups, in which women's ideas, values, and feelings had been ignored, WSP insisted on collective leadership and local autonomy…Long meetings and long speeches were frowned upon; creativity, laughter, and playfulness were prized. This movement format, it has been argued, is most consistent with the feminist concepts of freedom and interdependence based on self-realization and support for others.[5]

Some Grannies had positive experiences with groups of women or with the concept and power of women-only actions. Lois Marcoux had warm memories of living with five girls as they moved off their farms to a nearby town in order to finish high school, an experience that expanded her world. Joyce Stewart, a WW2 veteran, credits the loss of her shyness to living in barracks with women who "discussed a lot of things." Hilda Marczak refers to the sisterhood feeling amongst women friends, which made the life of a housewife with young children more meaningful. When she and a friend felt "a bit put upon about the work we had to do [and] no one to share it with," they decided to become teachers so they would have rights too and not be only wives. Doran Doyle was at Greenham Common in 1983 and 1986, which was "a powerful encounter with the unstoppable force and inspiration of these women." In 1987, there was among them a growing awareness of women's oppression. Maybe what is true in Ethiopia is also true in British Columbia: "The most important evidence of articulate resentment, if not of active resistance, comes from songs, many of which show clearly that the people [are] well aware of their oppression."[6] The Grannies wrote a song about their changing views of women's roles.

*Figure 5. A simple graphic of the spirit of the Raging Grannies. Source: Lanie Melamed Collection.*

## The Bad Old Days

Refrain: We're the women who did the work, So men could get the credit

We said "Leave it all to us," And wished we'd never said it.

No, I don't mind staying late, I'll type another stencil
Can I bring your coffee now? Let me sharpen your pencil

I'm sorry that the baby cried, I'm sorry that she wet you
I'm sorry she threw up on you, I'm sorry she upset you.

Politics was not for us, We left that to our spouses
But now we know a woman's place, In Parliamentary Houses.

...

We're prepared to do the work, But we want more than credit
Equal pay for equal work, We'll sing until we get it.

*Tune: I'se the B'y. Victoria Raging Grannies.*

Finding the same patterns at home, at the office, and in the peace movement got them searching for other avenues of expression as they had explored the path of service to men enough for a lifetime. They recognise aging as a gendered experience:

## Oh Dear!

We've been attacked by the forces of gravity,
Fat has appeared where we once had concavity,
Nobody said life was fair.

Older men become more adorable,
Even though their figure's deplorable,
Their physique is always insurable,
With or without their grey hair.

Older women are thought unattractive,
They're shunned as if they were radioactive,

...

Well, these grey mares, We ain't what we used to be,
We've given up on respectability,
Don't give a fig for acceptability,
We're far too busy to care.

*Tune: Oh Dear What Can the Matter Be? Raging Grannies "Carry On" Songbook.*

Rheta Stephenson, a Regina Granny, feels that there is an inequality as women age. While older men escape the plight of negative stereotypes that older women face, they do not escape the lucid eye of the Grannies. By willingly exposing their vulnerability, the Grannies disarm the stereotype. They humorously suggest their search for "Grumbling Grandpas" or "Raging Granddads." Trying to imagine Raging Grandpas reveals the gender component to the Raging Grannies: rage does not suit men as they are identified with more direct expressions of anger. The Grannies focussed on street theatre in their search for effective alternatives to convey their message and educate the public on the presence of nuclear ships in the harbour. They created a group called NERT—Nuclear Emergency Response Team. As Mary Rose recalls:

> We were all just so fed up with going to meetings and lectures, not necessarily fed up because there were lots of really interesting people, that was great, but just that it didn't do anything publicly. It wasn't getting the message out to new people. So this seemed to be a relief to us in that we could release some of our depression and various feelings about…the nuclear expansion that we were worried about.

Dressed in lab coats and carrying makeshift Geiger counters, they tested puddles for radioactivity or dusted statues and explained to curious bystanders that nuclear submarines were coming to these waters and that they were insuring there was no radiation in the water. According to Fran Thoburn,

> Betty Brightwell didn't like dressing up [as NERT], she's pretty proper…so she would…pass out these pamphlets…that we made up. I did a lot of research and got actual quotes from the Department of National Defence about the danger of nuclear stuff. So everything on that was a direct quote produced by our government. It could not be argued with, people got very angry when they'd read it.

This was invisible street theatre for educational purposes. But in the spring of 1986, Chernobyl happened. Seeing people on TV doing the same gestures they had done, "running Geiger counters over posts, buildings," they decided to do something else. Chernobyl, says Doran Doyle,

> …brought a halt to fun and play in the common byways [and] the streets of Victoria and Esquimalt. And we went into despair almost at that stage. We had a big public meeting, 'When can we eat our broccoli?'

In June 1986, Doran Doyle, Hilda Marczak, Lois Marcoux, Moira Walker (myself) and a few others walked from Victoria to Nanoose Bay to raise awareness about the visit of U.S. nuclear warships and submarines at the Nanoose Bay military base. At that time, Moira wrote:

### 5-Day Peace Walk from Victoria to Nanoose

Money was pressed into our hands by passing motorists and by people who noticed us in restaurants. People waved from their front gardens, calling out that they had heard on the news of our coming. At a day care centre where we were implored to stop, we were served mugs of hot tea and entertained by children. Horses and cows abandoned their grazing to stare in silence as we passed. Motorists honked and truck drivers leaned from their cabs to wave to us. A municipal public servant in Ladysmith asked if he could find us billets and a pregnant woman, her baby due in two weeks, joined us for an hour, expressing sorrow at having to part from us so soon. A group of sisters in Duncan gave us sachets of salt and named us the 'peace pilgrims.' We carried a banner from Victoria to Nanoose on which the words, 'Walking for Our Lives,' were stitched. Our five-day trek was intended, in part, to be a re-dedication to, and re-affirmation of life. In addition, we hoped to encourage the hundreds of motorists who saw us to join us in the struggle to preserve our planet and all who live on it. In the words of the Greenham Common song, 'They can forbid nearly everything but they can't forbid us to think.'

Later that year when the Trident Submarine USS Alaska passed by Victoria on its way to the Trident base at Bangor, Washington, members of the local peace group and the University of Victoria Stop the Warships Club spooked the passing Trident submarine, a ritual used in the Middle Ages to dispel the Plague but in this case it was meant to be a "raising of the spirits of horror at the evil presence in our waters," explained Doran Doyle. They had the co-operation of the fire brigade because they used Bar-B-Q pits to make flames and they played funeral march music since it was around Halloween. The Grannies often "bounce off" festivals to select symbols for their actions. Betty Brightwell remembers another protest:

> Doran was terribly creative, I mean beyond creativity; some of the things she did were wild! (laughs) And sometimes very difficult to ferret out the meaning of it, why she was doing these things. What were we objecting to? I think there was a ship in and for some reason we went out to UVIC [University of Victoria] in the absolutely pouring rain and we spent a week tying pantyhose together. I have video pictures: in the pouring rain, and here we were with great lengths of pantyhose. Now, the connection between that and the protest about nuclear submarines was lost on a lot of people driving by. We knew what we were doing, Doran knew what she was doing, but! (laughs) So I mean that was funny. I went home [wondering], what am I doing this for? Soaking wet.

Doran Doyle recalls the same story:

> We measured out the length of the Trident [submarine] in pantyhose tied together between the lampposts at Bess' house. We measured out all these lengths of three football fields long. That was wonderful doing that.

Doran also recalls a workshop with David Diamond, who studied with Augusto Boal, the Brazilian creator of Theatre of the Oppressed, as a catalyst for would-be Grannies. Moira Walker wrote:

> As a participant, I was struck by the number of women present who were older than my mother. But they were struggling to learn a new art in order to better save a home, the planet, to which in the course of their long years they had become attached. The weekend was a great deal of fun and we hoped to be able soon to put into practice our newly learned skills.

That workshop was another thing that gave them confidence. A few months later, the Raging Grannies came to life with the Un-Valentine action. The first group had eleven women: Betty Brightwell, Doran Doyle, Jane Mackey, Lois Marcoux, Hilda Marczak, Bess Ready, Mary Rose, Linda Siegel, Joyce Stewart, Fran Thoburn, and Moira Walker. White, well educated, and mostly middle-class, they were like many in the peace movement. Jane and Moira were only part of a few actions but Jane, a brilliant songwriter, kept writing songs for the Grannies for sometime after her departure. Teachers, a librarian, homemakers, an anthropologist, counsellors, artists, and businesswomen made up the group.

*Moira Walker was part of the original Victoria Raging Grannies. She was seeking answers, but rage was not it. She describes her childhood as being "visited by a great deal of violence," a violence she was seeking to explain and counteract. The Raging Grannies was part of that search. She found friends in the Raging Grannies, and for someone who needed reassurance about human kindness, friends were essential. Not a trained singer, she found no pleasure or beauty in off-key singing. Not comfortable with her body, it made it difficult to use it as a vehicle for expression.*

*A member of Voice of Women in Victoria at the time, she went to their International Peace School in the USSR in May 1986. Working with the Greater Victoria Peace Group she found some explanations that connected personal and systemic violence. She also discovered that the counteracting agent of violence is beauty.*

*On a quest to rescue herself from the prior violence in her life, she found beauty in literature that brought together a presentation of the violence, and at the same time, a movement out of it, especially in the writings of African-American women. Her performance now takes place in college classrooms as she has chosen to teach literature that looks at ways out of violence toward beauty.*

*Figure 6. Moira Walker.*
*Source: Doran Doyle Collection.*

*Bess Ready grew up on a farm in Manitoba. She remembers her parents as very nice and her father as a hard-working man. She tells of daily afternoon tea with her mother and many visitors. She trained as a nurse and found much joy in her work. One of the most exciting and rewarding challenges was to work in northern Manitoba assisting women during childbirth. She then joined the army and was sent to Italy during the war. She has had quite enough of war.*

*She refused to learn typing so she would not have to do it for men; given that her future husband was a writer, it turned out to be a prophetic insight, otherwise she might have been enlisted as his typist! Bess had a sense of adventure and daring about her. After her six children were born, she became an artist. She believes everyone needs to have at least two lives—one to make a living and one for joy.*

*She became a painter and felt that painting was not just part of her life but was her life. She taught art for a while. From early on, she loved performing and making props for the Raging Grannies. Bess is very hospitable and likes company. Her house was always a beehive of activity and for years she had an art group meeting there. The Raging Grannies were also born at her house where they continued meeting and making their props for quite a while.*

*Figure 7. Bess Ready.*
*Source: Doran Doyle Collection.*

All, except Moira, had children, and most had grandchildren. They ranged in age from 46 to 67, but Moira and Jane were in their thirties. Two were World War II veterans, one the wife of a retired military officer, and another married to a refugee from Nazi Germany who joined the Canadian army and is a veteran of WWII. Half the group were either immigrant/refugee themselves or had immigrant/refugee parents. Strong willed, they held diverse political views: most disagreed with peace-through-strength and one maintained the importance of the armed forces. But all agreed on the need to protest nuclear arms and have fun in the process.

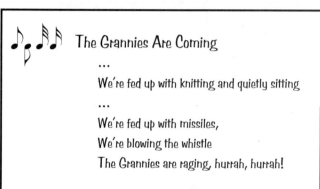

♪ ♪ ♪♪  The Grannies Are Coming

...

We're fed up with knitting and quietly sitting

...

We're fed up with missiles,
We're blowing the whistle
The Grannies are raging, hurrah, hurrah!

*Tune: The Campbells Are Coming. McLaren & Brown.*

*Figure 8. Not Amused: Victoria Raging Grannies.*
*Source: Doran Doyle Collection.*

## A Catchy Name

The Raging Grannies originated in Victoria, a place of good taste and decorum and the retirement capital of Canada where seniors represent a large proportion of the population. To associate *Grannies*, often representing loving care, with *Raging* offers a challenging image to a stereotype that would have older women as sweet and inoffensive. The name embodies a characteristic of the Raging Grannies, namely their ability to use paradoxes and ambiguities, a skill honed to superb mastery. The idea of rage in people perceived to be polite and loving is jarring and the unusual juxtaposition attracts attention. For Doran, there is a cultural component to raging:

> To be raging in New Zealand or France or Britain is not so appropriate because people are more comfortable with expressing in a forthright way their feelings. Whereas in Canada, I love the experience of how tolerant and how gentle people are, but then, there are times when you think why don't they…get more aggressive.

"There is a certain amount of controversy about who invented the name, but that's neither here or there, it did happen," said Betty Brightwell. Mary Rose says that "it wasn't my idea, that's for sure, because there's a great argument about who started it." One unlikely version of how the name came about was reported in an article:

"Most of us were grandmotherly types, but one of us said, 'I refuse to be a knitting, pie baking Granny…let's be angry Grannies.' That's where the Raging Grannies idea came from."[7] Doran Doyle acknowledged the controversy surrounding the name, but her feelings about it are quite different:

> Raging Grannies clicked in my head. I think I was in the car…I had been thinking a lot about rage, and Granny Boo [her grandmother] was always there. And we brought it to the little meeting we had at Bess' because we were trying to follow up from the David Diamond [Theatre of the Oppressed] workshop, and we knew that the drama was working, theatre in the streets and stuff. So it took a little bit of persuading in the group.

The granny part came from Doran's Granny Boo, a loving, strong, popular woman who took the unusual step of coming to live with her daughter-in-law to help care for Doran and her sister after the parents divorced; she provided a positive presence in Doran's life. Joyce Stewart remembers being in the car with Doran when the name came up as they discussed the need to do things differently and "the need to show our outrage" at nuclear ships. Moira Walker recalls Doran persuading others because *raging* generated hesitations: there is a stigma attached to women's anger. Fran Thoburn's memory is similar but slightly different:

> We just evolved from a peace group into a group. We were doing street theatre and we looked around our meeting and realised we were all women and Doran suggested that we change our image; then she suggested we all became Grannies because most of us were old and there was some balking at that. I can remember thinking, 'Granny? Who wants to be a granny?' I said, 'well, we're not gonna be Grannies that sit and knit and cook cookies.' And she said, 'raging!' I said, 'it has to be more than that…has to be something with real anger to it,' and Doran said, 'Raging Grannies!' And wow, we were gone. She was reading Mary Daly at the time. I'd read it too…and so it really clicked.

Doran made a collage with these words from Mary Daly, words that inspired her:

> Rage is not 'a stage.' It is not something to be gotten over. It is transformative, focusing Force. Like a horse who streaks across fields on a moonlit night, her mane flying, Rage gallops on pounding hooves of unleashed passion. The sounds of its pounding awaken transcendent E-motion. As the ocean…rhythms into every creature, giving sensations of our common sources/courses, Rage too, makes sense come alive again, thrive again, thrive again. Women require the contest of Be-Friending both to sustain the positive forces of moral Outrage and to continue the Fury-fuelled task of inventing new ways of living. Without the encouragement of Be-Friending, anger can deteriorate into rancour and can mis-fire, injuring the wrong targets. One function of the work of Be-Friending, then, is to keep the sense of outrage focused in a biophilic way.[8]

For Doran, the fact that there was recognition for songwriters but not for the authorship of the name was hurtful as she feels women have been denied so much authorship. This shows one challenge of history and how multifaceted the 'truth' of events can be. This issue of origins arose because the press wanted to know how the name came to be. Had they not been successful, there would have been no issue: success has its price, especially for women. It is significant that this conflict happened around naming, something so essential to feminism.

*Doran Doyle grew up in New Zealand and came to Victoria in 1968. Her father, an amateur actor and a Quaker, wrote* World Without War. *Her mother, a gifted and intelligent woman, faced tremendous challenges as a Danish immigrant and single parent working full time. A saving presence was Granny Boo, her paternal grandmother.*

*A thread of spontaneous and playful theatricality runs through Doran's life. Creative, she was something of a clown, doing fun things in public and putting on plays at school. Activism is another thread: at nineteen she delivered a petition against nuclear testing in the South Pacific to the Prime Minister of New Zealand but felt ill-prepared for his cynicism and glibness. She then searched for new ways to reach out for change.*

*She raised four children. Trained as a teacher, she worked with Native children and with people with disabilities or psychiatric problems. She founded a community association, started a teen activity centre and a job bank, a community soup kitchen, and helped seniors find housing. She was chair of the Catholic Social Justice Commission in her diocese. Every week for ten years she joined an ecumenical peace vigil. Her personal life also provided fuel for change: "There is a long period where I just exploded inside because of my personal life, and learning about this world, this beastly world, militarism…It all came together while reading Mary Daly about rage. I had already discovered for myself that anger was very releasing." An artist, she is now also a farmer and lives on Vancouver Island. Although not a member of a Raging Grannies' group anymore, she remains concerned and active on environmental, peace, and women's issues. She has done civil disobedience and been arrested numerous times.*

*Figure 9. Wearing a skeleton robe and banging on a garbage can lid, Doran joins Cache Creek residents in protest against the shipping of garbage to their region.*
*Source: Photo John Colville.*
*Published in The Province, March 10, 1989.*

Hilda and Moira suggest Margaret Laurence also provided inspiration: "As we grow older we should become not less radical but more so." Hilda still has Laurence's "Old Women's Song." It is interesting how feminist writers and the written word had such an influence on the definition of the character of the Raging Granny and helped crystallise experience into concepts.

> I see old women dancing, dancing on the earth
> I hear old women singing, singing children's birth
> great is their caring
> strong is their measure
> dancing and singing
> life's frail treasure…
>
> …
>
> I am one among them, dancing on the earth,
> mourning, grieving, raging,
> yet jubilating birth.[9]

## Raging Grannies Not Born, Made: Spinning Threads Out of Memories

Aside from the local nuclear threat and the experience of sexism and ageism in the peace movement, the individuals' personal histories also played a role in becoming Raging Grannies. When asked about the origins of their participation they offered a variety of interpretations. Lois Marcoux credits her involvement to a personal friendship with Doran Doyle, a co-worker on the Catholic Social Justice Commission. Friendship also led Joyce Stewart to new activities.

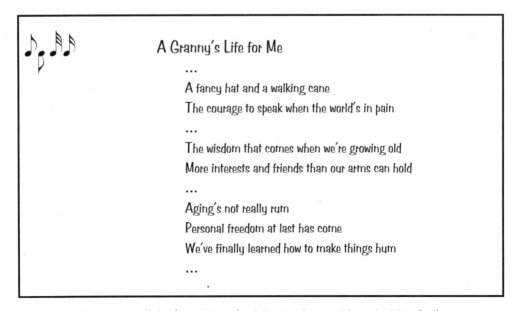

**A Granny's Life for Me**

…

A fancy hat and a walking cane
The courage to speak when the world's in pain

…

The wisdom that comes when we're growing old
More interests and friends than our arms can hold

…

Aging's not really rum
Personal freedom at last has come
We've finally learned how to make things hum

…

*Tune: Fox and Cat from "Pinocchio." Raging Granny "Carry On" Songbook.*

*Joyce Stewart was part of the first group of Victoria Raging Grannies. Her parents were immigrants from Europe and she recalls her father, a teacher, being very positive about Canada's ethnic diversity. He conveyed the message that people from other cultures were worth knowing. He was involved with the Co-operative Commonwealth Federation (CCF) and when Japanese people were imprisoned he, along with a few others, opposed it and unsuccessfully tried to convince the government they were making a mistake.*

*She is a WWII veteran: she was in the RCAF for two years but worked in a control tower and never went overseas. While living in Calgary, she was active and involved in helping new immigrants settle and she received the Queen's Medal for her work. She then worked with Native people and was inspired to go back to university to get a BA in Anthropology once her three children were grown up. After moving to Victoria, she got involved with the peace group. In January 1986, she joined the Central America Peace March in San Cristobal Las Casas in Mexico. Until recently, she volunteered at the Victoria Global Village store. Joyce is compassionate and capable of healthy indignation at injustices.*

*Figure 10. Joyce Stewart.*
*Source: Doran Doyle Collection.*

For Hilda Marczak "becoming a Raging Granny was inevitable." When asked how it happened, she goes far back:

> I'll go back a little bit because I really think that the Raging Grannies evolved...because of the experiences or interests that we, later on Raging Grannies, had had. In my case, the reason that I was very socially conscious goes right back to my very earliest days.

Hilda coherently and chronologically traced the history of her activism from childhood. Like an informant of the oral historian Alessandro Portelli whose long life was all meaningful to him so he could not identify one single event as a starting point, chronology proved the easiest organising factor for Hilda. Born in 1920 in Russia, she was one year old when her parents came as refugees to Montreal, where she grew up during the depression:

> My very earliest experience that I remember being really impacted by was when some of our neighbours were put in the streets because they couldn't pay their rent. Sometimes there were babies involved...with whatever is called furniture, which were a few sticks. I remember crying as a very young child because I couldn't understand why they would do that.

She wants to leave a legacy of hope and wrote the following poem:

> *A Raging Granny Says*
>
> No thanks to environmental destruction,
>> injustice, fear,
>> nuclear madness,
>> war!
> Not for me denial,
>> despair,
>> numbness,
>> "I don't care."
>> ...but what can I do?
> Dare to be aware—
>> cry out—
>> act, write, sing—
>> do something!
> Care enough to challenge myths
> that deny ecological pillage
>> justify injustice
>> commend complacency
>> glorify war.
> Care enough to dream of what could be:
>> accept the challenge—
>> change the course—
>> leave a legacy of
>> hope for change and survival
> We can do it alone and together.

*Hilda Marczak's social consciousness was raised early by her parents' visible compassion for others less fortunate. Her first action was one of defiance and solidarity. In grade eight she and a handful of students joined a picket line to support striking poor students at another high school in the inner city who were protesting having to pay for text books they could not afford.*

*She later became a Rosie-the-Riveter, joined a union for the first time, experienced shift work, strikes, and volunteered at a drop-in centre for refugees and immigrants during weekends. She married a refugee from Nazi Germany, the sole survivor of his family, and they had three children. She sent her children's baby teeth for a study on the effects of radiation. She later trained as a teacher and enjoyed working with children. She became quite active in the teachers' union because she felt it was the right thing to do and experienced strikes.*

*She got 10,000 names on a petition to support nuclear disarmament and the World Peace March in New York on June 12, 1982. She made a video on what kids were thinking about the nuclear situation, and leafleted for the local disarmament group. Travelling to Mexico and Guatemala in the 1980s, she saw links between poverty and militarisation.*

*Figure 11. Hilda Marczak.*
*Source. Hilda Marczak Collection.*

Like Hilda, those interviewed have rich lives of struggles and commitment, pain and joy, care and solidarity. Interestingly, the thread of immigrant experience goes beyond the first group. Many of the thirty-six women interviewed were immigrants to Canada or children of immigrants, seven having come from the U.S. in opposition to the Vietnam War. Eleven say they grew up in difficult situations, in families of divorced parents at a time when it was shunned, or with an alcoholic, violent, or troubled parent. One lost her mother very young and another had a difficult pioneer family life in a remote region. When experiences of immigration and difficult early years are included, twenty women have experienced feeling "other," or dealing with difficulties early on. It is tempting to suggest that their early experiences of being different or dealing with troubled parents may have contributed to their sensitivity to injustice and compassion for victims, as well as given them the strength to stand up and dissent. In an article published in *The Globe and Mail*, Rose DeShaw describes some of her childhood:

The other students spotted the gap between their suburban lives and my mining-camp background before I did. Not just bad haircut, wrong shoes, worse clothes, no table manners, different vocabularies and old army rations instead of homemade cookies in the mail. We didn't seem to meet on any points at all…I wore black and they wore a lot of pink and talked about things from radio and television; my only reference points came from the sanitised classics and the Bible. Maybe loneliness and geekiness don't seem a lot to be suicidal over, even throwing in my belief that it would be like this forever. But it mattered then. Returning home certainly wasn't in the cards. I didn't think I'd manage to escape it twice. And so with no place to run, I decided that ridding the world of me was a worthy goal. God didn't enter into it, despite the fact that my studies were theological. The deity was kept strictly between Genesis and Revelation and not invited to meddle with any part of my daily life.[10]

Rescued from her suicidal project by a student, she adds that he was "nobody official, just a noticer…And I could see he was serious, that it mattered to him." So Rose makes a point to notice:

I'm always looking for over-burdened mothers so I can say, 'You're doing a great job with those children' because you can just see that need, that isolation…I just want them to feel 'You've got support.' So as much as possible with the Grannies I try to be out in public. When the weather is good we meet down at city hall on the steps…And people come up and talk, because they need to. So many people are so lonely and so hurt. It doesn't mean you're not lonely and hurt, but it's just that there is that one-on-one opportunity. We sat down in the sunshine and were available to people to come and talk because we wanted them to talk and they can sense that, especially young mothers. They come by with the babies and they want to talk and I want to hear them, you know.[11]

From the pain of living she has since learned that:

Keeping on makes it tolerable. That some day joy will seep through the cracks in the wall you've built around yourself, the joy of lover, children, cats, dogs, sunsets, memories, and that supreme joy when you suddenly find you were designed for some purpose in this world and that the design is not a faulty one. Knowing what I was made for was like discovering myself a hinge on a heavy door, capable of swinging it open to more surprises than I ever knew existed, certainly enough to keep the pain at bay for a long time. Not that I can forget the face of the pain, but now I have some ammunition.[12]

*A professional with a Masters in counselling, Linda Siegel grew up in a middle class Jewish family in a working class milieu in Rhode Island, U.S., and moved to Toronto in 1975 after working for two years as a counsellor at the American University in Iran. In Toronto she loved working in an adult high school where students were mostly immigrants. In 1986, she moved to Victoria. Her social conscience developed early. Interestingly, Rhode Island, with apparently the highest number of Catholics per capita in the U.S., is where the campaign to impeach Nixon started. Married to a working class Irish-American man she learned about class struc-ture and witnessed the racist treatment of African-Americans. She has always identified with the underdog and sees herself as the outsider everywhere, which makes her a critical thinker.*

*She has a long history of activism. Present at the first meeting of the U.S. National Organisation of Women in Providence, Rhode Island, she was shocked when she could not use the appellation of Ms. on her cheque when she came to Canada. She took part in U.S. civil rights marches and actions, like pretending to look for an apartment after blacks had tried to rent it to reveal the racism at play. A member of Voice of Women at some point, she was also a member of the Victoria Everywoman's Books, a feminist collective.*

*Figure 12. Linda Siegel.*
*Source: Doran Doyle Collection.*

*A speech by Helen Caldecott and the movie "If You Love This Planet" inspired her to join the Greater Victoria Disar-mament Group (GVDG). Upset at the presence of nuclear ships, she was part of the original group of Raging Grannies in her search for ways to attract people's attention to the dangerous situation. No longer a member of the Raging Grannies, she is still active with the Council of Canadians and the Greater Victoria Seniors group. Never wanting to be a lady, she feels she is getting even more radical about her ideas. She feels no need to try and keep everything nice: otherwise, how will we move forward? She is dismayed at the increase of poverty in BC, the lack of pensions for many women, the war in Iraq, the missile defence build up, the breakdown of infrastructure in Canada and the U.S., the abuse of women and girls, and the eroticisation of violence. A for-mer storyteller, she does not have stories that inspire people now, does not have the positive mes-sages that need to be woven into the tapestry of our lives, and feels an acute need for stories that help women face aging. Of the Raging Grannies' impact, she concedes that the name, Raging Grannies, had an empowering influence, a branding of sort that gave women permission, and points to the power of psycho-linguistics. Always a seeker, she does not believe we are our brothers' and sisters' keepers but that we are brothers and sisters.*

The Raging Grannies share similarities as well as differences. While most describe themselves as middle class, a few insist they are from the working class, and one says she was raised in a very wealthy family. They seem unusual by their level of education as many have university degrees, including Masters and Doctorates. Most share an enduring commitment and active engagement with peace and social justice. Meeting each person was the highlight of the research, given their vibrant spirits and the determination and persistence with which they invest their days. It is inspiring and deeply humbling to realize the scope of their individual and collective achievements, to sense the passion, the courage and the daring that abide in each of these unique women.

## The Web Spreads, Catching a Defiant Spirit in the Land

Like a trail of fire, groups of Raging Grannies sprung up across the country. Each group has its own history. Some met Grannies or were recruited into existing groups; others heard of them through other activities or from the media. Saltspring Island, the second group, started shortly after the protest at the BC Legislature. Jean McLaren started the third group on Gabriola Island (BC):

> I was at a [peace] rally in Victoria and I saw these women walking around—you know how everybody is in a rally, they're in jeans and a packsack on their back or whatever—and I see these little old ladies with hats on and they looked quite conservative actually when they first started. And they had the little Victoria coats from the thrift store and patent leather bags and little hats and gloves: 'What are these women doing at this rally?' And then they got up on stage and started to sing! I said, 'I want to be one of them!'

Lorna Drew from Fredericton heard them on *Morningside* (CBC Radio) and she:

> …kept waiting for somebody else to start it and nobody did, so I finally started phoning people and I got most of my recruits from the Unitarians and the Voice of Women [around 1997]. We are pretty professional women: poet, artist, social worker, sociologist, and four university professors.

Rose DeShaw, a Raging Granny who encouraged Kingston-raised Lorna Drew, describes the Kingston Grannies' beginning:

> A friend of mine was the secretary for the union and she was in charge of giving the money to the people doing the Bread and Roses parade and organising events just for women. They were really pushing her around and she's Native, she was just beginning to understand her nativeness and she said, 'will you come with me? In case they start trying to push me around you'll be there.' I said, 'Oh sure.' So I went, and…this woman stood up and said she was organising this—where you get to write songs and wear funny hats. So the next week I went to her house. We were all supposed to write songs and bring them to the group: none of them had…and I had written fifteen! It was funny. So they sat and sang them and it was really quite nice.

The woman who initiated the group was a substitute teacher and felt that if she was seen as a Granny she would look too old to substitute, so she quit. But Rose wanted it to go on: a lifelong love of singing and the chance to be an activist at the same time was too good to pass up:

> It was just sitting in there, waiting for me, grannying was. I don't mean to brag but I know so many songs. My parents didn't like music. They really hated music and they never let radios be on in our

house so I didn't hear music except in church, and that really wasn't too much. It was just a little country church. So whenever I heard a song, I knew I'd better memorise it because I might not hear it again, so I memorised hundreds of songs, well, I'd say thousands. I know so many songs. And I was thinking, just before the Grannies, I'll never be able to use all that. I used to think maybe I'll get stuck in an elevator somewhere and I can sing. (laughs!) I had no outlet for that and I'd gone through menopause, menopause is wonderful! It makes a big difference. It put me back to when I was a kid and I could run and climb trees. I am a really shy person but suddenly I wasn't shy anymore. It was so great, those two things happening.

Rose had already been involved in a similar type of protest.

Kingston is such a damned polite town. It's very British, very polite, very old boys. My boys went to the Cathedral church here which had a choirmaster, who was a pedophile. CBC did a film called *The Choirmaster* on it and I picket in it. He was a terrible man, so we picketed. That was before the Grannies. I picketed the Cathedral with the mothers…It was a horrible, horrible, horrible thing and two of the boys killed themselves…You know the church was just furious that we would impinge on the church; it's still like that. They're saying, 'Oh it was such a nice choir, it's a shame a few people had to spoil it,' meaning the parents who complained. It's very painful. I can't talk about it without getting just enraged. That would have been the sort of things that Grannies, if there had been Grannies then, would have really given support. So when I was doing that, I made signs every single day. I made St George, I made the dragon, I made all sorts of dragons. I made a choirboy, everyday, because they were constantly filming and taking pictures and so I just did all these really vivid signs and made songs then too.

Having no contact with other Granny groups, they were excited to hear the Toronto Grannies would be at a gathering in a Kingston convent and dispatched Rose, who returned with Betsy Carr's phone number. That was before Google!

Betsy Carr, the founder of the Toronto group, heard through the Voice of Women that Victoria Grannies were coming east and she offered them hospitality. Soon they suggested she should start a group and they would give her songs which, according to Betsy, is

…a principle of the Grannies, that we help other groups get started by giving songs on current issues. That's the way I started out. I let it be known…that I was thinking of getting a group together…around the testing of cruise missiles in northern Ontario. The Dutch and Great Britain and other countries were sending their pilots over here to train so we thought it would be a good idea to have a demonstration at the Dutch consulate. It was a freezing day. We got out there on the streets and we started to sing. We were all shivering and shaking and we didn't know the songs…I don't even know if we were wearing Granny hats, I forget. I think that probably we knew enough to identify ourselves. So we gave up pretty soon and all piled into a restaurant to get some coffee! (laughs) That was the first event and it was in November. I thought, I'm gonna leave this till January, this is the wrong time of the year to get going…In January 1990 I started again.

The Ottawa Grannies also started after the Victoria Grannies protested in Ottawa.

The Montreal Raging Grannies' first appearance took place on Earth Day in April 1990, the initiative of Joan Hadrill and Barbara Calvert Seifred. Ten years later, a French-speaking group, Les Mémés Déchainées, became active. The two groups co-operate when possible. A bilingual member, Angela Silver, participates in both groups and was important in nurturing the French-speaking group. In Edmonton, the repeated appearances of the Victoria Grannies at the Fringe Festival led women involved in the environmental movement to start their own group in the spring 1992. In 1996, in Halifax, at the age of 87, Muriel Duckworth, a founding member of the Voice of Women and of many other organizations, felt the need for the Raging Grannies' brand of protest for the G-7 summit and Parallel People's Summit taking place in that city:

> When the G-7 was coming here it did seem obvious that we had to have some Raging Grannies to meet them and sing to a lot of people in the Commons…It wasn't hard to do because a lot of women in the Voice of Women were eager to do it.

New groups keep forming. In Regina they have Raging Grannies and Daughters. A recent group involved women on both sides of the border in the Windsor-Detroit area who call themselves the Cross-Border Raging Grannies, taking part in actions on both sides of the border. There are many groups in the U.S. now: Rochester, Boston, New York City, San Francisco, Seattle (and others). They were very active in their opposition to the U.S. administration's war plans against Iraq. They took part in the large rallies in Washington and have been prolific songwriters against the war.

According to various articles, Grannies who were not interviewed also had active lives. Joan Hadrill (Montreal) went to El Salvador and Honduras with a United Church refugee committee in 1986, met with human rights workers and visited camps filled with families fleeing persecution. Alice Coppard (Vancouver) hitchhiked with a friend to Ottawa and Washington, DC, in 1969 with a petition against the Alaska Pipeline: they didn't stop it, but they delayed it! Alison Acker (Victoria) accompanied Guatemalans back to their villages from Mexico. Helen Riley (Toronto) was a retired economist. During World War II, Inger Kronseth (Victoria and Argenta), raised in Denmark and whose father was active against Hitler in the 1930s, joined the Danish resistance movement with her brother who was later murdered. Anne Moon (Victoria) traveled with her mother across the country with the Acid Rain Caravan to inform people and has been so politically active that she once belonged to three political parties at the same time. Freda Knott (Victoria) grew up in a household of activists and was a founder of the Greater Victoria Disarmament Group; as a child, she made placards to protest the raised cost of chocolate bars from 5 to 10 cents! Very early, Millie Ryerson (Montreal) was conscious of "too much unevenness" between poor and rich, spent a lifetime working for social justice and received the Order of Canada for her work. Anne Pask (formerly of Victoria) married for the first time in her 70s to a well-known ecologist in his 80s, had a colourful guard of Raging Grannies at the wedding, and went on a ten-day canoe trip for the honeymoon! Dr. Barbara Lacey (Lethbridge), a former Raging Granny, topped the aldermanic polls in her first run at civic politics. Cathy Hamel (Woodstock), volunteer Granny webmistress works shifts in a welding shop making trucks, has three children and is a member of the Canadian Autoworkers Union. Rheta Stephenson (Regina), told of a woman who drives 125 km to Regina to attend Raging Grannies activities!

Among Grannies we find the following present or past occupations (not an exhaustive list): bookbinder, editor, teacher, women's shelter worker, social worker, founder of an hospice, writer, actress, mature student, nurse, artist, archivist, art therapist, practitioner of acupuncture, housewife, professor of economics or English or women's studies, retired professor, historian, adult educator, activist, banker, business women, anthropologist, musician, librarian, "and just plain Grannies," said Rose DeShaw. No doubt many more interesting backgrounds would be found amongst other Grannies as well. At this point, I do not know how the backgrounds of American, Greek or Australian Raging Grannies compare to Canadian Grannies, but the mix of similarities in outlook, yet diversity of backgrounds, is a strength of their movement in Canada. It is as though the spark that the Raging Grannies provided found fertile ground in women already passionately, at times courageously, involved in social justice.

*Figure 13. Millie Ryerson, Montreal Raging Granny.*
*Source: Eva Munro Collection.*

## Notes

1. Joseph F. Zygmunt, "Movements and Motives: Some Unresolved Issues in the Psychology of Social Movements," in R. Serge Denisoff, ed., *The Sociology of Dissent*, pp.41-57. New York: Harcourt Brace Jovanovich, 1974: 45.

2. Betty Brightwell, "N-Sub visit is spurned," *Esquimalt Star* (Victoria), February 22, 1989.

3. Cited in John Farrell, "Nuclear submarine captain sounds nuclear alarm bell." *The Daily News Extra* (Prince Rupert), August 28, 1991: 3.

4. Betty Brightwell cited in Sandra McCulloch, "Victoria's Raging Grannies lead the battle against war," *Times-Colonist* (Victoria), December 1, 1991: 18.

5. Bruce Kokopeli and George Lackey in Amy Swerdlow, *Women Strike for Peace: Traditional Motherhood and Radical Politics in the 1960s* , Chicago: The University of Chicago Press, 1993: 241.

6. Jenny Hammond, *Sweeter Than Honey: Ethiopian Women and Revolution: Testimonies of Tigrayan Women,* Trenton, New Jersey. The Red Sea Press, 1990: 31.

7. Lucinda Chodan, "Raging Grannies combat war with comedy, song: Kazoo-playing troupe would rather needle politicians than knit, sew," *The Gazette* (Montreal), August 26, 1989: H3.

8. No source was known for this quote, except that it is Mary Daly's.

9. Margaret Laurence, "Old women's song," in *Dance on the Earth: A Memoir*, Toronto. McClelland and Stewart, 1989: 225, 228.

10. Rose DeShaw, "Making a promise for life," *The Globe and Mail*, October 28, 1997: A 24.

11. *Ibid.*

12. *Ibid.*

# Chapter Two

# GOOFY HATS, SONGS OF CHEEKY IRREVERENCE, AND HUMOUR

## Creation of the Raging Grannies

### "An Old Bunch of Hats": To Be Seen To Be Heard— Outlandish Costume Confronts Invisibility

The Grannies protest using irreverence and humour in the service of their serious commitment. But first, they get the attention with colourful clothes: without a dramatic and group approach, women's resistance tends to suffer invisibility. The Grannies are known for their distinctive costume: disarming smiles, outrageous hats, pink running shoes, gaudy shawls, frilly aprons, and colourful vintage clothing. According to Temma Kaplan, the women involved in the Love Canal environmental battle, mostly mothers, realised that they had to be seen in order to be heard and recognised the importance of dramatic creative actions to make themselves colourful for the media. Granny Joan Harvey agrees:

> Middle-aged women become invisible because they're not seen as possible sex partners, so men and women start to ignore middle-aged women, menopausal women, and post-menopausal women. Older women are completely transparent and invisible: you try to go anywhere to do something, and you can stand there for hours and you're not there. For the most part in our culture…older people are not revered and respected, they are ridiculed, 'get out of the way old woman,' you know. I can't remember who said it, which of the Grannies, that the only way we're going to get anyone to notice us and pay attention is to dress ridiculously. 'Now that we have your attention, listen to what we have to say.'

We've put on our hat
Our apron and our shawl
Cause we'll never grow
Too old to dream
Of justice for one and all.

*Edmonton Raging Grannies.*

*Figure 14. Montreal Raging Grannies. Source: Barbara Calvert Seifred Collection.*

In their first actions the Grannies did not dress ridiculously but looked rather proper and conservative, as Jean McLaren pointed out earlier. They were obviously wearing a costume, of bygone fashion that emphasised matronly dignity. Joyce Stewart remembers: "We dressed very nicely in those days, we wore nice hats and clothes and we tried to look nice, but funny." Betty Brightwell says that at times they wore long white gloves and patent leather purses to convey the idea of proper older women.

Outrageous hats brimming with a cacophony of bright colours have become a trademark of the Raging Grannies. In an article she wrote Rose DeShaw displays the Grannies' typical humour:

> Yes, the hats get competitive. Every granny gig, somebody has a new one. But with rumours of a life-size pheasant being stitched onto someone's headgear, we're probably going to have to set a weight limit on the decorations.[1]

*Figure 15. Victoria Raging Grannies in the early days. Distinguished, dignified costumes. Source: Doran Doyle Collection.*

*Figure 16. The level of colour and outlandishness quickly increased.*
*Victoria Raging Grannies in their finery. February 24, 1990. Source: Joyce Stewart Collection.*

In an another article she describes her hat as follows:

Three tiny flags: gay pride's rainbow, Quebec's, Canada's;
plastic bicycle horn in purple and orange for rowdy rallies;
pin from the Dicken's house—reminder for whom we fight;
pin from Bread and Roses—reminder of our need for unity;
three birds: canary—reminder to sing my best,
Canada goose—reminder of where I am, a white dove of peace spreading its wings;
bunch of violets—remembering Grannies who have gone before;
tiny plastic wonder woman action figure—reminder to be strong, well-costumed and a
little silly; all of which is quite enough for one small black felt pillbox.[2]

*Figure 17. Such glorious hats. Montreal Raging Grannies.*
*The Un-convention in Kingston, June 2002. Source: Carole Roy.*

*Rose DeShaw grew up in Alaska in a pioneer family, studied at a theological college in Oregon, and immigrated to Canada with her husband in protest of the Vietnam War. She now lives in Kingston, Ontario. A prison librarian, published writer, journalist, and bookstore owner, she ran a professional resume service and worked with inmates and troubled youths. For twenty years she wrote a national column for an Anglican journal.*

*She is involved in supporting women who work/have worked in prisons and is a member of many groups: a swim group, a dog owners group, a writers group, and a booksellers group. And of course, the Grannies, "Fellow gnashers, eschewing the more traditional pleasures of grannydom—fiddling with your children's marriages, splitting church congregations and helping old Boy Scouts across the street—in order to mock the current condition" (1997: A20). Rose has become a prolific songwriter. She discusses the on-going dilemma about Grannies' singing (in Kingston most of the social politics are around the choirs): "So if you're a real high class person you get into the high class choir so the grannies had to be up to snuff." She adds, "Well, who cares? I don't care as long as the words are clear so they can hear them…there'll always be a battle" to get the Grannies to be a choir.*

*In spite of serious health issues she is very active: "I know that I'm gonna be sick, so when I'm well or when I'm able to walk around I really use the time…I'm involved with people and it's enjoyable."*

*Figure 18. Rose DeShaw and her collection of cardboard Grannies, reconcilers in the land. Un-convention, Kingston, June 8, 2002. Source: Carole Roy.*

The media like to comment on the Grannies' image. While Rose DeShaw suggests they dress like Suffragettes, others say they dress like cartoon grannies, like the stereotypes of older women, by wearing quaint shawls and bonnets decked with all manner of flowers—artificial and otherwise. Phyllis Creighton acknowledges that the way they dress makes them vulnerable and that they can easily be made a joke of, which is not enough for them to go away or mince their words. Moira Walker suggests that their willingness to divest themselves of the artificial notion of decorum and dignity and make fools of themselves help make the stereotype visible for all to see, a useful contribution as stereotypes keep the population regimented and controlled. In the Canadian Theatre Review, John Burns wrote that the Grannies reverse "cultural expectations by empowering themselves within a society which belittles their experience and point of view"; the Granny figure transcends her limitations by becoming a court jester of sorts and the audience identifies with her attempt to defeat adversity and stereotypes (21, 22).

Anna Louise Fontaine and Louise Edith Hébert-Ferron of the Mémés Déchaînées say that the costume makes them more approachable and signals to the audience that they are using the absurd and going beyond the intellectual level. In an article by Morelle Saindon, Kathleen Foy, a 90 year old Montreal Granny, agrees that such ridiculous clothes are more funny than threatening and allows them to go further than they would otherwise. Anna Louise, who lives in Montreal, wears her Granny clothes from her home because she finds people are willing to engage with her as she travels by public transit to the protest sites. Invariably, people along the route tell her it is not Halloween, but also come to talk to her. This is prime time for her educational work:

> It allows me to talk all along my route. The whole travel time someone is talking to me, many youth, many older people. It's obvious that I am disguised and not mentally ill. Generally, people are not attracted to talk to the mentally ill, but they approach me without fear. Just by the way we dress we already are not behaving in ways people expect. So already there is something, they don't reason the same way and they approach us differently…Already they are entering our play when they talk to us, becoming accomplices in a way.

*Anna Louise Fontaine heard of the Raging Grannies a few times but could not contact them until they appeared on French TV. A phone call put her in touch with the Montreal English-speaking Grannies, who were delighted by her interest, having tried for years to spark interest in the French-speaking community. She is a member of the only French-speaking group.*

*A former practitioner of acupuncture, she is the mother of two teenage sons and works with the elderly at a neighborhood community center. She is one of the younger Grannies. She found two women to join her and they call themselves "Mémés Déchainées" [literally meaning Grannies Without Chains] which they chose because of two aspects: "déchainées" as unstoppable, a word often used to indicate the uncontrollability of storms, and also meaning to take off the chains that restrict and silence.*

*Anna Louise remembers her love of disguise in childhood and to this day, she is very aware of the power of clothing to express her state of mind. A sensitive idealist with an analytical mind and a great capacity for self-discipline, she believes in a better world, which she saw briefly during the 60s. She feels identity based on nationalism must evolve to a planetary sense of identity. This requires solidarity and a willingness to sustain discomfort. It requires that we do not forget what unites us. For her, the collective is a way to train ourselves to live up to our values. She came to the Raging Grannies because of the absurdity of the present agenda's obsession with the bottom line.*

*Figure 19. Anna Louise Fontaine.*
*Source: Louise Hébert-Ferron Collection.*

It is an interesting phenomenon that as the Grannies disguise themselves and stand out by their difference, they become more approachable and people feel free to engage in conversation with them. Wearing a costume is a sign of play and allows the breaking down of barriers. Taking people by surprise provides an opportunity for people to get out of predictable reaction patterns. Scott McKeen thinks that the costume allows Grannies "to lampoon a stereotype while, perhaps, catching many of us off-guard long enough to capture our attention." It is funny to see the Raging Grannies in their colourful clothes because it is unexpected of respectable women with credibility to dress in such a way. Lorna Drew feels that:

> If I were twenty-one years old and out in the streets singing I bet I would be in a lot more trouble than I am now…Age and privilege. If I were a bag lady I wouldn't be so untouchable either…It's economics, lots to do with economics. It's the middle class who is in the driver's seat of history, so you might as well drive.

There is a fine line. If they were bag ladies people would not approach them or find them funny, something Kathleen Dunphy is aware of: "We have to watch we don't get any bag lady kind of appearance." While Fran Thoburn acknowledges that the original group had concerns about the image that they might project, she offers another perspective:

> We got the idea of dressing as older women and really playing up the older woman part of ourselves and people were uncomfortable with that because of the fear of being disrespectful. I had no problem with it, no problem whatsoever. I was an older woman, I didn't mind acting like all the older women I saw carrying patent leather purses, wearing ridiculous shoes or coats that kept them from being able to really ride a bike or be active. So I had no problem at all in dressing as the other counterpart of my group that I saw on the streets every day. We talked about it a lot and we realised that it would work. It would work. And it has, it really has.

The impact of wearing a costume is not only on the audience: it has an empowering effect on many Grannies. The "uniform" gives them a sense of freedom, says Bonnie Doyle. Hats make them brave, says Hilda Marczak. Alison Acker told Sandra McCulloch that with her Granny hat on, she "can march right down to the legislature and walk right up to the front door."[3] When Rheta Stephenson puts on the dress she puts on an attitude: "I don't care, I'm old, I don't care what people think anymore." For Eva Munro putting on her hat and skirt is empowering:

> When we get together with the other Raging Grannies, and we're an old bunch of hats…put a hat on and my long skirt on and then I feel like a Raging Granny…I can really rage then…the uniform helps, it gives me a power for getting in front of other people.

Barbara Calvert Seifred admits the costume allows her to do things she would not normally do and talks about the impact that being a Granny has had on her life:

> There is a real dotted line in my life. Before, I was a very shy person and living under a stone and then I got out of that…When I put on my costume I consider it my protective uniform, it makes me much braver than I would be without it.

A friend noticed. When requested by that friend to ask some questions at the meeting she was to attend, Barbara was hesitant and "a little timid about confronting," so the friend told her: "Put your Granny clothes underneath your clothes!" conveying the empowering quality of the Grannies' costume. Barbara continues: "I was always basically very shy, painfully shy when I was younger so somehow it [costume] turns me into a different person and then I feel able to speak out."

Rebels in Disguise
    I looked like a granny
    I felt like a granny
    I thought like a granny
    Then I got wise
    Now I'm a rebel in disguise
    ...
    I learned it was canny
    To protest LOUD

*Tune: You're a Devil in Disguise. Raging Grannies "Carry On" Songbook.*

Yet the costume, or uniform, has been a point of discussion in the Grannies' newsletter. Barbara wrote:

> A woman from Boston told me that they did not wear costumes, just hats, so perhaps it is a good time for a reminder about FULL UNIFORM. (Ed note: Granny uniform is hat, skirt or dress, shawl, apron.) I hate to be critical but I think it is important and something that links us together. Though it sounds strange, our outlandish appearance lends credibility. One look at us and y' know we must be serious. And that's why we are here. Got to have commitment to risk looking so serious in our thrift shop veneer! Just wearing funny hats makes us look somewhat eccentric. The full kit and caboodle is a VERY STRONG STATEMENT. After all, Canada's finest in uniform have an image to uphold. And look at the media attention it has brought us—to say nothing of the RCMP attention! [Who labelled the Grannies a low threat to Canada's security for the APEC summit and later graduated them to subversives].[4]

In the next issue of their newsletter came this letter from Fran Thoburn, one of the original Victoria Grannies:

> I would hate to see us become one of those trite female clichés that clutter our culture. In naming our uniform as being 'hat, skirt or dress, shawl, apron,' we are becoming that cliché, that cutesy little old-fashioned person. True, we speak out and we are humorous, but I believe that we speak most strongly when we are clothed in whatever garb that inspires our power. Originally we adopted a look that parodied the little old ladies you see on our streets here in Victoria. Dark woollen overcoat with fur collar, patent leather purse, dowdy hat with unexpected trimming to catch attention, pink running shoes. So if the Boston tribe wants to don hats and protest—good! If another group wants to wear bonnets and feels powered by bonnets, apron, whatever, good! My favorite attire is a pair of tights and a top with spangles of all colours that clash marvellously with the red boa and blue insects on my hat. Boots, running shoes, hiking shoes, whatever suits my activity of the day complete the costume. Skirts and shawls get in the spokes of my bike, aprons are for the kitchen where I spend as little time as possible, having raised 4 kids and two husbands. Let's concentrate on empowering our-

selves and each other and leave what we wear up to each individual. It's our hearts and courage that make us Raging Grannies. PS: When I read this letter to our meeting, the other grannies wanted me to add several items. Betty Brightwell reminded me of the time we appeared on the main street downtown wearing bikinis (with hats) to bring attention to the depleting ozone layer…[Someone] brought up our decision to seriously consider appearing nude (with hats) should we feel an issue that desperately needs public attention is not getting serious consideration.[5]

Wearing a costume brings some people back to their childhood. Many Grannies point to a like of disguises and dressing up in childhood—Doran Doyle, Rose DeShaw, Anna Louise Fontaine, Angela Silver come to mind. But Fran talked about the solace and excitement she found in the outdoors as a child and connects the idea of costume with limiting women's role rather than with the freedom and creativity of childhood games.

The point Barbara makes about the strength of a recognisable visual presentation cannot be dismissed. The outlandish and colourful clothes are an important trademark that paradoxically lends credibility to the individual Grannies as they identify with a character with a corporate identity of sorts, suggesting they are not alone. Whatever costume Grannies wear, Barbara Calvert Seifred sees a sweet irony in her antics:

> One of our dearest members was an old friend of mine; I hadn't seen her for years. We'd been in touch a little bit when we were first married but I had known her at designing school in my teens. We always used to laugh over the fact that our fathers had sent us to fashion design school and we went out on the streets looking like…in our wild costumes!

Although the costume is an important part of the Grannies' image, it is a tool they use with appropriate consideration for the purpose of the specific activity. Now that they have a reputation and a recognisable image, due in large part to their colourful costume, they can rely on that reputation and appear in different outfits if they need or want to. For example, a Montreal Granny sometimes wears a baseball uniform with the backward baseball cap like young boys do: on a sixty-something-year-old woman the effect is comical by the unexpectedness. One Regina Granny wears a night gown, a granny wig, and a night hat. The Kingston Grannies wore long bright flannel night gowns over drab winter clothes for an outdoor gig, which made them look cute and helpless, belying their real intent. There have also been times when they left their outlandish clothes at home. When the Victoria and Saltspring Island Grannies appeared at the BC Legislature to present their views on NAFTA, Marg Simons said:

> We deliberately decided not to dress in our usual outlandish clothes. We took our hats but only put them on when it was our turn to speak so that others making presentations wouldn't be distracted.[6]

The Ottawa Grannies made the same decision when appearing at a citizen's panel discussing police actions during the protests of the G-20 meeting that took place in Ottawa in the fall of 2001. It is undeniable that the Grannies' look is an important part of their effectiveness. Barbara has the following analysis:

> We used to do peace demonstrations and peace marches and things on the street. Lots of people would stand there and argue…or they'd back off, they didn't want to know anything about it. But with the Grannies, because we look so funny, they kind of lean in instead of leaning out. You know there's a connection. They want to know a little more about what these crazy women are up to. So then they stop and listen and they're open. They don't generally argue with us too, too much…We put out a message, and crazy as our presentation is, people know that there is a serious message underneath it all. So we have fun while working on serious things.

*Fran Thoburn immigrated to Canada from the U.S. because of the Vietnam War and the civil rights movement: her phone was tapped, her friend "had a bomb thrown on her porch." She sees herself as having been a rebel, always. She moved to Victoria in 1985 from Peterborough, Ontario, where she had helped start a peace group and a radio program on peace issues at the local university. Reading Jonathan Shield's* Fate of the Earth *at the time of the birth of her first granddaughter created a sense of urgency to insure a future world, for her grandchild "to live to be old and die a natural death."*

*While her childhood appeared idyllic on the surface, she spent a lot of time alone in the outdoors trying to escape her alcoholic and confused mother and the beatings of a brother. A sceptic early in life, she has been motivated to find the real and true. Interestingly, she ended up adopting a fictional character, the Raging Granny, to tell the truth through satire. She reconciles this dilemma through what she sees as her role—that of an educator—and her ability to recognise "the door to other people's minds."*

*Earlier married to a U.S. Army private stationed in Germany, she defied the rules and went to live in Germany where she worked and had her first child. She LOVES the world and says it would be just too tragic to lose it all. She has held a variety of positions: teacher, file clerk, psychotherapist, salesperson, made and sold maple syrup, ran a bed-and-breakfast, and been on the board of the Citizens Counselling Centre in Victoria.*

*Figure 20. Fran Thoburn.*
*Source: Hilda Marczak Collection.*

## Creative Props: More Attention

Props are part of the visual statement the Grannies make. Symbolic props make it easier for the audience to relate to the satirical lyrics. They make masks of politicians, bang on pots with spoons, or use brooms, mops, or vacuums, like Mother Jones' successful army of miners' wives. Umbrellas, kazoos, plastic nuclear missiles, knitting needles, turkey basters and sieves, kayaks and canoes, all find their use. At times, Grannies have to sneak in their message through a judicious use of props. Jean McLaren went to the Nanoose Bay military base where banners are not allowed: "We took our umbrellas because it looked like it might rain and…went to the line up where the people were and stood there with our umbrellas up [with slogans]." The Kingston Grannies have a panoply of props: they wear false noses—with buckteeth or bushy eyebrows—when they wish to speak for the government and made an ambulance and huge shiny cardboard scissors to symbolise the cuts to healthcare and social programs in Ontario. Lorna Drew has a wooden spoon that has become an icon, "the sacred spoon!" Joan Harvey talked about Rose's flair for props:

> Rose DeShaw in Kingston, she's got a wonderful hat and at the back of it she has a little bicycle horn that you squeeze. If she's singing to a politician and they're distracted, she goes (sounds of horn) and they don't know where it's coming from, but all of a sudden they're paying attention again!

Rose waves her brolly for emphasis, dances in her hiking boots, and leads with a rubber chicken that she waves like a baton! She and her chicken even had an encounter with Prime Minister Paul Martin (then Finance Minister). She found herself

*Figure 21. Rose DeShaw with Paul Martin.*
*Source: Rose DeShaw Collection.*

…poking Paul Martin in the tummy with my rubber chicken. I really did it… though it was just me getting overexcited, not an act of violence. We were chatting. I had never seen such an expensive suit on anyone, man or woman, and I was gesturing with the rubber chicken with which I lead the singing ('Chicken Soup for the Soul,' etc.), and Paul graciously came over to talk…After singing Paul Martin our songs about the state of the country, his name in some, I got going on some aspect, I forget which, and when I came to, I was poking him emphatically, beak first, with the chicken. I remember gazing down at his cashmere waistcoat in horror. Paul was gazing down too. But he remained gracious and didn't try to duck us and said he'd read the songs over on the way home, though he didn't promise to sing.

**Cutbacks, Cutbacks**

Cutbacks, cutbacks, good old Tory Cutbacks
But we can remember those days of old.
When so many people were hungry and cold.
When no one could get any medical aid;
Till doctors were sure that the bills could be paid.
And children left school at an early age.
When we grannies were just little kids.

*Tune: School Days. Source: Edmonton Raging Grannies,*
*Press release by Ralph Nader (April 1998).*

The Ontario government cut the allowance designed to insure pregnant women on welfare adequate nutrition because Mike Harris said they bought beer with it. Kingston Grannies got their pillows out and put them under their dresses so they were pregnant to go to the social services office singing, "Going to social services and we're gonna get hassled." To their surprise, the staff cheered and applauded. Rose DeShaw remembers she was

…wearing a really awful dress. I mean, when you find a really awful colour you know that's the dress for you, and I had that underneath. So there was a picture of me on the cover of the paper, and I'm sure they were doing it to embarrass me: my whole self from top to bottom with my mouth open, this dress, and I was pregnant. You know it was really awful! I mean, just looking at it made you laugh.

She once put a picture of Mike Harris, professional golf player, then Ontario Premier, in a bicycle wheel and woke him up to the consequences of his cuts by hitting him with a golf club:

It went clear across Canada because it was a slow news day…it shows you that if you get in a crowd and everybody has signs that are all printed [you need something different to attract attention]…Words are great but graphics are so wonderful…to make people pay attention. It's art for a purpose.

In Edmonton, the Grannies prefer not to use props. But in their fight against Ralph Klein's provincial government, who openly advocates private for profit health care, they presented a "brief" during the Parklands Institute on health care. They had "a gigantic pair of men's boxer shorts with the message KEEP MEDICARE PUBLIC on one side and NO PRIVATE PARTS on the other," wrote Shelley Mardiros. Grannies remember fighting for medicare once. They have historical memories.

*Figure 22. Rose DeShaw pounds a golf club onto a caricature of Mike Harris during a protest against workfare in downtown Kingston, July 30, 2001. Source: CP PHOTO The Whig-Standard/Michael Lea.*

Marg Simons lives on picturesque Saltspring Island in British Columbia. She is an artist and an art teacher. Marg is a catalyst and helped start the community centre on the island. She feels an especially strong bond with younger activists, possibly because "Grannies do silly things and are off the beaten track."

She recalls a Raging Grannies Un-convention in Vancouver during a time of tension due to the U.S. submarines affecting the fish run at Dixon Entrance. They decided to take action and while one group of Grannies made a cardboard submarine another group zipped down to China Town to get dry fish. They then met at the busy Granville Island Market on a Saturday morning and sang and got people to send letters and dry fish to Prime Minister Brian Mulroney—postage was free so they had a huge pile of letters on the way to the parliament in Ottawa! Marg created the Granny logo "Knitting the World Together," which she made as a banner, and her husband, Art Simons, also an artist, designed the Granny with the brolly logo.

*Figure 23. (Above) Marg Simons wears a sweater with the Raging Granny logo.*

*Figure 24. (Left) Marg designed the Raging Granny logo, "Knitting the World Together," which she used to make this banner.*

*Source: Marg Simons Collection.*

*Figure 25. Saltspring Island Grannies take part in the 1995 Sea Capers Parade with their "cow"*
*to make a statement on the use of growth hormone on dairy cattle. Note the clever use of the glove.*
*Source: Marg Simons Collection.*

*Figure 26. Grannies go quietly? Victoria Raging Grannies protest against provincial government*
*cuts to medical services. The newspaper reported that the Grannies occupied the Ministry of Health*
*building in Victoria and while the title suggests the Grannies went away quietly, both Grannies' mouths*
*suggest otherwise. Source: Debra Brash, Times-Colonist, May 31, 2002: C1.*

## Not A Church Choir: Special Harmonies and Not Exactly Grandmotherly Lyrics

*Figure 27. Members of the Toronto Raging Grannies practising kazoos.*
*Source: Phyllis Creighton Collection.*

## Not Entertainment

Without songs Mary Rose believes the Raging Grannies "would have never come to be what it is now because street theatre is one thing but this is something quite different." The idea of the Raging Grannies using familiar tunes with satirical lyrics to communicate a message is credited to a gifted songwriter, Jane Mackey, who was a Granny only for a short time but wrote Grannies' songs for a while. Jane remembers the discussion before the first Raging Grannies action in Victoria:

> We came up with this idea of an Un-valentine…Part of the imagery was the nuclear umbrella…a term that was around a lot, 'We're under the nuclear umbrella of the United States defence system'…Our opinion was that the nuclear umbrella had holes. So we got these umbrellas…all ratty and broken down and cut holes in them…They would be shown to have very little protective ability…We did the hats and the coats and the purses…We were sitting [and talking]…"What are we actually gonna do? We should do something, we should make a speech or something," and we came up with the idea of a song. We sat around and tried to come up with something and we couldn't. It just didn't gel. But it put the idea in my mind. When I got off on my own and started playing with it, it just kind of came…So at the next meeting I shyly took it out. Everybody loved it because it was a focal point.

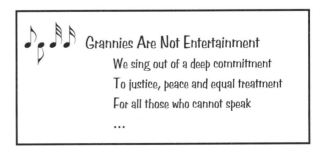

Grannies Are Not Entertainment
We sing out of a deep commitment
To justice, peace and equal treatment
For all those who cannot speak
…

*Tune: Dumbarton's Drums. Kingston Raging Grannies.*

The Raging Grannies use old familiar tunes, which make it easier to tolerate the harsh message: "All our information is so terrible, we need to have this kind of strategy to protect ourselves as well as the public," said Doran Doyle to John Burns (22). The irony in the songs acts as a mechanism that includes and distances listeners at the same time (Burns 22). The tune is familiar but the lyrics are not, which requires participation from the audience in the decoding of the new lyrics. For example, the song "Take Me Out To The Clearcut" to the tune of "Take Me Out To The Ball Game," a tune of strong American resonance, requires the audience to concentrate on the lyrics and move from a passive to a participatory role in order to get the irony (Burns 22). The audience has to make connections between environment, corporations—MacMillan Bloedel—investors, jobs, and themselves who need air, earth, and not an oven to live in. The incongruity of a picnic on tree stumps makes people laugh because the absurdity is obvious. Their image of a chainsaw that is stuck with the switch on is a strong one. They challenge the claim that BC tree farming licences are environmentally viable as they first and foremost seem to cultivate corporate profits and greed.

### Take Me Out To The Clearcut

Take me out to the clearcut
We'll picnic on a few stumps
I want you to know I'm a tree farming nut
Who thinks like a chainsaw that's stuck in a rut!
Mac Bloedel gets a Hip Hooray!
They make black picnic grounds pay
So it's ONE gets you TWO, dear investors, thank you:
...
The timber's been tidied away.
It's been sold down the stream
In a businessman's dream
It's swell to stand here in a landscape so clean!
It's off to lumbering elsewhere,
...
It's the buzz of the mill that produces the thrill
Worth a million trees, So take me out to the clearcut,
Who needs tall cedars, I say?
The air is depleted, and so is the earth
...
Let's all get into the greenhouse,
...
If God wanted trees, he'd not make it so ea...sy
To whack them away!

*Tune: Take Me Out to the Ball Game. Victoria Raging Grannies.*

*Jane Mackey lives in Victoria and was a Raging Granny for a short time, but continued writing witty songs for a while. A graduate student and mother of a young child at the time, she was considerably younger than most. Born in the U.S., she immigrated to Canada. She came from a "fairly musical background, of people who were thwarted in their ambition to be musical." She wanted to be on stage but needed encouragement that never came. From early on, she had the ability to make up songs: "For some reason this ability with doggerel was always there...I had a huge repertoire of songs." But the first time she came up with a song for the Grannies: "There was something about this process that just kick-started this whole thing...The fact that people liked it was great but it was more that I wanted to be able to do this activity and here I had a vehicle and a group of people who were receptive and it contributed something. It fulfilled a lot of different criteria all at once."*

*At the time, like many people, she felt isolated and absolutely devastated by the nuclear arms race. She woke up in the night or simply could not sleep. She was: "Absolutely paralysed with fear...Oh my God! You mean, my kid is not gonna get to grow up? It just felt so frightening and horrible and that's...why I wanted to get involved because I found the whole thing so huge, so frightening and so horrible." She had been an activist earlier: "My first picket line I was sixteen. It's just that my family was political." She was a radical while in college, took an active part in the women's movement, started a women's centre on campus, and joined the protests against the Vietnam War. After finishing graduate school, she worked as a child care worker, then as a policy advisor for the provincial government, sitting in on cabinet meetings. She also got involved in neighbourhood and municipal politics.*

*Figure 28. Jane Mackey.*
*Directing the "choir" at the first action.*
*Source: Hilda Marczak Collection.*

Singing is empowering. Under adverse circumstances, it gives a sense of freewill, provides a possibility of dignity, and sends the clear message that the singer will not be silenced. At times, singing is a victory over fear as it rekindles and strengthens one's determination and commitment. Jean McLaren says: "When I've been scared, or worried about something, or a couple of times when I've been arrested—I've been arrested nine times—so at any one of those times I'm sure I sang."

Ava Louwe recalls singing during the demonstration at the G-20 meeting in Ottawa where there were many unpleasant and scary encounters with the police:

> There was a group behind us who started singing and they spurred us on, and we began singing. And I know one of the reasons I was singing was just to dissipate my own distress, my own discomfort with what was happening…I think it also helped keep a sense of calm…In the area where we were it ended up being a really nice energy, developing a real sense of solidarity that we were there on a peaceful mission. And that's the best thing we could do, hold the peace, be witnesses.

Alma Norman agrees: singing can defuse tension or potentially violent situations. Alma believes that at the G-20 demonstration singing itself was what mattered: it allowed people to join together and feel part of a collaborative and co-operative action. At that moment, singing became a much needed instrument of unity and solidarity; the songs themselves did not matter as much as joining one's voice with that of others. For Jane Mackey: "It's no big surprise that most people get energised when singing. There's something about singing and doing music together that gives people a feeling of being together, raises the feeling level."

Phyllis Creighton, invited to Japan to deliver a speech for the commemoration of Hiroshima and Nagasaki, started a song that "created quite a mood, quite a sense of unity, of caring…a sense of being together" among a group of people of diverse cultures and languages. In an article by Stephen Chase, Phyllis suggests that music taps into the deepest feelings, things that we may not even be conscious of. She adds:

> The medium is the message in a profound way…When you sing a sad song or a powerful song you may, by the intensity of emotion, seed the sense that this is sad, this is important, this is deeply wrong, and by humour you seed the feeling that this does not make any sense and we've got to stop it and we can, this is absurd.[7]

Phyllis suggests that Grannies use music to reach below the intellect right to the gut and said to Sarah Jane Growe: "If you touch their hearts, you'll release energy so that they'll do something."

Political music has been used since the eighteenth-century to "evoke or reflect a political judgement by the listener."[8] The Raging Grannies understand the power of satirical songs. "What we really are is singing cartoonists," says Alma Norman. Once they get the attention, they sing to educate leaders and the public. The songs take an unorthodox look at current issues in the hope that people will think seriously about the subjects raised says Betsy Carr, but they try to avoid a preachy tone. It is easier to reach out through songs than speeches: "If we came in and gave lectures, people's eyes would glaze over and they would leave or turn off. Instead, we want to get them to think more about the issue," suggests Sylvia Campbell, a Lethbridge Granny. Jean McLaren agrees: "People can yap and yap and yap and nobody listens to them, words are words. But when you sing it, they kind of listen and I think that's the difference, they do listen."

Eva Munro of the Halifax Grannies believes that "a good song, performed in the Grannies' finest form, can be worth 10,000 words at least!" Barbara Calvert Seifred agrees: "It takes longer when you're talking and discussing, but when you're focussed as tight as a song it delivers the message." Songs allow the expression of emotions in public settings in a way speech rarely does: rage and outrage are always challenging to express in a constructive way, but singing makes it more acceptable than ranting.

Music has played an important role in social movements, but Phyllis Creighton recalls a recent conference of environmentalists, most under forty years old, who did not realise that songs have been at the heart of resistance in many struggles. Given the reliance in our society on commercial entertainment, it is not surprising that the power of singing is undervalued. Betty Mardiros, a Granny in Edmonton, remembers "the most militant days of unionism" when "very strong unions were supporting the songs, a pity it has not continued because it brings people together and gives some sense of solidarity." Shelly Romalis (1987) says that the Greenham Common women, arrested for entering the military base, often sang to keep their spirit up and were known to clap and sing in court and prison, creating "disturbances" and "breaching the peace," making a mockery of the proceedings. In a similar spirit, the Raging Grannies use any opportunity to make themselves a "nuisance" and crash receptions, hearings, meetings, or parties that are related to their concerns. Phyllis Creighton has seen an increase in Grannies' appeal: "Ever since things turned bad in Ontario with Mike Harris, we've been in more demand. People need the energy, they need the hope, they need the laughter…it's empowering for us too."

Although they sing, Grannies repeatedly make a point: "We are not entertainment," says Muriel Duckworth. When a well-meaning columnist made such an assumption, Rose DeShaw wrote a letter to the editor:

> Call us activists if you will but we simply do not have time for entertainment…The raging is a cry from the heart…Being a persistent nuisance would be a more flattering description than billing us as entertainers, however well-meant. The heedless policies of our misguided provincial leadership are creating critics in the most unexpected places. We are proud to stand and sing among them.[9]

As Alma Norman says, their aim is not to frighten but challenge people to think; to prick consciences in Joan Harvey's words. "Singing acapella, we're often off-key even with a pitch pipe and putting the most tuneful grannies closest to the mikes!" wrote Rose DeShaw (A20). Jean McLaren was told, "Oh, it's wonderful how you deliberately try to sing off key!"

> Our singing is so awful, it is a riot, just a riot. Oh God, absolute innocence…We were so lucky we weren't a singing group before we started, otherwise people would not have joined. Other groups—most of them sing in tune because they knew they were going to be a singing group…So we say we have unique harmonies![10]

A report by Lucinda Chodan in the local newspaper has Fran Thoburn of the Victoria Grannies making clear their priority: "We just start on any old note, and our singing is incredibly awful; we have people who can't sing a note. The issues are what is important."

*Figure 29. Cartoon by Trevor Bryden about the Victoria Raging Grannies. Source: Trevor Bryden.*

Although some would take exception to this, for many Grannies non-professionalism is not an issue: "We pride ourselves on not being professionals, we're not musicians…we're just having fun," said a Granny who wished to remain anonymous. They see their appeal as being ordinary people. This attitude toward singing makes it possible for many to join. Pearl Rice, in Regina, had quite a good voice, sang in a choir, and still sings with the war brides at the local veterans' ward. But she is happy for this opportunity: "my voice has changed in the last few years, going down as I'm getting on. But this is the thing about the Grannies, you don't have to be a great singer, you just come and join in like you're around the campfire." Some groups sound good naturally. Fredericton Grannies even do harmonies. A few groups do care about how they sound but for most the priority is for their message to be heard clearly.

Singing with the Grannies is not without challenges, according to Betsy Carr: "This isn't a church choir!" [Some say] "Don't sing too fast…yet others feel then it's dragging." The task is harder because their songs are topical and the issues come and go, so they do not get the chance to sing the same songs often so memorising is of little use as the songs quickly become obsolete. They constantly have to come up with new songs as the range of issues they address requires continuous song writing. Muriel Duckworth explains:

> You can't go to sing at a health meeting the same things you would sing for the miners. You have to have material that is related, therefore you have to know the situation, you have to believe in the situation, and then you have to write the words.

Recycling of tunes over and over also offers challenges: sometimes they can't sing some songs at the same gig because they have the same tune, although they address different issues.

## Crafting Songs: Inspiration, Analysis, Collaboration

One of the remarkable features of the Raging Grannies is the discovery for some women of a passion and talent for song writing. Grannies' songs are individual as well as collective creations. Sharon Wurmann, a Granny from Kelowna, "finds song writing an exciting and creative way to remain involved in social justice issues." The Oxford Grannies claim that song writing has therapeutic effects and that the opportunities to raise their voices are limitless. Those who have discovered a passion for song writing report a high degree of spontaneity in the process. Phyllis recalls the impact of her first song: "The first time it happened to me it was totally out of the blue. I got off the subway train and realised, 'Ohhhh, I just bought a new subway pass and I left it on that train.' That's how absorbed I was."

Lanie Melamed said Barbara Calvert Seifred is "moved to write anywhere and anytime." Barbara admits: "Some days are crazy. I'll write four or five songs. It's a surprise to me." About the first song she says:

> We worked so hard to put down a few lines and it was just laborious. And then, all of a sudden, it just started to roll and fall onto the page. Now of course it's become a ridiculous obsession: the minute I get an idea I have to write up something else. There's no way we could ever use a fraction of the ones that I write but that's fun. I figure if I don't write them, the well may dry up.

Barbara has written more than 1100 songs on Grannies' role and social change, anti-war and weapons trade, environment and anti-nuclear, and globalization and government. She knew it had become an affliction when she started to rhyme grocery lists! Although she has some understanding of the process, it still puzzles her: "Once you get a few words you want to write about or use, they have a rhythm and suggest one tune or another. Something I wrote recently just had its own tune. Really, they just happen. I don't know how. It's fun."

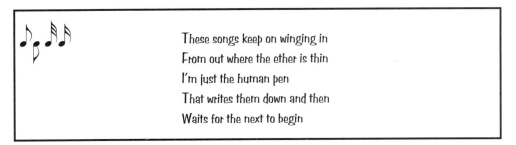

These songs keep on winging in
From out where the ether is thin
I'm just the human pen
That writes them down and then
Waits for the next to begin

*Tune: Original. Barbara Calvert Seifred Collection.*

Phyllis Creighton, who led a song writing workshop at a Grannies' Un-convention, says of the process:

> It takes time to write a song…I don't know what the process is. I know that…you require information…it has to be fed into your brain and you have to allow time for the sifting to go on and then if you have enough faith…You just got to let it go, you've got to believe you can do it…You put it in the back of your head that you need a song about x or y and when you need it…Very seldom do I have to push it at all. Before it's due, I get a moment where I think, 'Gosh, I got to get a piece of paper and a pencil and I got to start writing.' I don't know where it comes from but I do know you couldn't [do this] unless you had a reasonably broad range of information and knowledge.

Phyllis' comment clearly shows the connection between knowledge and creativity. Although the process is experienced as spontaneous, it does not happen without some prior knowledge. This resonates with the Raging Grannies' emphasis on the importance of the research they do on the various issues they take a stand on. The Grannies take pride in the research they do on issues, which is absolutely necessary to their humorous brand of commentary. Having the facts right is important: "When you make an ass of yourself you have to be serious about it!" says Mary Rose. Betsy Carr agrees: "Grannies don't assume, they make sure of their facts." "There is no point in our going and singing terrific songs when we're talking nonsense or what is half-assed. We HAVE TO KNOW! [Otherwise] people can laugh at you and brush you off, so we have to do our homework," says Alma Norman. It is important to have a serious message to deliver once they have "broken through the ice," says Barbara Calvert Seifred, and adds that they need to back it up with real knowledge of the issues they are targeting. "If this was an organisation that wasn't pretty careful about knowing what we're doing I wouldn't be part of it," says Kathleen Dunphy, a former reporter. "The group in Victoria is very careful…about figures and information so they can't be accused of just blowing off a lot of hot air. So statistics and all that have to be accurate," says Mary Rose. Karyn Woodland reports that "with the help of the Sierra Legal Defence Fund, they unearthed the fact that the province was renting the seabed of Nanoose Bay to the federal government [military base], a fact then-Premier Glen Clark used to his political advantage in the salmon dispute. Citizens research is behind a lot of what we do," says Fran Thoburn.

Invited by the government to attend a conference on health in Ottawa in the early 1990s, Fran thought they made good use of being in the national capital:

> There we were, in Ottawa, lobbying like crazy. We'd just find the dignitaries and tail them. We followed Mulroney into the House of Commons. They wouldn't stop us 'cause it would look really bad if the security guard started wrestling with old ladies.[12]

In an article she wrote, "They're coming," Granny Alison Acker reveals that officials from the Department of Defence admitted that Grannies were accurate with facts and figures. The Sunshine Coast Grannies sang at the Federal Commission on Fisheries:

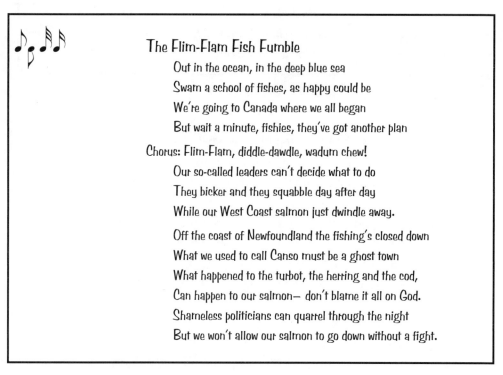

The Flim-Flam Fish Fumble

Out in the ocean, in the deep blue sea
Swam a school of fishes, as happy could be
We're going to Canada where we all began
But wait a minute, fishies, they've got another plan

Chorus: Flim-Flam, diddle-dawdle, wadum chew!
Our so-called leaders can't decide what to do
They bicker and they squabble day after day
While our West Coast salmon just dwindle away.

Off the coast of Newfoundland the fishing's closed down
What we used to call Canso must be a ghost town
What happened to the turbot, the herring and the cod,
Can happen to our salmon— don't blame it all on God.
Shameless politicians can quarrel through the night
But we won't allow our salmon to go down without a fight.

*Tune: Three Little Fishes. Sunshine Coast Raging Grannies. The Granny Grapevine.*

Doing careful research and having their facts right frees them for creativity. Barbara Calvert Seifred says:

> You have to back it up…It has to be based on something real, then you can present it in a humorous way, which will make people laugh until they understand what's underneath it. It's great that we gained respect because they know that we know what we're talking about and we can be as crazy as we want in delivering the message!

Sometimes songs require collaboration. "Once a song starts to take shape it needs a decent critique," says Rose DeShaw (A20). "After a brief heartfelt appreciation," new songs rapidly get "rubbed, chewed, kneaded, and polished into a shape comfortable for the whole group to perform," wrote Margaret Ford in the *Raging Grannies "Carry On" Songbook*. For new songwriters, collective input can be intimidating. Lorna Drew talks about the openness and courage it took initially to submit her songs to the group:

> There is a shyness connected to it too. I'm not afraid to show my songs to our Grannies now, not at all, but I was. Because I didn't know them very well, some I didn't know at all, maybe they wouldn't like it: translation, maybe they won't like me for having written that stupid stuff. But you get used to that. I think that operates with a lot of people, because your words are who you are and if they're rejected that's painful. Especially if you've gone through academia at all and know how it feels to have something you have written, not made fun of but trivialised, maybe not good enough. There's all

this hype about writing, 'the writer, the great writer, the great male writers mostly,' and nothing ever measures up to genius, which tends to be transmitted through the male line, which is all crock. But you know, you internalised that stuff. So when you write, that's precious stuff. I've learned that you can put it out there, it's okay, doesn't have to be great poetry. Not everybody has to like it either. It can be changed, it's not written in the living rock.

This experience is similar to Jane Mackey's first song for the original Raging Grannies.

Then I came up with this song and I was, 'Oh gosh, what will everybody think? And am I being too presumptuous or will they think it's stupid.' Oh, what will they think sort of thing. I actually called Doran and told her, 'I've done a song, what do you think? She thought it was great and she was very supportive and enthusiastic. It wasn't great art but it made the point.

They translated the effects of chemicals on health and environment, the gap left by a media vision of life, the complicity of our consumerism, and society's obsession with appearance that can deeply hurt future generations into a song.

### Polychlorinated Biphenyls

Po-ly-chlor-i-na-ted bi-phe-ee-nals
Will fry your brain and rot your adre-ee-nals.
Concentrating in our fatty ti-ish-ue
It's not a very glamorous i-ish-ue.
But may be if they bury it deeper in the ground,
By the time it kills somebody, we won't be around!
Chlor-o-flour-o-car-bon production
Is causing oZone layer reduction.
When ultraviolet rays have seared us to the bone,
We won't get much relief from using coppertone!

Disposables pursue us no matter where we roam—
Who could contemplate a life devoid of styro-foam?
We all want our comfort and convenience,
Which leaves us sitting squarely right on the fence.
These things are very difficult to believe,
It's not the way that life's portrayed on our TV.
Our kids might all get cancer, and have defective genes,
But they will be the best-dressed mutants that you've ever seen!
Oh! Po-ly-chlor-i-na-ted bi-phe-ee-nals
La la la la, la la la la la la la...

*As a Rap or make up a tune. Victoria Raging Grannies.*

Exposing new songs is a vulnerable moment, but finding support and a receptive group is empowering. Eva Munro in Halifax suggests it is essential for Grannies "to allow your songs to be changed by the group." Betsy Carr adds, "as soon as it clicks, we all know it and then we change our words." That attitude prevails not only within each group but also between groups across the country, and beyond. From the beginning, Grannies freely gave their songs and it has become a principle. They exchange songs through the Internet and each group modifies them to suit their local situations: "There can be no ego involved. Whoever writes a song knows that some words may be changed," said Betty Mardiros. The Edmonton Grannies sent this message through the *Granny Grapevine* (Fall 1996): "We appreciate the generosity in the sharing of these gems and the tolerance of the creations being changed and mucked about to suit our needs." The principle of free exchange is interesting: "Nobody owns Grannies songs. They're in the public domain and there is no author. Anybody can use anybody else's material," says Lorna Drew. Others are more protective and do not like to pass songs to outsiders as they do not want them used for purposes they do not agree with, says Alma Norman. Still, "plural authorship challenges a deep Western identification of any text's order with the intention of a single author"[13] But not all songs are written by Raging Grannies: on Saltspring Island, Raging Grannies

> …have several supportive husbands who may be seen at many of our gigs but one deserves special mention. Andy Gibson has a way with words and a keen sense of humour: Andy doesn't seem to mind if we alter words, rearrange verses or slightly rewrite the songs to fit different occasions. So here is a tip of the hat to Andrew Gibson, writer of subversive, pertinent and very funny songs.[14]

Some songs daringly court controversy. The Halifax Grannies were advised not to sing a song they wrote, "The Crotch Man," at the courthouse. Eva Munro adds: "[It] was pretty daring. As women, we had to make sure that certain people weren't in the audience."

### The Crotch Man

How many times can a man grab a crotch
Before he's committed a crime?
Yes and how many times can a man force a kiss?
Is it crime this time?
How many complainants does it take to make a case
When defendant's a…family man?
These questions, my friends, are not before the courts
But the answer is blowin' in the wind.

We learn as a child "Keep your hands to yourself"
It also applies to a man
Yes and how many girls does it take to complain
When defendant is called a great man?
How many times was it all covered up
Till too many people have lied?

*Tune: Blowing In the Wind. Eva Munro Collection.*

But controversy is also within: "They are still looking for songs they all agree are funny. Humour is not universal, but [thankfully] Grannies don't take themselves seriously," says Dorothy Fletcher. Some are vocal about their opinions:

> I was surprised to see several 'preachy' songs. I would like to see more of the satirical kind. It is tempting to tell the politicians, multinationals, whoever, what they ought to change but we find the satirical the most effective to get people's attention.[15]

Although satirical lyrics are their trademark, a humorous tone is not always appropriate, says Joan Harvey: "There are some subjects that you can never joke about; violence against women is not funny. You can't be flippant about disaster. Some things like that are not funny and there's no joking about them." Phyllis Creighton also believes that:

> There are situations that are intensely sad and you need to sing in that vein, otherwise you can't address that situation. There is a place for a whole range of human emotions [and] you can't write a funny song about some things. When you're confronted with the massive callousness of Mike Harris, the massive brutality of the bombing of Iraq, Afghanistan, you need to be able to play off grief and sorrow too.

She has written a few such songs. One is a passionate appeal for Mordechai Vanunu's freedom, a nuclear whistle-blower and now prisoner of conscience in a jail in Israel for more than a decade:

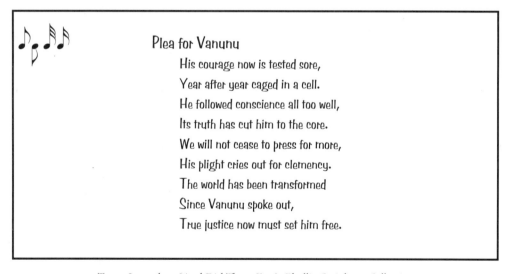

Plea for Vanunu

His courage now is tested sore,
Year after year caged in a cell.
He followed conscience all too well,
Its truth has cut him to the core.
We will not cease to press for more,
His plight cries out for clemency.
The world has been transformed
Since Vanunu spoke out,
True justice now must set him free.

*Tune: Jerusalem (And Did Those Feet). Phyllis Creighton Collection.*

*Phyllis Creighton describes her childhood in Toronto as wealthy, privileged, and difficult. As a student, she was the recipient of the Governor General's Medal and many scholarships. She pursued graduate studies in history in France before moving into ethics and becoming an expert on reproductive technologies. She served for seven years on the Health Canada Advisory Committee on Reproductive and Genetic Technologies. She was awarded the Anglican Award of Merit for her work and dedication to a variety of causes including fighting the reinstatement of capital punishment, reproductive technologies, mental health, peace, and low level flights over the Innu lands. She has been happily married for 47 years, has four children and 6 grandchildren.*

*She is very articulate and has been on numerous boards of directors including Project Ploughshares and Science for Peace. She was one of two Canadian delegates to the Washington hearing of the Independent Commission on Population which culminated in the Cairo Conference. Phyllis worked on the Dictionary of Canadian Biographies and wrote briefs for the Ontario Law Reform Commission. In spite of her high profile and achievements she felt the limited effectiveness of conventional means. She had already started thinking about street theatre: "It's fine and dandy to pass motions in parliamentary bodies, write briefs, write long letters, argue with people but maybe that's not the only way that you build awareness. The problem with the issues has always been how do we get it up front and public, so I saw that as a way to reach out." A deeply spiritual and creative person, she has discovered a passion and talent for song writing. She movingly talked about how love is at the center of her motivation for all the work that she does.*

*Figure 30. Phyllis Creighton.*
*Source: Phyllis Creighton Collection.*

There are other sobering songs about the Gulf War, the Montreal Massacre, and September 11, pieces at times angry and full of rage, at times mournful.

## Montreal Remembered

Where is now their beauty?
Where is now their drive?
All the love they were born with
In the massacre died.
We remember their ventures
Honour their minds and hearts.
We will not forget them,
Fourteen women apart,
We will cherish their memory
Fourteen women apart.

They are not alone,
Women and children die too,
In our land men kill them
By knife and blow and gun.
We remember their beauty,
Lives cut short by hate.
All the love that is in us,
Dedicate to redeem,
Change the hatred and violence
Into love, healing pain.

*Tune: Land of Hope and Glory. Raging Grannies "Carry On" Songbook.*

## Abolition 2000

Must we serve a god of doom,
Born to destroy the web of life?
Must nuclear terror rule the world
— Or will humanity win with grace?

*Tune: Jerusalem (And Did Those Feet). Phyllis Creighton Collection.*

In a song written for a Take Back the Night march, they sang:

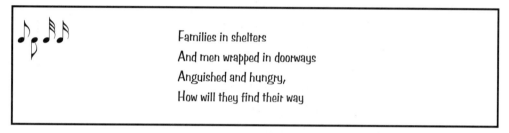

**We'll Walk Down the Streets at Night**

We must take the night into each hand

Embrace it and let it be ours

We've got to become a large band

To fight for the right to see stars!

*Tune: How Much Is That Doggie? Raging Grannies "Carry On" Songbook.*

Some have poetic lyrics. During an election, the Calgary Grannies sang:

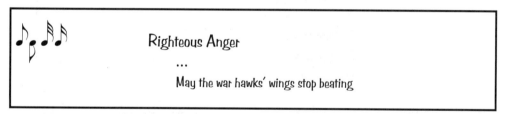

Families in shelters

And men wrapped in doorways

Anguished and hungry,

How will they find their way

*Tune: My Favorite Things. Calgary Raging Grannies.*

**Righteous Anger**

...

May the war hawks' wings stop beating

*Tune: Clementine. Phyllis Creighton Collection.*

The Raging Grannies' songs publicly articulate and collectively express their point of view. They will not be deterred or, as some said, will not shut up. Humour is recognized as a lubricant for smooth social interactions as well as a way to express hostility and aggression, wrote Mahadev Apte. In *Introduction to Satire,* Leonard Feinberg suggests that while institutions are not likely to be influenced by satire, individuals are. Political humour is a way citizens have to counteract "the state's efforts to standardize their thinking and to frighten them into withholding criticism and dissent," says Gregor Benton. Although they often sing to educate, at times their singing becomes an act of protest and resistance. Grannies use their credibility subversively to gain entrance to all kind of places without being noticed, until they get into action. During the U.S.-Canada Free Trade talks, they crashed the Empress Hotel in Victoria to greet the then Federal Minister of Trade, Pat Carney. They lined up and, smiling, she shook their hands as she came by, assuming they were part of a receiving line. But then, they broke into a song written for the occasion:

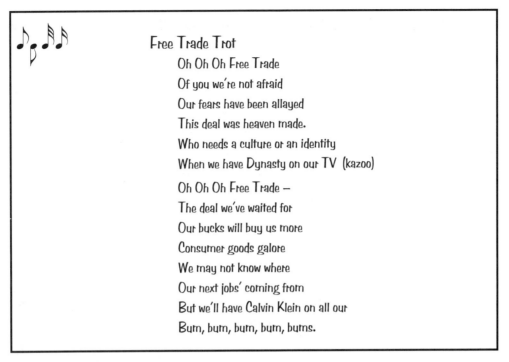

### Free Trade Trot

Oh Oh Oh Free Trade
Of you we're not afraid
Our fears have been allayed
This deal was heaven made.
Who needs a culture or an identity
When we have Dynasty on our TV (kazoo)

Oh Oh Oh Free Trade –
The deal we've waited for
Our bucks will buy us more
Consumer goods galore
We may not know where
Our next jobs' coming from
But we'll have Calvin Klein on all our
Bum, bum, bum, bum, bums.

*Tune: Playmates Come and Play with Me. Victoria Raging Grannies.*

Acidly, Ms. Carney told them, "your singing is a hell of a lot better than your logic," (Stuckey) to the delight of the Grannies who appreciate a good line and like to recount the story as part of their lore.

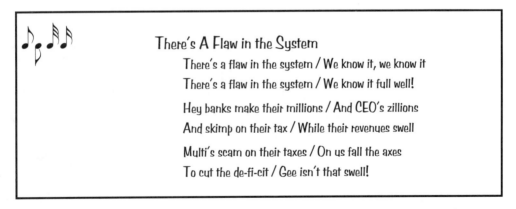

### There's A Flaw in the System

There's a flaw in the system / We know it, we know it
There's a flaw in the system / We know it full well!

Hey banks make their millions / And CEO's zillions
And skimp on their tax / While their revenues swell

Multi's scam on their taxes / On us fall the axes
To cut the de-fi-cit / Gee isn't that swell!

*Tune: There's A Hole In My Bucket. Parliament Hill Mob (Ottawa Raging Grannies).*

*Betty Brightwell, one of the original Grannies, taught, was a private secretary, raised Hereford cattle, and ran an antique business. She got involved after her husband retired from the Department of Defence. "He was certainly dead against it," given the media coverage Grannies got. She believed she came from a "totally respectable family, a belief tempered by the recent discovery that her grandfather had been involved in the 1837 farmers' rebellion." She also thought the government could do no wrong" (in Woodland 82). But when she realised U.S. nuclear warships were visiting the base she looked for emergency plans.*

*When she phoned around the city to the various emergency programs, she was horrified to learn that not only had no one been informed of the nuclear submarine visit, neither was there any clear plan should something go wrong. This was unbelievable, unacceptable, and "outrageous!...What should we [civilians] do if there was a nuclear accident in Esquimalt." [16]*

*But Betty has a keen sense of humour. A year after Grannies publicised their desire to get a Navy of their own, an article, "Stripped, worn warship too messy for Grannies," reported Betty's comment:*

*"The Raging Grannies found it 'too messy' so they won't bid on it for their navy... 'We found it needed a tremendous amount of housecleaning...It was just too dirty for us. It has been stripped and was covered with a lot of bird...and rat dirt. It would need an awful lot of scrubbing, so we decided it would not be satisfactory for us'...She said the Grannies wanted to look at the ship for possible inclusion into its navy now in the making...We have a couple of thousand of dollars and we thought we might put a down payment."[17] When Allan Fotheringham interviewed Grannies on TV, they offered to make him an honorary Granny; when he replied it would require a sex change, Betty told him he could be a granny-in-drag (Gibson B1).*

*Figure 31. Betty Brightwell.
Source: Doran Doyle Collection.*

## Deadly Serious Kazoo Playing Troupe: Singing Warriors Inflict Giggles and Laughter

Humour and unpredictability make for good press. Betty Brightwell sees humour as the successful factor of the Grannies: "There were some very serious subjects that were sort of taboo…to treat them with humour and with silly little old ladies who were fireproof, the combination" was a winning one. Humour is often a sign of rebelliousness; laughter can defeat the fear of the unknown and is related to freedom, says Jo Anna Isaak in her book, *Feminism and Contemporary Art: The Revolutionary Power of Women's Laughter.* Isaak mentions Bakhtin's idea that laughter is not used by authorities or in violent situations, but rather as tools against those. According to Gene Sharp, who wrote *The Methods of Non-Violent Action,* there are times when humour and satire become more than verbal dissent and turn into public acts of protest. While the idea of presenting a broken heart on Valentine's Day was humorous, to present it to an MP because he failed to challenge the presence of nuclear vessels in the harbour was clearly a public act of protest. Isaak suggests that humour can be a metaphor for transformation as well as a communal response of sensuous solidarity as it implies common understanding with others. When the Grannies showed up at the BC Legislative Building carrying a basket full of women's "briefs" to present to the parliamentary hearings on uranium mining, the crowd responded to a common perception of parliamentary hearings of "briefs" as seemingly pompous and pretentious. The same basket of women's briefs would not likely have elicited laughter and cheering from those who supported uranium mining.

From the beginning the Raging Grannies demonstrated a dynamic and humorous imagination. They grasped the educational uses of humour. As Ava Louwe says, "something humorous and satirical has much more punch than something that is serious and analytical." Alma Norman agrees:

> We are more likely to respond to ridicule than to head-on attacks because nobody likes to be laughed at. So if you present something in a satirical way and ridicule…it's easier to get under their skin. Whereas if you come on seriously and you say, 'well, you did this and this and this and this and this,' very analytically, then what you might get is, 'oh yes well, but this is the explanation, and this is the reason, and this is the background.' Then you're into one of these pointless arguments.

Their use of humour has a purpose. "It isn't just for fun," but allows them to "get the point across perhaps a little more gently" as people take it in "a little better than when you just give it to them straight," says Angela Silver. "Humour, there is no doubt about it, is a way to teach," says Muriel Duckworth, a long time adult educator and activist.

Humour is easier for the audience to hear but also provides the Grannies themselves with a way to cope with the situation in the world. Lorna Drew suggests the need for humour is greater in difficult times as well as "in groups from the margin." Humour is "a survival mechanism that helps one handle such exceedingly tragic material. Because it's so depressing…you've got to have black humour to survive the stuff you find out about, really, you've got to laugh at it, the ridiculousness of what's going on," says Fran Thoburn. Dorothy Fletcher agrees: humour "originates in despair," in a search for "ways to deal with the terrible problems of the world." "Most humour comes out of pain…personal pain, group pain," says Rose DeShaw, who thinks laughing is important to prevent the many burnouts she has seen. Humour indicates "an active and assertive orientation… and perhaps an impatience with negative affects such as anxiety and depression," wrote Herbert Lefcourt. Kathleen Dunphy looks to her experience of nursing and sees humour as a resource:

Humour can lighten and make it easier to get through difficult things. Humour is used in medicine to help you through pain. It doesn't lessen the gravity of the situation but it helps you through it, and we all need that. We could be frantic over some things we think are so important, such as what's happening right now with American involvement worldwide. But we have to be able to sort of laugh at them too in a way, make jokes not at the people they're killing but, 'Are they gonna take over us?'…All those kind of jokes, a nervous kind of laughter. We have to have that laughter. You have to have some way of expressing your concern in a way that doesn't devour you and doesn't immobilise you. If you become immobilized, you think what's the point, what good is it, we can't do anything…[But] you can laugh and it lightens you a little, so you say, "okay, I guess I'll go on, I guess I'll do it."

Barbara Calvert Seifred also points to the sustaining power of humour: it is probably "the only thing that keeps you going through bad times." Mary Rose holds a similar view:

Don't you think that sometimes when people are almost hysterical that they laugh instead of cry? I think maybe that's part of it. Because if you thought about some of the things that are going on you'd be weeping all the time, and if you don't relieve it you just can't go on. So you have to break up the tension I guess and laughter does it.

Pearl Rice, who lived in England during World War II had this reflection:

Introducing humour kind of gives a break. You're still giving a message but it' s more fun than being serious all the time…During the war lots of sad things happened during bombings…Quite often during something really serious, something that was getting you down, somebody would make some remark and it might have been silly but it kind of broke things. And you had a laugh and it lightened things up you know, so I think humour is quite important.

Ava Louwe also sees a connection between the challenging times and reactions of most audiences to Grannies' humour: "I think the times are so stressful for people that when they listen to Grannies singing songs of humour it gives them a chance to vent some of their own stress through laughter…It's non-threatening to the audience." But Ava goes further: "Humour," she says, "seems to open avenues of con-nection" with the audience. Humour requires common ground. Joan Harvey suggested that the last six years of massive cuts by the Harris government have provided lots of common ground in Ontario. At times, it is the anticipation of what will happen that makes people laugh. When the first Victoria Grannies stood on the stairs of the BC Legislature ready to go in to present their "briefs," what the crowd reacted to was the anticipation of the surprise, shock, or discomfiture of serious-looking self-important politicians. The laundry basket was pok-ing a hole in the persona of the pompous politician. The fact that the crowd spontaneously laughs together without having to discuss reveals a common understanding of the situation and creates a sense of together-ness. "People will laugh if they're in tune with it, but if they're not in tune they're not going to laugh," says Kathleen Dunphy. Their laughter connects them instantly. Barbara Calvert Seifred agrees: "Humour breaks down barriers…[and] eases the interactions. We're basically preaching in a way, but not in a preachy way…I think they're disarmed a little bit at first, then they understand the message and it's too late." The politicians in the legislature would likely have a different reaction, but at times power is not enough to win the contest of wit. Could one be arrested for laughing? How could they stop a crowd from laughing? Ava Louwe suggests:

Laughter by its very nature changes your perspective on things. It takes you to a higher plane. When you're in a certain frame of mind and something strikes you as funny it automatically opens you up and elevates you and you get a new perspective.

Regina Barreca, professor of Women's Studies at the University of Connecticut, writes on humour and has written almost the same thing: "Not only does humor allow for the elevation and exploration, rather than denigration, of feelings and ideas, at its best it encourages us" to continue fighting against injustice while having fun. She continues:

Humor doesn't dismiss a subject but, rather, often opens that subject up for discussion…Humor can be a shortcut, an eye-opener…to get to the truth of the matter. The best humor allows…for joy, compassion, and a new way of looking at a very old world. Seeing humor as a way of making our feelings and responses available to others without terrifying our listeners can free us to take ourselves less gloomily, although not less seriously…When we can frame a difficult matter with humour, we can often reach someone who would otherwise withdraw.[18]

Opening up subjects for discussions, allowing new perspectives on issues, and freeing themselves from gloom are part of what the Grannies achieve with their songs and actions. They make us see that we can broaden our thinking in ways unexpected, a key to finding solutions as it allows us to state problems anew and perceive connections previously not recognised.

The process by which they come to their ideas is "mysterious" as Joan Harvey calls it. Elinor Egar Reynolds suggests: "You really have to be in groups that are thinking and talking about this…It doesn't just happen with one person…It has to be mulled over and gone through, it's a process." It's not a linear process and it requires "turning things around, looking at things in a different way, turning something to the absurd," suggests Angela Silver. There is an element of spontaneity to that creative process, as Joan Harvey understands it:

A joke happens, very often it's a pun, a wry observation…some people invite jokes. [Mel] Lastman [then Mayor of Toronto] for instance, and some of the statements politicians make are just so absurd that they write them themselves and we just pick up on them. What they do is a joke, or sometimes the things they say are so silly.

Barbara Calvert Seifred agrees: "Politicians write their own satire anyway. They do such outlandish and stupid and ill-advised things." Alma sees potential humour in "Bush being recommended for the Nobel Peace Prize, that's a wonderful beginning for a song, redefining peace!" At times, distance from the event is needed before it can be seen with humour, says Lanie Melamed. Six months after September 11, Eva Munro suggested that:

In the alternative budget, maybe we could do Bush saying, 'Spend, Spend, Spend, Get Out to the Mall and Spend.' That was his cry after September 11, 'Spend, Spend, Spend, Go to the Mall and Travel and Spend.' So I'll have to see if we can work that into a song.

The Raging Grannies understand the role of the unexpected and the element of surprise in humour, a creative act that requires "digging" within one's mind to find an angle, a thread that sheds light on a particular situation says Louise Edith Hébert-Ferron. Humour requires analysis of facts but it also demands new metaphors to reveal new perspectives, different connections between facts. Humour creates an atmosphere of possibility. When people can see an alternative perspective they might also have the creativity to imagine new solutions, go beyond analysis, envision new scenarios and innovate. Grannies, says Alma Norman, take "something serious and turn it around so that people may not laugh uproariously but will giggle or grin or step back and say, 'Right!' "

At times, Grannies struggle with the dilemma of daring and attracting attention, or being appropriate so as not to offend potential supporters. It is a balancing act. Another challenge is the possibility that satirical lyrics can be misunderstood, a fear expressed by Betsy Carr. Jean McLaren warns: "Just have enough, a few lines, then you have to get your point in. If it's completely satirical then people just don't understand, they think you're for it. You have to be careful." After the APEC conference in Vancouver, Lorna Drew wrote a song: To Lorna's surprise somebody actually thought they were against protesters:

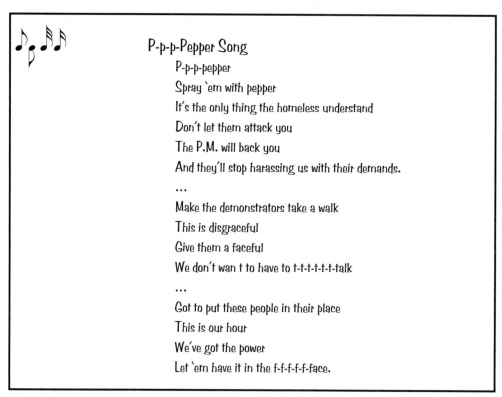

P-p-p-Pepper Song

P-p-p-pepper
Spray 'em with pepper
It's the only thing the homeless understand
Don't let them attack you
The P.M. will back you
And they'll stop harassing us with their demands.

...

Make the demonstrators take a walk
This is disgraceful
Give them a faceful
We don't wan t to have to t-t-t-t-t-t-talk

...

Got to put these people in their place
This is our hour
We've got the power
Let 'em have it in the f-f-f-f-f-face.

*Tune: K-K-K-Katy. Lorna Drew Collection.*

They missed the whole thing. In rehearsal I remember one of the Grannies said, 'what if they don't get it? What if they think that's what we're at?' And I said, 'Nonsense. They'll get it.' But no, you have to be careful with irony. Now wherever we sing that song I usually say: 'This is from the point of view of the government, this is not what we believe.'

Lorna sees the Grannies in a larger context, and as creators themselves of a context that allows humour:

The political meetings are about some hideous happening in the world…landmines or the environment is going. I mean, it's just going worse and worse. I'm not sure we're gonna make it. It's not something you can go to a meeting and start laughing about. You've got to have a context for it and I think the Grannies provide that context. It's black humour and that's an old tradition, gothic tales…it takes the dark side and brings it out, so that you're not repressing all the time, and then makes it funny.

Through the contrast between colourful, outrageous costumes, the biting satire or the humour in songs, and their deadly serious intent, the Grannies manage to captivate the attention as they engage the audience visually, musically, and cognitively. That very contrast between intent and appearance is at the heart of their identity. But that identity has two purposes, education and protest, which will be examined in the next two chapters.

## Notes

1. Rose DeShaw, "Goofy-hatted reconcilers in the land," *The Globe and Mail,* April 10, 1997: A20.

2. Rose DeShaw, *Granny Grapevine* (Kingston), Winter 2001: 27.

3. Sandra McCulloch, "Victoria's Raging Grannies lead the battle against war," *Times Colonist* (Victoria), December 1, 1991: 18.

4. Rose DeShaw, *Granny Grapevine,* (Kingston), Fall 2001: 3.

5. Fran Thoburn, *Granny Grapevine,* Rose DeShaw, ed., (Kingston), Winter 2002: 6.

6. Alison Gardner, "The Grannies are coming, watch out, watch out," *Maturity,* 13(3) 1993: 11.

7. Steven Chase, "Word to the Grandmother," *The Gazette* (University of Western Ontario), December 4, 1991: I, 8.

8. David Dunaway cited in Shelly Romalis, *Pistol Packin' Mama: Aunt Molly Jackson and the Politics of Folklore,* Chicago: University of Illinois Press, 1999: 160.

9. Rose DeShaw, reprint, *Grannie Grapevine,* Fall 1997: 12.

10. Fran Thoburn, personal communication, May 13, 2002.

11. Karyn Woodland, "The Raging Grannies: Tackling serious issues with satire," *Focus on Women,* 11(1) 1998: 84.

12. Woodland, 84.

13. Clifford cited in Margery Wolf, *A Thrice Told Tale: Feminism, Postmodernism, and Ethnographic Responsibility,* Stanford, California: Standford University Press, 1992: 120.

14. *Granny Grapevine,* Summer 1995: 12.

15. Kronseth, *Granny Grapevine,* Fall 2001: 3.

16. Betty Brightwell, "N-Sub visit is spurned," *Esquimalt Star* (Victoria), February 22, 1989.

17. Bill Cleverley, "Stripped, worn warship too messy for Grannies," *Times-Colonist* (Victoria), April 24, 1991: B1.

18. Regina Barreca, ed., *The Penguin Book of Women's Humor,* New York: Penguin Books, 1996: 10.

*Pearl Rice grew up in Scotland, came to Canada as a war bride, and lives in Regina. She is also a war veteran. A past provincial vice-president of Voice of Women, she is a member of the Council of Canadians. She has always been involved in community development, starting public libraries where none existed and workshops for the handicapped that had no access to schooling. She first got involved as a high school student by collecting cans of food for older students who had joined the International Brigade in Spain. During those years, she went out at night with buckets of whitewash and painted slogans in the streets. It was common for people to demonstrate in Britain and she was surprised at the lack of protest in Saskatchewan.*

*During the war, she worked in a protected job, learned a great deal, became a troubleshooter in the factory where she worked, and was later put in charge of purchasing for 70 branches throughout Britain. But when her house was bombed two nights in a row she asked for release so she could join the armed forces and encountered a block: "No, we're not going to release you Pearl." She continues: "They hated people going in late so I started going in ten minutes late. The manager, never said anything, and staff would say, "How are you getting off with this, we get heck for coming in late." So I went in twenty minutes late. When I went to collect my paycheque…[the] manager said, "I know what you're doing, but it won't work." So I started leaving early as well! After some months he finally said: "You're really determined, aren't you?" I said, "yes I am." So he said, "okay we'll give you your release." I guess I was a bad example for the rest of the staff. So I joined the forces and I served on an all-women gun site east of London." Her duties were key to rescuing pilots in distress looking for a landing site or those who fell in the ocean.*

*More recently, Pearl was involved with a group of older women from the Unitarian Church called Raging Chromosomes, later called the Raging Crones, who sang to young women because there had been incidents of young girls being attacked physically and sexually, one of which was murdered. They were partly inspired by hearing about the Victoria Raging Grannies.*

*Figure 32. Pearl Rice.*
*Source: Bonnie Doyle Collection.*

Chapter Three

# CULTIVATING THE SOIL OF CHANGE
## Humorous Education, Singing Support

Social change will not come to us like an avalanche down a mountain.
Social change will come through seeds growing in well-prepared soil and
it is we, like the earthworms, who prepare the soil.       —Ursula Franklin

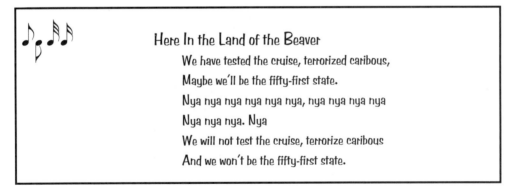

**Here In the Land of the Beaver**
  We have tested the cruise, terrorized caribous,
  Maybe we'll be the fifty-first state.
  Nya nya nya nya nya nya, nya nya nya nya
  Nya nya nya. Nya
  We will not test the cruise, terrorize caribous
  And we won't be the fifty-first state.

*Tune: Original tune—make one up. Brightwell, "I am a Raging Granny."*

## Rebels in Disguise Debunk Myths

Outrageous hats, colourful clothing, cheeky songs, and humour are woven into Grannies' actions to educate on various issues, support other groups, and confront authorities. Like the Love Canal protesters who challenged stereotypes of motherhood through what Temma Kaplan called spirited, dramatic, and colourful actions, the Raging Grannies demonstrate a dynamic imagination for creative, non-violent, and often newsworthy, actions. They engage with a wide array of subjects. While all of their actions and songs have an educational goal, some are more explicitly so, while others are more definitely daring and confronting of authorities and institutions. In this chapter I will focus on their educational use of humour in actions and songs for cultivating the soil for social change. The Grannies disseminate information as well as extend themselves and support groups already involved in a variety of struggles. The Grannies are activists, but they are also educators. Education becomes a political action. They give expression to Freire's words: "Radicalization involves increased commitment to the position one has chosen. It is…critical, loving, humbling, and communicative."

*Figure 33. Victoria Raging Grannies become "beavers" to protect Canada's sovereignty.*
*Source: Doran Doyle Collection.*

## Earth's Beauty Fading: Grannies' Singing Brigade to the Rescue

The initial impetus for the Raging Grannies was the nuclear threat, but since then their range of concerns has expanded considerably. The next major focus to develop was the environment: "We are the Western Nations/ And we don't respect the Land" (*Raging Grannies "Carry On" Songbook*). They translate technical information into songs, as in this short cheer:

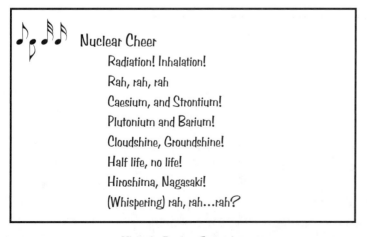

**Nuclear Cheer**

> Radiation! Inhalation!
> Rah, rah, rah
> Caesium, and Strontium!
> Plutonium and Barium!
> Cloudshine, Groundshine!
> Half life, no life!
> Hiroshima, Nagasaki!
> (Whispering) rah, rah…rah?

*Victoria Raging Grannies.*

Whispering a cheer? Irony is conveyed. Whispers denote the secrecy surrounding the visits of U.S. nuclear vessels to Victoria. But other dangers lurk: the Earth's "beauty's beginning to fade…Cause garbage won't fade away" (*Raging Grannies "Carry On" Songbook*).

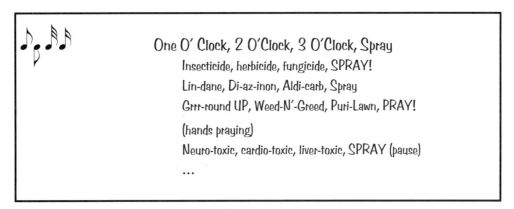

*Tune: One O'Clock, 2 O'Clock, 3 O'Clock, Rock!. Eva Munro Collection.*

Pig genes in the salad and square tomatoes are "re-arranging" and "estranging" (*Raging Grannies "Carry On" Songbook*). Corporations, war, agriculture and science are linked in an unholy alliance:

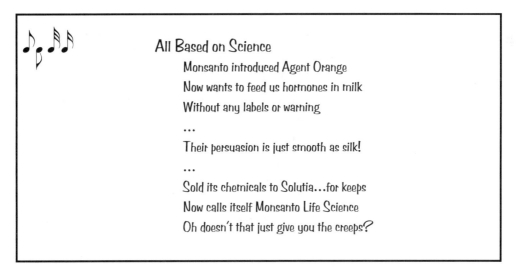

*Tune: My Bonnie Lies Over the Ocean. Barbara Calvert Seifred Collection.*

To raise awareness of genetically modified food, Fran Thoburn tells of the Victoria Grannies' supermarket tour in the *Granny Grapevine*. They picked up items likely to be modified and asked about the products to cashiers who did not know. Yes, probably modified, said the manager. Surprised, the cashiers suggested it should be labelled. "Tough regulations we have for our bridges/And specifications we have for our fridges/But labelling food products—not even smidges" (*Raging Grannies "Carry On" Songbook*).

The Gene Song

Now they're cloning sheep and piggies, And feeding pork to beans

Maybe it's time for grannies, To auction off our genes

Our joints are kinda creaky, Our livers are passé

The rest is kinda leary, But we still got DNA

We're not sure where to find it, But we're told it's quite unique

If genetic pirates want it, They will have to play hide and seek

Better still, let's veto, A science that's not benign

Do they know what they are doing? Remember Frankenstein?

*Tune: No One But a Logger. Alison Acker, Granny Grapevine, Spring 2000.*

They make fun of themselves, but have a definite point of view.

## No Taboo Topics, All Audiences Welcomed, and Plenty of Flair

The Grannies have moved beyond environmental issues to embrace social issues of all kinds. Because of their lively delivery, the Raging Grannies are often invited by universities and colleges to make presentations to students. Humour can enhance education and create openness about topics more difficult to approach:

> Surrounding very serious issues is that high-spirited sarcastic element that makes the Grannies so captivating. You don't often expect a group of elderly ladies in outlandish hats and ruffled aprons to be singing about safe sex, drug addiction, or the bomb. It's their shtick that quite often holds the attention of their audiences.[1]

Grannies have been asked to sing about safe sex and sexuality in later years to first year medical students, to medical professionals in the field of geriatrics, and to nurses. "I'm sixty, and I'm sexy…There is more to aging than getting old!" they sing. The Lethbridge Grannies issued condoms and sang "Safe Sex" at 8 a.m., in a class on the Sociology of Aging, and shook everyone awake!

Safe Sex

Hi Ho, Hi Ho, it's off to bed I go

We grannies smile because we know

Safe sex, it really is the best!

Hi Ho Remember Jill or Joe

AIDS isn't caught by chance, you know

Safe sex is very much the best!!

Hi Ho Life ain't no TV show

To unprotected sex, you say

Oh No, Oh No, Oh No— OH, NO!!!!!

*Tune: Hey Ho! Hey Ho! It's Off to Work We Go! Betty Mardiros and Louise Swift Collection.*

Jean McLaren recalls: "We all wore nightcaps. And when we go to bed we take our condoms…We actually sang to a bunch of nurses in Nanaimo and they just rolled on the floor. These little ladies put on these nightcaps…Yeah the unexpected."

**The Condom Song**

I used to wear a diaphragm,

I used to take the pill,

I smeared myself with every kind

Of contraceptive gel.

But times have changed since then

Old dear, so listen up to me,

It's your turn now for

Reproductive responsibility,

Sooooooo,

You'll wear a condom,

A big rubber condom,

And I'll wear a great big smile,

Cause it ain't gonna hurt ya

To don that gutta percha,

Now that safe sex is in style.

So take it out of your wallet,

Whatever you call it,

And stretch it for a mile,

And put on your condom,

…

*Tune: Where You Wore a Tulip. Vancouver Raging Grannies.*

This song made a strong impression on a journalist from *The Chicago Tribune* who watched their performance and planned to write an article about it, said Dorothy Fletcher. But such a topic is not immune to controversy within Granny groups says Betty Mardiros:

> It is not easy because not everyone has the same sense of humour. I come from Britain and I know there is a difference sometimes in what I think is funny. Others don't think of it that way…We've got several sex songs like "Safe Sex," and some feel it is not something to make fun of. There is some inhibition about that amongst a few Raging Grannies.

They hand out condoms to great laughter. "But it isn't funny," says Dorothy Fletcher, "it's because of AIDS, contraception, and overpopulation."

*Dorothy Fletcher is the archivist for the Toronto group. She came to activism later in life, after retirement. She worked as a museum curator and had no time for activism then. She was not involved in politics—just had an opinion.*

*As a member of Voice of Women and the Unitarian Church, she was aware of issues. Being a Raging Granny is also an expression of her spirituality and her concern for social justice. Contact with so many different groups has been a great learning experience for her. Joining the Grannies has provided relief from "feeling like an invisible woman…Very seldom did anyone ask for my opinion on any social concern. The Raging Grannies welcomed me and gave me the opportunity to spend time with a group of lively women of my own age with similar concerns and a desire to express themselves. Now, when I am introduced I say, "I am one of the Raging Grannies" and immediately there is a smile, a recognition and a statement—"I saw you on TV" or "I think you're great." "Put on a funny hat and you can be 'seen' in public; it's a way to express oneself."*

*Being older means she is not concerned with what others think anymore: "I had not realised how inhibited I was, trying to please husband, children, neighbours. There now have been many experiences that have enriched my life." She finds relief from despair by actively engaging with issues of concerns. One person she admires is Ursula Franklin for, among other things, walking out when the University of Toronto conferred a honorary degree on George Bush.*

*Figure 34. Dorothy Fletcher.*
*Source: Carole Roy.*

Peace issues are still central to the Grannies' actions. They often sing to audiences who share their point of view, but not always. The Edmonton Grannies, who sing "songs of social significance," make an effort to sing to audiences not already converted to Grannies' views. Betty Mardiros told of being invited to sing for women coming to the 50th year world reunion of the RCAF (Royal Canadian Air Force) in the summer of 1999:

> They were from all over…Canada, New Zealand, Australia, U.S., 6,000 of them. So we had to give considerable thought to what we were going to sing and, we had a very good program for them, and it went very well. We got a standing ovation. It went very well, and we were relieved! They gave us a problem because that sort of group you have to think of how you can be persuasive without being provocative and put them off…[But] We don't want to be co-opted; we do not change our songs in any way.

They received warm applause and laughter from the audience, yet,

> There was a slight cooling of enthusiasm when we sang our anti-war songs. But after the perfor-mance a number of the military wives came up to us and quietly said, "It was wonderful to hear these songs against war; when we say that sort of thing to our husbands, they don't seem to get it."[2]

Many women asked for copies of the songs, a receptivity which suggests the Grannies were successful in their choice of program. They did not antagonise a crowd that could have easily been less than open to a Granny view of things. It is their ability to use humour with all kinds of audiences that makes them such welcomed educators. Freire's words come to mind, education is communication, education is dialogue. The Grannies are willing to engage with everyone, and make efforts to reach out with actions which takes courage at times.

*Figure 35. Gaggles gathered at the Un-convention in Kingston, June 2002. Source: Carole Roy.*

*Betty Mardiros is the founder of the first group of Edmonton Grannies. Born in Britain, her father was a coal miner in Wales and used to say, "you have to be a moron not to be a socialist." According to Betty: "[That] certainly wasn't an exaggeration because the oppression, the repression, the conditions that miners faced in those days when they went down the pits often killed them. It was absolutely appalling, so they had to unionise; they had to become active against the system. So I got it through osmosis."*

*She married a professor who taught social philosophy at the university and shared her views: "He wasn't just an academic, he was an activist," says Betty. She was a founder of the Voice of Women in Alberta. In June 1982, Betty went to New York for the demonstration of one million people for nuclear disarmament and peace. She is a strong believer in the educational potential of the Grannies: "We sing songs of social significance…think of how you can be persuasive without being provocative" and put people off. She suggests that "ridicule is quite a good thing as a political strategy."*

*As Raging Grannies, they were part of a large committee fighting the Alberta government cuts to health care, Friends of Medicare, with United Nurses of Alberta and other unions and the churches. Being a Raging Granny does keep them up to date as they "are always on the look out for something of significant concern" to make a song and communicate their concerns. In the end, she sums up their commitment: "This is the reason: the continuity of this planet."*

*Figure 36. Betty Mardiros.*
*Source: Photo Shaughn Butts. The Edmonton Journal.*

## Their Own Christmas Carolling: Challenging and Transforming, Always

Christmas has become a prime time to encourage shoppers to give educational toys rather than toys that normalise war and violence. At times the Grannies' carolling gives rise to unforeseen and unintended but funny consequences. Shelley Mardiros wrote the tale Sylvia Campbell told the Alberta Grannies about the Lethbridge Grannies' attempt to protest war toys on December 7, 1996—a protest that got them banned from the mall:

> The group had gone to the mall to sing songs against war toys when the two young guards rushed over and told them to leave. As the Grannies made their way down the mall toward the exit, they began to sing as they walked, and the security guards promptly decided to detain them…the "keystone cops talking to each other on walkie-talkies from about eight feet apart, while trying to herd six garrulous Grannies through a maze of winding passages in the bowels of the mall to the security office," then noticing that two of the original eight Grannies had "escaped" (having been ahead of the main group and unaware of the "arrest"). The remaining Grannies crowding in and around the tiny office couldn't contain their giggles at the officious puffery of the young guards, who telephoned the police for back-up. When the guard told the desk sergeant that they had the Raging Grannies in custody, the guffaw of laughter coming over the telephone line could be heard across the room. Someone in the mall had taken photographs of the arrested Grannies and alerted the *Lethbridge Herald*, which published the story…CBC picked it up and interviewed the Grannies, who told such an amusing tale…on [the program] As It Happens, broadcasting their campaign against war toys across the country. [They sang:]

GI Joe, GI Joe is back in the stores again
Telling kids that Might is Right, And war is without pain.

*Tune: Jingle Bells. Edmonton Raging Grannies. In S. Mardiros.*

The one year ban was later rescinded by the mall authorities and "full apology and pardon" were offered.[3]

However, the incident was not over for the Parliament Hill Mob as Pat Howard reported:

> We sang right outside Toys 'R' Us but nobody called the cops. Imagine our envy when we heard a Lethbridge Granny's account on "As It Happens" [CBC] about police being called and dire warnings issued to stay away in future. Where did we go wrong? We're dangerous too! Could be the sliding door kept out much of our message from the store itself.[4]

There are many traditional Christmas songs with Granny words. Sometimes the new lyrics offer a response to the original lyrics, as in their version of "God Rest You Merry Gentlemen":

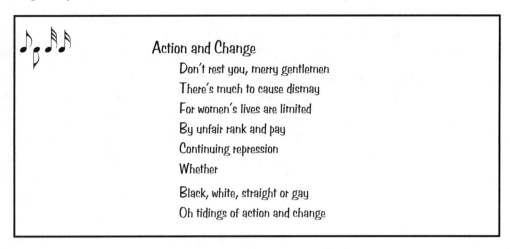

**Action and Change**

Don't rest you, merry gentlemen
There's much to cause dismay
For women's lives are limited
By unfair rank and pay
Continuing repression
Whether
Black, white, straight or gay
Oh tidings of action and change

*Raging Grannies "Carry On" Songbook.*

Christmas' economics of global toy making and the many injustices it generates are examined and the analysis put to "Jingle Bells":

**The Toycott Song**

Jingle bells jingle bells
Lots of toys today
Made by little sweatshop kids
Who never get to play hey!
...Santa's going to be
In western chimneys everywhere
Except where toys are made

Dashing through the malls
In a hurried, merry way

Hearing money fall
Jingling all the way
Far east kids will sweat
Through the night and day
To give us all the toys we want
For which they don't get paid
...

*Phyllis Creighton Collection.*

Now the bells are jingling for the cuts to social services by the Ontario government.

> **Jingo Bells**
>
> Cutting through our dreams
> With their axe and razor blades
> Through our town they go
> Laughing all the way
>
> Banks and brokers sing
> Keeping profits high
> Oh how much they love to push
> The corporate market lie! Eh!
>
> ...
>
> Banks and brokers sing
> Keeping profits high
> Oh how much they love to push
> The corporate market lie! Eh!

*Woodstock Grannies. Raging Grannies "Carry On" Songbook.*

*Figure 37. Grannies join the Ontario Coalition Against Poverty and sing. Source: Dorothy Fletcher Collection.*

## Grocery Lists, Menus and Corporate Agenda: Analysis of Poverty in Songs

One of the Grannies' main concerns is social justice. Granny Sue Davidson-Brouse wrote of the Oxford (Ontario) Raging Grannies' protest against the cuts to welfare benefits. They brought rolls of toilet paper stacked upon silver trays to their MP's office and announced that it was their way of helping out, since Mr. Harris's bottom line did not include money for basic necessities. A letter to be presented with the rolls was sent to alert the Toronto Grannies to the action:

> We can see that our government is having a difficult time making ends meet because your bottom line does not include toilet paper on Mr. Tsubouchi's $92 grocery shopping list. We'd like to help out. We don't have a bankroll, but we do have an extra toilet paper roll we'd like to contribute. We are encouraging others, who share our belief that your government's 'bottom line' on social programs is hurting the people of Ontario, to bring a roll of toilet paper to their MP's office…Let's get this province rolling. Let's use common sense solutions.[5]

Our Favourite Things

Rightsizing, downsizing, rationalizing
Insourcing, outsourcing, pri-vatizing
Dis-entanglement, cutting the strings
These are a few of our favourite things

Off loading, downloading, re-engineering
Divest, restructure, promote volunteering
Tax cuts to fund our friends Florida flings
…
Housing's not part of this government's mandate
Vulnerable people just need a band aid
We won't give handouts, they need a hand up
Let's start by grabbing that fellow's tin cup

Improve education by inventing crises
Can't tell the difference 'tween values and prices
Close down more hospitals, costs are too high
Isn't it cheaper to let people die?

*Tune: Our Favourite Things. Peterborough Raging Grannies.*

For Grannies, exclusive reliance on free market ideology confuses value with price. Bringing moral issues to the level of price results in an orientation away from life: let people die; it is cheaper. The incantation of the "bottom line" as justification for decisions hides more than it reveals of the working of the market, which is supposed to exercise more fairness than human beings. The Ontario government's economic language is corporate and reveals another set of values. But some things do not have a price, according to Grannies:

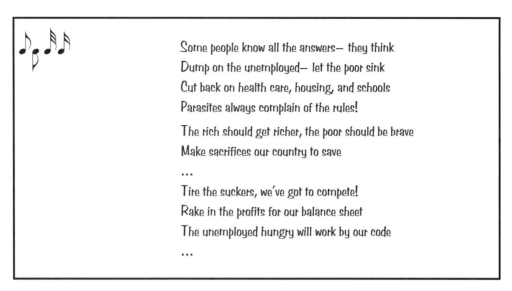

Some people know all the answers— they think
Dump on the unemployed— let the poor sink
Cut back on health care, housing, and schools
Parasites always complain of the rules!

The rich should get richer, the poor should be brave
Make sacrifices our country to save
...
Tire the suckers, we've got to compete!
Rake in the profits for our balance sheet
The unemployed hungry will work by our code
...

*Tune: Lavender's Blue, Dilly, Dilly. Parliament Hill Mob (Ottawa Grannies).*

The Grannies identify a problem with the corporate sector's power to set the agenda. "Old MacDonald's Farm" has new lyrics, and Grannies wear pig snouts:

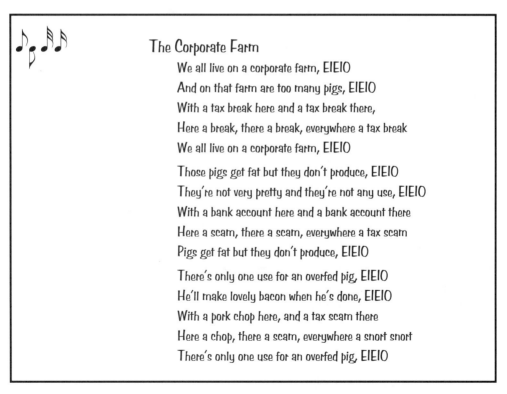

**The Corporate Farm**

We all live on a corporate farm, EIEIO
And on that farm are too many pigs, EIEIO
With a tax break here and a tax break there,
Here a break, there a break, everywhere a tax break
We all live on a corporate farm, EIEIO

Those pigs get fat but they don't produce, EIEIO
They're not very pretty and they're not any use, EIEIO
With a bank account here and a bank account there
Here a scam, there a scam, everywhere a tax scam
Pigs get fat but they don't produce, EIEIO

There's only one use for an overfed pig, EIEIO
He'll make lovely bacon when he's done, EIEIO
With a pork chop here, and a tax scam there
Here a chop, there a scam, everywhere a snort snort
There's only one use for an overfed pig, EIEIO

*Tune: Old MacDonald's Farm. Victoria Raging Grannies.*

During the Ontario provincial elections, Kingston Grannies were annoyed that the government used tax money for their ads. So they wrote new lyrics to a 1930's depression-era song, but the bluebird on the windowsill morphed into a vulture:

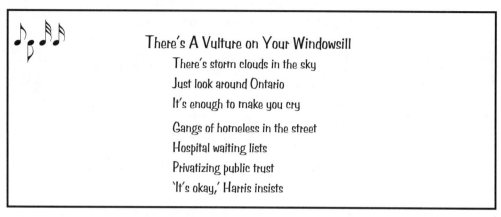

### There's A Vulture on Your Windowsill

There's storm clouds in the sky

Just look around Ontario

It's enough to make you cry

Gangs of homeless in the street

Hospital waiting lists

Privatizing public trust

'It's okay,' Harris insists

*Tune: There's A Blue Bird on Your Windowsill. Rose DeShaw Collection.*

Human agency, not natural processes, is responsible for poverty, according to the Grannies, especially bureaucrats who do not think critically but follow orders. Those running the deep cuts for the Ontario government are said to have:

### Little Tiny Brains

Little tiny brains

That we have in government

They wobble to and fro

Where 'ever they're sent

When they cut us back

They are showing their

Little tiny brains

*Tune: Do Your Ears Hang Low? Kingston Raging Grannies.*

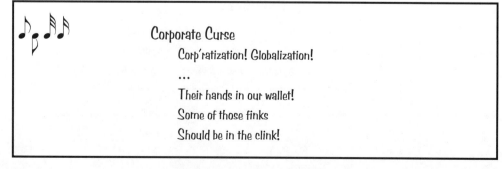

### Corporate Curse

Corp'ratization! Globalization!

...

Their hands in our wallet!

Some of those finks

Should be in the clink!

*Tune: Frère Jacques. Barbara Calvert Seifred Collection.*

As is obvious, Grannies don't mince words. Governments are quick to extend their hand and rescue large wealthy corporations but quickly disregard the effects of their actions on the most vulnerable. The misguided policies result in unnecessary misery and hardships.

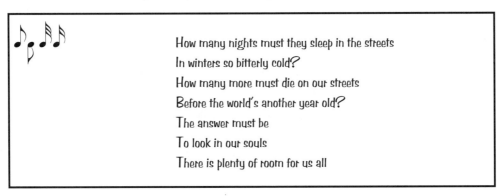

How many nights must they sleep in the streets
In winters so bitterly cold?
How many more must die on our streets
Before the world's another year old?
The answer must be
To look in our souls
There is plenty of room for us all

*Tune: Blowing in the Wind. Toronto Raging Grannies.*

Suggestions made by government officials about how to cope with the consequences of their cuts are, at times, impractical and lacking in compassion. For example, a direct outcome of the cuts by David Tsubouchi, Minister of Social Services in the Ontario government, is a new, mean, and lean cuisine.

### Lean Cuisine, Mean Cuisine

Tsubouchi is planning a menu
For 69 cents a great deal
Find tuna all dented and marked down
Or just say,
"Clerk, Let's make a deal!"

Chorus: Lean cuisine, mean cuisine
It all smells so fishy to me, to me
Lean cuisine, mean cuisine
It all smells so fishy to me

Palladini heads public transport
For the disabled he has a scheme
Take a hike, ride a bike, hitchhike
He yells from his long limousine

Mike Harris as master chef
With Robin Hood he never would bake
The poor and the old folk get dry bread
To the rich he will give the cake.

*Tune: My Bonnie Lies Over the Ocean. In "Tuna protest."*

In the early days, the Victoria Grannies also wrote about poverty:

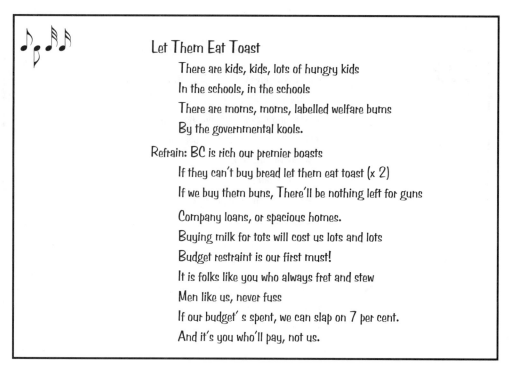

**Let Them Eat Toast**

There are kids, kids, lots of hungry kids

In the schools, in the schools

There are moms, moms, labelled welfare bums

By the governmental kools.

Refrain: BC is rich our premier boasts

If they can't buy bread let them eat toast (x 2)

If we buy them buns, There'll be nothing left for guns

Company loans, or spacious homes.

Buying milk for tots will cost us lots and lots

Budget restraint is our first must!

It is folks like you who always fret and stew

Men like us, never fuss

If our budget' s spent, we can slap on 7 per cent.

And it's you who'll pay, not us.

*Tune: Quartermasters' Store. Victoria Raging Grannies.*

Some songs use a maternalist discourse as a tool of resistance says Shelly Romalis (1999). Women are especially sensitive to food given they often take care of the health and nutrition of their families. Leaders are questioned for their convenient omissions and their definition of what being a rich province means. On the International Day for the Eradication of Poverty in 1996, the Ottawa Grannies sang in front of large banks:

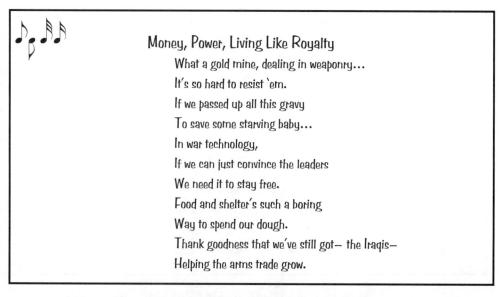

**Money, Power, Living Like Royalty**

What a gold mine, dealing in weaponry...

It's so hard to resist 'em.

If we passed up all this gravy

To save some starving baby...

In war technology,

If we can just convince the leaders

We need it to stay free.

Food and shelter's such a boring

Way to spend our dough.

Thank goodness that we've still got— the Iraqis—

Helping the arms trade grow.

*Tune: A Bicycle Built For Two. Victoria Raging Grannies.*

> ♪♪ ♪♪
>
> ## Poverty is Great
>
> O poverty is really great, our numbers grow and grow
> And it's a corporation's fate to profit don't you know
> So as we struggle and make do with used and second-hand
> We sympathize with millionaires
> Gross spending must be planned
>
> They struggle with their profit shares
> And bank / stock reports and so
> They don't get stuck with too much tax,
> That's such an unfair blow
> We're lucky that we only need to worry 'bout the rent
> We laugh our way to the food bank,
> Our lives are heaven-sent

*Tune: Auld Lang Syne. Parliament Hill Mob (Ottawa Raging Grannies).*

Poverty and injustice do not stop at the border. Grannies are concerned about global issues, including exploitative working conditions around the world. The Montreal Grannies are regularly invited to CEGEP Vanier, and other institutions, to make students aware of various issues. In the fall 2001 I assisted at the fashion show, borrowed from Project Ploughshares Maquiladora project, which they presented to students in social work. Each Granny dressed with a piece of clothing made under sweatshop conditions and sold by a well-known corporation. One after the other, Grannies twirled and posed on stage, some with walking canes, making a parody of parading and being "fashion models." Two commentaries were read, one giving information on the particular corporation, their location, profits, and executives' salaries while the other listed the horrific working conditions in which the clothes were made, the meagre wages and lack of decent working conditions. The audience, some wearing the trendy clothing sported across the stage, learned of clothes made in Toronto by workers paid 65% of the minimum wage. In El Salvador, workers get $0.15 U.S. per pair of pants that sells for $16.96 U.S., are forced to work 11 hours a day six days a week, and women are obliged to take pregnancy tests and are fired if they test positive. In Myanmar, clothes are produced under ruthless military rulers who use sweatshops to finance their repression. In Indonesia, women workers make $35 to $42 per month, not enough to cover basic necessities. In California and Mexico, there is evidence of forced labour, child labour, and unsafe working conditions. In Guatemala, the wealthy owner closed the only unionised factory with a collective agreement the day before Christmas.

Their fashion show was very effective. The expressions on students' faces were in turn shock at the information and delight at the humour Grannies can rescue from even such terrible subjects. At the end, the Grannies did not suggest a boycott, which should be initiated only by the workers affected, but asked students to be aware of the issues and support the efforts of workers all over the world to improve working conditions. They certainly held the attention of the audience as no one could predict what they would do or say. In this case they made use of something developed by someone else, yet the way they made people laugh was very much their own style. The Grannies constantly balanced on the edge between being funny and irreverent, and getting a serious message across. They had a song fitting the occasion.

> ♪♪ ♫♫  **Walking Billboards**
>
>    Don't be a sucker, don't be a label, Or a walking billboard for a clothing line
>    Just be your own self, be independent, Don't be conformist, it's a bind!
>
>    Clothes made in sweatshops and they ain't pet shops!
>    A leap backward to time gone by,
>    They're simply debt shops with workers under locks,
>    Time to kiss those brands goodbye!...
>    With your unmarked sneakers y' can kick the habit!
>    And let your own personality shine!

*Tune: You Are My Sunshine. Barbara Calvert Seifred Collection.*

In this age of mass media, corporations need the support of public relations firms to spin the news surrounding particular events to control the damage that might threaten corporate image and profitability. In a way that keeps up with the times, the Grannies make sure the complicity of public relations firms is raised.

> ♪♪ ♫♫  **Burson Marsteller Rap**
>
>    When gas kills thousands / in Bhopal
>    Who do you call? Burson Marsteller
>    When Exxon oil / spills from Valdez
>    Who do you call? Burson Marsteller!
>    ...
>    It's nice to know / when disaster strikes
>    There's someone to turn to / to make it look right
>    Damage control / is their game
>    Burson Marsteller is their name
>    ...
>    The Chiapas revolt / came as no surprise
>    Their crops and farms / were to meet their demise
>    The free trade agreement / so carefully managed
>    Gave comfort and aid / to the powers that damaged
>    ...
>    Now, who do you guess / for a fee of 8 million
>    Was hired to quell / news of rebellion?
>    Burson Marsteller / that king of spin doctors
>    Made Mexico look / like a garden of flowers
>    ...
>    The forest industry / and Vancouver Sun
>    Use this firm / when they're on the run
>    When they need to fake it / for whom do they holler?

*As a Rap or make up a tune. Vancouver Raging Grannies.*

## Cultivating the Soil of Social Change: Singing Support

> My heart is moved by all I cannot save:
>> so much has been destroyed
> I have cast my lot with those
>> who age after age, perversely,
> with no extraordinary power,
>> reconstitute the world.
>
> —Adrienne Rich[6]

Many groups of Grannies seek to support groups already involved in various struggles and working on environmental, peace, women, human rights, or social justice issues. Muriel Duckworth, a long time activist and adult educator, is very clear that supporting other groups is fundamental to her vision of the Raging Grannies:

> Being ready to support causes openly on the streets and getting attention on the media. You know, the Raging Grannies get a lot of attention. You go out to shopping centres or you go out to the streets or you go to where something is happening…We spoke to the annual meeting of social workers, and you might wonder why we do speak to an annual meeting of social workers? Because…they asked us to and they don't get a lot of real solid support from people who really believe in what they're doing. They don't get the attention they deserve for what they're doing. So to go and sing to social workers was good for us, and you could tell by the expressions on their faces as you're singing that it means something to them, and we're not good singers! (laughs) Nobody listens to us for our music, but I think it's a question of conviction and commitment…When the CBC staff was on strike we went on the street corners with them. When miners came in from Cape Breton we were on street corners with them.

Grannies find ways to express support appropriate to each group and situation. At times, says Muriel, they even choose silence:

> Lately we're doing silent vigils because they're lots of words being thrown at people…Silence, especially when they began bombing Afghanistan, it was really important to have those silent vigils. And then there was a coalition, which did things on the streets but that faded. But the Voice of Women and the Raging Grannies go on forever!

But the Halifax group is not always silent. They showed up to support people who asked them to sing at the meeting with bank managers coming to announce the closing of their bank. Eva Munro recalls,

> Someone was smart enough to say, "Dorothy, you grab the microphone first after the big wigs finish speaking their spiel about how convenient these machines are going to be; just get your card and we'll show you how to use it, and you won't have to do anything but use your card." So Dorothy got up to the mike and said, "I live in this area and I have something to say about moving the bank, and I brought some friends to help me say it." So we jumped up, sang our song, quite a few of us, and poor bank fellows, all men, in their nice suits and ties didn't know quite what to make of it in front of this huge crowd of people. They said, "well, I guess they said everything you people want to say." [But people] jumped up and down in front of all the microphones. Afterwards the social worker that works there laughed…She was quite happy we jump-started the meeting.

Such appearances loosen up people so that they can say what is on their minds. This reveals the ability Grannies have to strategize from experiential knowledge. To bank managers they sang:

**Dear Bank**

Chorus: My eyes are not dim, I now can see
I know something about the economy
I know something about the econ-o-my

1. There are suits, suits, exploiting the grassroots in the world, in the world…

2. We have poor, poor, who have a sad future in the world, in the world…

3. There are corporate forces, plundering resources in the world, in the world…

4. They invest, invest, and democracy divest in the world, in the world…

5. We want work, work, lots of full-time work, in the world, in the world…

6. Countries can't get out of foreign debt in the world, in the world…

7. We pay tax, tax, while the rich relax in the world, in the world…

8. We have choice, choice to change, we have a voice in the world, in the world

*Tune: Quartermasters' Store. Eva Munro Collection.*

*Figure 38. Halifax Raging Grannies. Source: Eva Munro Collection.*

*How does one write about a woman with more than six decades of activism? Ninety-three-year -old Muriel Duckworth founded the Halifax Raging Grannies six years ago! She is an inspiration to many and has become a national institution. A Quaker, she has been working for peace through many organizations and was a member of the Voice of Women since its inception. In a video,* The First Thirty Years of the Voice of Women, *she is brilliantly pointing out the gender barrier of a panel with twelve men and no women. Yet she recalls her first action with Voice of Women: "The first time I went on the streets I could hardly stand it. It was in the very early days of Voice of Women, the early 60s, and we decided to have a national street action. We had little umbrellas [used in children's birthday parties] and attached little tags…that the nuclear umbrella will be no more use to you than this… We did it on one of the main streets in Halifax—and I can't believe this now—but when I saw a woman that I knew I crossed the street rather than face her and give her the umbrella. I'd rather give it to someone I didn't know!"*

*Muriel is "an extraordinary woman who thinks she is an ordinary woman" (Borden). She founded seventeen provincial and national organizations, was active on the national board of OXFAM, participated in a Central American Mission for Peace organized by NGOs in 1985, received the Order of Canada in 1983 as well as the UN Association of Canada's Pearson Peace Medal in 1991. She was granted eight honorary doctorates from universities across Canada and was featured in a 1985 NFB film called* Speaking Our Peace. *She is now very concerned, amongst other things, about the U.S. government's assertion that they have the right to arm outer space.*

*Figure 39. Muriel Duckworth.*
*Source: Eva Munro Collection.*

♪ ♪♪♪

**Person's Day**

In 1928 Canadian persons all were men

Their wives were their possessions

...

They couldn't vote, own property

Their lives, their husbands ran

Till five brave women saw they'd better

Take this thing in hand

Chorus: Irene Par-l-by, Henriette Muir Edwards,

Louise Mc-Kinney, Emily Mur-r-phy

And there was Nel-lie McClung

Names that should be sung

We owe our personhood

To what these five have done

In 1929 they went to England where they asked

Privy council to ensure a law would soon be passed

In legal language making women persons with all rights

...

What are we doing with the rights

For which they fought and won?

...

Do we stand up strong and

Speak our minds when trouble's on the way?

I'd like to think their work was not in vain today

*Tune: Open Up Your Heart. Kingston Raging Grannies.*

Grannies remind us of historical struggles and honour those who worked for justice in the past. The Regina Grannies pay special attention to women's issues, so when local librarians went on strike the Grannies went out to support them. Most librarians being women, the Grannies saw this as an equity issue. In Lethbridge, Grannies picketed and sang with childcare workers who "walked out with paper bags over their heads and blank signs, afraid for their jobs." A fear well justified: "The media discovered child welfare supervisors, hidden in a parkade across the street, noting names" (*Granny Grapevine* February 1998). On such occasions, there is a sense of safety in numbers; people are strengthened by a show of support from others.

The Toronto Grannies participated in a fund raising event organised by Polish Gays and Lesbians for children with HIV/AIDS in Poland. Dorothy Fletcher, one of the Grannies in attendance that night, recalled the warmth of people welcoming them as well as the drag queens and other "strange performers." The irony of a bunch of Granny types who don't like smoky environments in the seedy side of town late at night is a measure of their commitment. The ex-mayor of Toronto was there and talked about the importance for other groups in the community to offer recognition, like the Grannies were doing. There was an enormous crowd who warmly applauded. Dorothy adds, "We were pretty tame really—no safe sex song!" Betsy Carr recalled the evening as quite an adventure. But she was surprised at the reactions of people who were quite puzzled that the Grannies would accept such an invitation: "Well! The Grannies can be a bit offbeat but this was really beyond belief!" according to some. In spite of these reactions, she went downtown at night to the bar and found it "quite an education." Kathleen Dunphy was also part of the group at that event and wrote: "It was a grand night and we were received like Royalty. I was met by a huge drag queen as I went in, who said, 'Oh, here's another Raging Granny.' 'Not at all,' I said, 'I'm a drag queen!' For Kathleen the evening was especially important:

> I worked in Casey House [for AIDS patients in Toronto] so I was back to my old stomping ground. We were glad to do it. We sat at the bar and many came and talked to us and I really liked that. They were really interested in what we were doing. And I thought, I hope they remember this when they're seventy because they fought many battles already and I hope that they remember too that they can keep on and can find people to do it with them. I honestly think that will probably be our biggest contribution.

And, being asked to participate was meaningful:

> The mere fact these groups will call and say, "We're having a rally will you join us? Will you do that?" You know, you sit there and you call the groups that you feel care about things…You recognise people who are fighting the same battle and you're always so happy, "Oh there's somebody who cares."

Being asked was recognition for the Grannies, and by participating they offered recognition back.

*Kathleen Dunphy lives in Toronto. In earlier years, she worked as a reporter and at times as an ESL teacher. The mother of nine children, she is full of energy and wit. At fifty-five she "was a geriatric nursing student." She then worked in psychiatric nursing, was on the board of a house for hard to house HIV street people, and worked at Casey House Palliative Care for AIDS until she was 71—"and they made me quit!"*

*A life long activist, she feels that "if you have a family, you have a commitment to the community and to your children and to schools and the neighbourhood and the town and the world." She and her family were picketing grocery stores in Toronto during the California farm workers' grape boycott in the 1970s. Over the years she saw the Raging Grannies at many of the events she attended: "I always had in mind that I'll get hold of them one of these days, and I did."*

*She raises the issue of diversity within the Grannies: "We're seen as white Anglo-Saxon middle class women, which we are. People see us for what we are...I just sort of brought it up several times and others talked about it...The women in the Black, East Indian, Pakistani, or Sri Lankan communities...often they're people who are activists. There's sure plenty to do without getting out singing silly songs...And their time is well taken up in this society, existing and making a life for themselves and their families...I suspect they're busy women."*

*In this photograph, Kathleen looks meek, which to anyone who knows her is a huge surprise: she is anything but meek. Maybe it is her hat—borrowed from the kettle—that disguises her strong and vibrant personality.*

*Figure 40. Kathleen Dunphy.*
*Source: Carole Roy.*

In Fredericton, Lorna Drew remembers the Grannies' "Closets-are-for-Brooms" protest:

Our mayor refused to have a gay pride day and some friends in the lesbian community were protesting [so] we went out and sang in front of city hall. We were joined by the mayor, whose picture appeared in the paper with us singing, but he was clearly abashed and dismayed by the notion that we would actually do this. We had people on the streets clapping, which really "skewered" the mayor and his homophobic attitude…We checked it out with them [gays and lesbians] first before we got them in any more trouble. They were just delighted…We had some people shouting obscenities at us and many…clapping and delighted…I was terrified. I remember walking around city hall and coming out on the public square and singing and having people there who actually approved of what we were doing, because we didn't know if they would. A couple of years after that there was a gay bashing, and we went out downtown at night as part of a larger protest group. We marched through the bars, singing, handing out leaflets…to combat homophobia.

Their public advocacy offered support and legitimised the issue. Letters to editors on their action and on homophobia kept the issue alive. Shortly after that Lorna Drew got a phone call:

I got a call from somebody…who couldn't tell me her name but who just wanted to thank me. I was so moved by it. She seemed to be in fear and trembling while she spoke with me on the phone. Wherever she was and whoever she was, she was scared to death. Maybe we can help people to not be so afraid, to let them know that there's a possibility for change and people are working at it.

*Figure 41. Supporting Gays and Lesbians. The Raging Grannies sang and marched on city hall in Fredericton, N.B. in support of gay and lesbian rights. Mayor Brad Woodside has refused the gays and lesbians the right to have their parade in the city for the past decade. Source: CP Photo/ Fredericton Daily Gleaner/Bob Wilson, 1998: July 8.*

*Lorna Drew, a former nurse and now university professor of English, lives in Fredericton. She has been an activist for years. In the 1970s, she started one of the first women's groups in Montreal. In Fredericton she worked with immigrant women.*

*Figure 42. Lorna Drew and her mother, Mabel Drew, one of two mother-daughter Grannies. Source: Rose DeShaw Collection.*

*Feminism is key to her vision of the world. Talking about the Grannies, she says: "Old women are invisible in this culture and I thought it was such a great idea to be in the face of citizens who thought we weren't there, and so what we do is to be old over the top, old with a vengeance. We still have the vote, we ought to count for something! Part of the Granny mandate I think is to say, 'Okay, yeah, I'm old and I can do this.' If we can do it, then there's hope." The Grannies have a good time being activists and it's a break from political meetings, which tend to be arduous as they deal with difficult issues.*

*Among other things, she has "developed a high bullshit meter," something quite useful for a Raging Grannies as they sort out facts from fiction. To be the wise fool means taking risks, taking the risk of being vulnerable, says Lorna.*

The use of humour has numerous benefits, including enhancement of learning. Some studies found that humour provides greater co-ordination between right and left brain hemispheres; laughing "stimulates both sides of the brain simultaneously...producing a unique level of consciousness and a high mode of brain processing," (Harvey 1998: 58), which would enhance learning. It is clear that the Grannies' ability to produce humour makes it easier for listeners to be open to new information. Humour is known to help release tension when people experience fear, anxiety, sadness, or anger, suggests Linda Harvey, and, at times, it can break through grief and despair, wrote Herbert Lefcourt. It helps prevent our being overwhelmed by stress. Humour also improves creativity, says Harvey.

Lefcourt identifies another characteristic of humour that bears directly on the work of the Raging Grannies: its ability to help "create feelings of community and closeness" (2001: vi). Humour has "the power to unite people so that they do not feel isolated and forgotten" (2001: 139), promoting greater group cohesion which fosters flexibility. When people laugh together it indicates that they "share common views without having to discuss it," which is especially important when dealing with uncomfortable or controversial topics, says Linda Harvey (1998: 68). As Henri Bergson wrote, "laughter appears to stand in need of an echo...Our laughter is always the laughter of a group" (in Morreall 1987:119). This dimension is especially important when people try to build movements for social change.

As much as laughter forms a bond, it also draws a line, suggests Lorenz (1987: 254). This dual capacity of humour makes it an excellent tool for the Grannies' dual purpose of education and protest. Historically, wit has been used as "an effective tool for explaining ideas and an effective weapon for attacking opponents" wrote Leon Harris (1966: 14). This dual possibility in the use of humour results in Grannies' ability to generate a sense of togetherness while also remaining critical of authorities. Humour is participatory and represents freedom: no one can force another to laugh suggests Kazlitt (in Morreall 1987: 70). The audience needs to use critical faculties to decipher and decode the message as it relies on the unexpected; this also creates curiosity and interest. Contrary to rites, which seek to order collective life in predictable patterns, Mary Douglas thinks "humour disorganizes...[and] destroys hierarchy and order...Joking does not affirm dominant values, but denigrates and devalues them" (in Mulkay 1988: 154). In *Laughing Feminism,* Audrey Bilger suggests that while "radicalism is not inherent in comic expression...comedy can serve as an excellent vehicle for making radical ideas palatable to an audience that might otherwise be offended by them" (1998: 9). Michael Milkay suggests that "humour can be used to challenge the existing pattern, as we saw in the case of the women's movement—but only when it is given meaning in relation to criticism and confrontation that is already under way within the serious realm" (1987: 177).

In the case of the Raging Grannies, the peace, environmental, women, and social justice movements provide the context of meaning in which their humour is embedded and given meaning. The effectiveness of humour and satire was recognised by the Roman Emperor Augustus, who "passed a law against satires and lampoons, the punishment for offenders being death by whipping," wrote Elliott (in Feinberg 1967: 259).

The humorous actions and songs such as the Grannies produce require what John Morreall calls "conceptual flexibility, an imaginative use of unusual perspectives" (1987: 2), an ability to look at things in new ways and shift mental gears. Morreall also associates "tolerance for disorder and ambiguity, acceptance of the unfamiliar, critical thinking" as part of that flexibility (in Lefcourt 2001: 73). Such mental flexibility allows the Grannies to constantly come up with interesting ways to communicate their message. Humour is memorable. Lefcourt, a professor who has developed a course on humour, noticed that "many students could recall these [humorous] events in minute details despite the length of time that had elapsed since their occurrence" (2001: 15). Humour production suggests an active stance: humor is rebellious; not resigned…it is rebellious, and contains a liberating element, according to Freud. But the essence of true humour is not contempt; it is love, says Richter (in Greig 1969: 252). Humour can often defeat obstacles better and more forcefully than can serious words, says Morreall. Like poetry, wit can sometimes go to "the heart of the matter and concisely present real issues," says Harris (1996: 15). While serious discourse tries to eliminate "ambiguity, inconsistency, contradiction and interpretative diversity," these are essential to the humorous mode and its reliance on what Michael Mulkay calls "opposing interpretative possibilities" (1988: 26). Arthur Koestler defined humour as the result of juxtaposition of self-consistent but usually "incompatible frames of reference" (Mulkay 1988: 26-27). But it requires risk taking, the risk of rejection or of looking foolish, says Linda Harvey.

Interestingly, some literature makes a link between humour, aging, and gender: while men use humour less as they age, women use it more, and the humour used by women appears to be more conducive to social cohesion than humour shared by men, wrote Lefcourt. Humour requires "doubleness of vision" (Greig), which may be a reason why women increase their use of it as they age: how can one survive in a patriarchal system without doubleness of vision? In the last three decades there has been a "significant emergence of female humorists…in parallel with the women's movement in western advanced industrial societies" (Powell and Paton 1988: xx). The Grannies are one expression of this development. Interestingly, "elderly women's relative freedom of speech and behavior has been noted in many ethnographies" (Apte 1985: 79). Acting together, they chart new paths of political expression: "When women act collectively, many of the behavioral constraints that they must observe as individuals are disregarded" (Apte 1985: 78). Their challenge of norms encourages the audience to rethink conventions. The Raging Grannies are providing us with an example of the educational power of humour in movements for social change. At the same time, they reflect the learning that can happen for those actively involved in social movements. The Raging Grannies are educators and activists who have developed a particular approach that is both education and resistance. With wit and humour they transform our understanding of many serious issues, empowering people to think critically about what is happening and providing us with moments of mirth as we discover the latest Grannies' mischief. Unfortunately, humour "has only recently come to be regarded as a legitimate topic of interest," says Lefcourt. Clear-eyed, sharp tongued Grannies understand that "a straw thrown up into the air will show how the wind sits, which cannot be learned by casting up a stone" (Selden in Harris 1966: 13).

## Notes

1. Laurie Graham, "Grannies rage on," *The Gateway* (University of Alberta), December 1, 1998.
2. Betty Mardiros cited in Shelley Mardiros, "Raging gracefully," *Alberta Views,* January/February 3(1), 2000: 28.
3. *Granny Grapevine,* February 1997: 5.
4. *Grannie Grapevine,* February 1997: 18.
5. Oxford Raging Grannies, Letter, October 30, 1995, Dorothy Fletcher Collection.
6. Adrienne Rich, "Natural resources," *The Dream of a Common Language: Poems, 1974-77.* New York: Norton: 67.

# Chapter Four

# SPEAKING TRUTH TO POWER
## Pesky, Mouthy, Old Wrinkled Danger

 Grandmothers' Squawk

The Raging Grannies squawk
And do much more than talk
'Cause there's so much work to be done
There's the question of peace
While weapons sales increase
And foreign aid keeps you going

Our leaders of course
Show no shame or remorse
Supporting the slaughter called war
So we'll bitch, rage, and roar even more
Till we change our country's course

They say hi-tech war is good for trade
But notice how craftily
They chop and slash from our social economy

Education and health
Now get less of our wealth
Hungry kids are a bloody shame
...
Let's all rock the ship of state
Together we can channel our rage

The poor always pay
Politicians increase their own wage
They must clean up their act
Or we'll give them all the sack
We must be very much on our guard
While we bitch, rage and roar even more
Peace and justice shall be our reward

*Tune: Grandfather's Clock. Toronto Raging Grannies adapted by Edmonton Raging Grannies. Granny Grapevine, Summer 1996.*

*Figure 43. Rose DeShaw with one of her creative props.*
*Grannies' Un-Convention, Kingston. Source: Carole Roy.*

## A Persistent Nuisance: No Protection, Even for the Military

*Figure 44. Grannies ride in style on their way to the naval base.*
*Source: Doran Doyle Collection*

Saturday afternoon saw an unusual procession through Esquimalt heading for the gates of the Dockyard. The Raging Grannies, who are against nuclear weapons, wanted to get into the dockyard and lay bouquets of flowers on the guns of the ships stationed here. Not surprisingly they weren't allowed into the military complex and had to content themselves with singing anti-nuke songs from their carriage that had been halted by M.P.s [Military Police].[1]

The original Grannies from Victoria have an unending stream of innovative ideas for protests. Initially their focus was the military base. To ride in elegant style, they rented Belgian horses. The inoffensive horse-drawn carriage and the cheerful, spirited group of older women provided vivid contrast to the danger of the nuclear submarine at the base: they delivered their message in a lively manner, expressed dissent yet were obviously no threat. The Grannies' ability to create ambiguity for their opponents is captured in an account, in a local newspaper, entitled "Grannies ride in style": "Officials…[at the base] had to confer for quite a time about the request…Finally the word came that the flowers couldn't be taken onto the base." Dissenting with smiles confuses people prepared to react to threats. Grannies' actions often create a space where the people confronted have to question their roles. Unexpected and creative avenues of expression disturb complacency, and challenge routines, established roles, and non-questioned assumptions, the very aim of non-violence.

With their approach, the Grannies grab the attention, surprising media and the public, not to mention the military. For example, this ad, which was to appear in a local newspaper:

---

### Hi Sailor!

Why not join us for tea & tantalizing talk?

Learn all about it from yourRraging Grannies

About What? You need to ask.

Come along, sailor. You'll find out.

Where? Under the Captain Cook statue across from the

Empress Hotel on Government Street

When? Saturday, March 24- Noon to 2 PM

---

This invitation and an explanation were shared in the *Granny Grapevine* Spring 2001:

### CFB [Canadian Forces Base] Esquimalt Nukes Grannies

At first it seemed harmless enough. Victoria Raging Grannies invited sailors from the 3,000 strong nuclear-powered aircraft carrier USS Abraham Lincoln, for tea & talk with anti-nuclear Raging Grannies. The Raging Grannies wrote this ad for Esquimalt's weekly newspaper *LOOKOUT*. It [the invitation] was accepted and then the commander rejected it. The grannies have organized similar events. 'U.S. sailors are typically friendly,' says Granny Betty Brightwell. 'They all want their pictures taken with us. However, when a plainclothes security man is present, the sailor's behaviour changes. In the presence of security, sailors and their families often give the Grannies a miss.'[2]

The Grannies have the audacity to contact the "enemy" and play on stereotypes of sailors looking for women, but in this case the women want to discuss nuclear arms in a very public and central location. This never became public. Although the local newspaper accepted the ad, the Base Commander rejected it, indicating his power in the community. Victoria Grannies' witty approach is revealed again by Alison Acker:

Our banner flying—a scarlet Raging Granny brandishing an umbrella—the Victoria Grannies turned the tables on Ottawa by expropriating a federally owned island to match the threatened expropriation of the Nanoose testing base on Vancouver Island. With tent, deck chairs and provisions, we clambered over the Esquimalt cliffs and onto the island we had proclaimed *Pacifica*—the land of peace—no military, no police. Tea-time delicacies arrived by kayak from a sympathetic veggie restaurant. Visitors were issued visas, and the local press made the best of an ideal photo op. Apparently the Canadian navy wasn't quite so enthusiastic. We were later told they had consulted the terms by which our island had been loaned to Esquimalt for *recreational purposes only*. 'Your invasion was certainly more political than recreational,' the Base Commander told us, 'but we don't know what to do about it.' Luckily for him, we had agreed to relinquish our claim, temporarily of course, when the tide began to come in and the water was getting too deep for us to wade home. But we'll be back![3]

*Figure 45. Cartoon by Trevor Bryden. Base Commander cannot ignore Victoria Raging Grannies. Published in Esquimalt News. Source: Trevor Bryden.*

Their ability to identify appropriate targets for their irreverence and educational efforts is remarkable. The Commander's, "we don't know what to do about it," is quite an admission for a military officer. Is there grudging admiration in his comment? If nothing else, creativity and humour allow the Grannies to keep protesting: it provides fun and adventure in an otherwise rather serious and exhausting struggle against nuclear arms.

*Figure 46. Another activity of the Victoria Grannies was to hold a tea party on the deck of U.S. warship. They were quickly and unceremoniously evicted. Cartoon by Trevor Bryden. Published in the Esquimalt News. Source: Trevor*

The use of nuclear energy for arms and energy production remains a concern for Grannies across the country. In 1997, the Toronto gaggle hosted the biennial Un-Convention, the only opportunity for Grannies from across the country to meet, discuss, share songs and ideas, and act with a much larger group of Grannies than usual. By a wonderful coincidence, the Pickering Nuclear Power Plant was holding an open house the same weekend, an opportunity too good to pass up. A tongue-in-cheek poster by the Toronto Grannies announced:

---

### The Raging Grannies

### Still Raging After All These Years

### Sixty Grannies To Storm
### Pickering Nuclear Power Plant's Open House

### 2,000 visitors expected— but Hydro says
### no room for 60 elderly shawl-bedecked songsters

### The Grannies are going anyway.

A busload of Raging Grannies from across Canada will interrupt their 10th Anniversary Un-convention— a weekend of workshops, stories, lies about their grandchildren— long enough for a visit to the troubled nuclear power plant at Pickering...A Convoy of Grannies will disembark...flowered hats held firmly on their grey heads, sing about the expensive, forever dangerous nuclear mess in Canada. They may keep us out of their invite-only Open House, but they won't stop our songs from crossing over the gates.[4]

---

The media came and reported that the Grannies,

> '...didn't want to do something orderly,' said manager of Hydro's common systems and services. He was stationed at the gate to the site, asking visitors to make sure they had no gums or mints. 'Radioactive material might get on something they might later consume,' he said.[5]

This is a startling comment for an employee of Ontario Hydro to make. The presence of media probably provoked the plant authorities to reconsider and change their decision: Grannies could come in, but only one at a time! This just added to the humour of the situation. Not wanting bad publicity for refusing harmless women to an "Open house," the authorities were obviously worried of what Grannies might do once inside, but felt confident they could tackle them one at the time. That sort of restriction speaks to the effectiveness of the Grannies. They made the news: sixty Grannies in colourful garb in a great display in front of the Pickering nuclear plant:

> Ontario Hydro pulled out managers and public relations staff at its Pickering nuclear power plant...to make sure the busload of garish grandmothers didn't get on to the site...The 58 members of the satirical singing protest group were told the party was off-limits to them. Members had come

from 17 cities across Canada and the United States for the 10th annual UN-convention…Brandishing bonnets and banners, the Grannies stood in the parking lot…and sang 'What have they been smoking at Ontario Hydro to let management skills sink below sub-zero?'…'If my home was in a mess like that, I wouldn't be having any open house,' said Sue Davidson-Brouse, a Granny from Woodstock.[6]

*Figure 47. The Raging Grannies, not allowed into an open-house at the Pickering Nuclear Power Plant, stand in the parking lot behind a yellow tape that says: Attention/Danger—Raging Grannies at Work. Source: Dorothy Fletcher Collection.*

Grannies take advantage of any situation: had they been allowed into the open house, they would undoubtedly have found a way to make their point. The media reports add to the action and to the humour: having a manager guarding the entrance and asking people to remove gum or mint to insure radioactive material does not get onto something they might later consume reveals why Grannies and others should be concerned about the Pickering Nuclear Plant. The report depicts Pickering authorities as quite silly, suggesting an image of rather ignorant people at the helm of such a potentially dangerous plant. The Grannies successfully managed to hijack the publicity surrounding the open house, and the authorities of the Pickering nuclear plant came out with ruffled feathers, at least in some media reports.

One of the funniest, most spirited actions took place in November 1989 and shows the Grannies' crafty use of ambiguity. The first arms trade show of the Armed Forces Communications and Electronics Association (AFCEA), which deals in high-tech military products, was planned to take place in Victoria. The organisers were trying to keep it secret because they were:

'A little concerned about the peaceniks,' said Bill Sargeant, secretary of the AFCEA, because 'they were a problem in Ottawa at ARMX 89…There will be American uniformed officers there, and it makes them feel ill at ease.'[7]

To Sargeant's chagrin, peaceniks, including the Raging Grannies, showed up. Entrance to the trade show was free for those wearing military uniforms so the Grannies, having a few WWII veterans in their ranks, opened old trunks and resurrected uniforms while others fashioned themselves new ones with things at hand, including dusters and decorations made of cellophane. The ragtag gang reminiscent of a Sergeant Pepper's procession showed up demanding free entrance to the trade show. Predictably refused admission, they haggled long enough at the door to allow cameras to reveal Mr. Sargeant's little secret on the evening news.

*Figure 48. Raging Grannies seeking entrance to the Arms Trade Show, November 4, 1989.*
*Source: Doran Doyle Collection.*

*Figure 49. Not allowed in? Victoria Raging Grannies serenade them anyway.*
*Source: Doran Doyle Collection.*

As people see the Grannies' uniforms, they know at once that these are supposed to be military uniforms yet are not military uniforms but a parody. This ability to use ambiguity and create situations where two realities become visible at once is remarkable. A year later they wrote the following song:

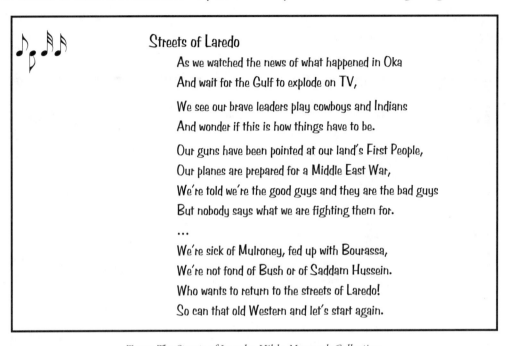

### Streets of Laredo

As we watched the news of what happened in Oka
And wait for the Gulf to explode on TV,

We see our brave leaders play cowboys and Indians
And wonder if this is how things have to be.

Our guns have been pointed at our land's First People,
Our planes are prepared for a Middle East War,
We're told we're the good guys and they are the bad guys
But nobody says what we are fighting them for.

...

We're sick of Mulroney, fed up with Bourassa,
We're not fond of Bush or of Saddam Hussein.
Who wants to return to the streets of Laredo!
So can that old Western and let's start again.

*Tune: The Streets of Laredo. Hilda Marczak Collection.*

Militarisation at home and abroad, race, politics, propaganda and economics are linked to make hidden agendas more visible. War is, among other things, a class issue: the rich make decisions and get richer, the poor get killed. The Grannies make hidden agendas more visible.

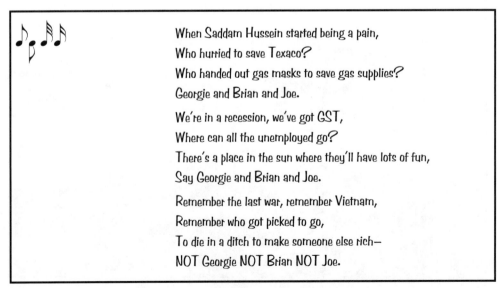

When Saddam Hussein started being a pain,
Who hurried to save Texaco?
Who handed out gas masks to save gas supplies?
Georgie and Brian and Joe.

We're in a recession, we've got GST,
Where can all the unemployed go?
There's a place in the sun where they'll have lots of fun,
Say Georgie and Brian and Joe.

Remember the last war, remember Vietnam,
Remember who got picked to go,
To die in a ditch to make someone else rich—
NOT Georgie NOT Brian NOT Joe.

*Tune: Unknown. Hilda Marczak Collection.*

To highlight their concern with the escalating threat of war in the Persian Gulf, the Grannies resurrected their "uniforms."

*Figure 50. Doran Doyle.*
*Source: Doran Doyle Collection.*

*Figure 51. Kate Mortimer. Source: Doran Doyle Collection.*

Then they went to the Armed Forces Recruitment Office to sign up for service. Having already lived long and full lives they thought it was unnecessary to risk young people's lives for oil.

*Figure 52. Raging Grannies*
*Volunteer for Service at the*
*Army Recruitment Centre.*
*Raging Granny in military*
*uniform-Kate Mortimer.*
*Source: Times Colonist.*

Unable by law to ask the Grannies their age, the baffled recruiters ploughed through the necessary paper work straight-faced; one Granny was even invited back for a math test! Back we were a week later with knitting needles and wool. We sat down for an hour, chatting and knitting scarves and comforts for the troops![8]

Again, the Grannies use ambiguity to their advantage. While the officers, no doubt, realised that these women were in their 60s or 70s, they were forced to take in their applications, which made for excellent press and served to highlight the dangers of the looming war. It made many people smile at the incongruity of these women offering to be soldiers. Invited back for a chance to qualify as a maritime officer, Betty Brightwell responded in typical Grannies' style:

I'm certainly prepared to go in any capacity they send me…I wanted to go as a person who is experienced in conflict resolution. I qualify because I lived with a man for forty years and brought up children.[9]

This comment brought the following letter, "Grannies: Ship' em Out," to the local newspaper:

Am I alone in being underwhelmed by the latest cutesy episode in the continuing saga of the Raging Grannies ('Grey power platoon,' Nov. 3)? Such unique credentials they offer: 'living with men and raising kids.' I suggest to the Department of National Defence that it lower its standards temporarily, recruit the old girls and ship them out to the Persian Gulf. When the Grannies have squared away presidents George Bush and Saddam Hussein, the military might well employ them elsewhere. How about a 10-year posting to Antarctica, to establish a Canadian presence there?[10]

A few months later another letter appeared "Anti-Saddam Weapon?"

We should all applaud the idea of the Raging Grannies going to the Persian Gulf, that land of sand and prickly heat. To make the trip worthwhile, perhaps they could arrange to take the place of hostages. Canadians on both sides of the Atlantic would benefit from such a gesture. There is also a chance that once Hussein hears the Grannies' off key singing, he may withdraw to avoid further punishment.[11]

The writers of these letters express their disagreement in as humorous a tone as the Grannies express their own dissent. Such spirited responses indicate that humour can engage opponents. Ava Louwe suggests humour opens avenues and creates bridges. Such exchanges enliven public airing of different views.

*Figure 53. Cartoon by Trevor Bryden that makes fun of the Grannies' protest against the war. Published in the Esquimalt News. Source: Trevor Bryden.*

*Figure 54. Cartoon by Trevor Bryden that pokes fun at the Victoria Grannies but also at the Prime Minister. Published by the Saanich News. Source: Trevor Bryden.*

In spite of some opposition, these two actions inspired a trail of similarly spirited actions across the country. In 1991, Grannies in Vancouver carried on their own version of protest against the Gulf War and held a Knit-In For Peace outside Vancouver Beatty Street Armory and knitted themselves to a large military tank. As I asked Grannies in different regions what had been their most creative or humorous actions, Montreal and Toronto Grannies recounted going to army recruitment offices, inspired by the Victoria action. Barbara Calvert Seifred recalls the experience in Montreal:

> We heard that there was a special Armed Forces recruitment day to be held at the Olympic Stadium. It was a last minute decision and we could only get 3 Grannies, but off we went. We got dressed when we got there and tried to get in. They confiscated our *pancartes* (signs) saying they were dangerous! (Not as dangerous as their weapons, though.) But we got in and said we were there to enlist in order to save our grandchildren from having to go to war. We even had special camouflage shawls for the occasion! They were pretty jovial about our request but we did not meet their age requirements, even when I reminded them it was unconstitutional to discriminate on the basis of age!

But the Grannies are well known to find microphones irresistible, Barbara continues:

> They had a small stage with a military band playing and I sat down beside a young officer to chat. I asked if we could go on stage when the band took a break, assuring him we were good singers! He grinned but was obviously a little uncomfortable. They don't have anything in their training manual to prepare them for an assault by Raging Grannies commandos! Finally the band left and we rushed up, hijacked their stage, and started singing 'There is No Business like War Business.' A very large woman in uniform came up and tried to push me off, but I just leaned back against her and took a chance that she would not use brute force on old ladies! We stood our ground and sang two songs. They were very glad to see us go, but we had a great time!

*Kate Mortimer was born in Philadelphia, but also spent some of her childhood in the peacefulness of the country. Her father owned a small business. Her grandfather was an Irish immigrant, one of twenty children and no sets of twins! The oldest of five, she remembers the "blackout pudding" of wartime, pudding that would take on a blackish hue due to the windows being blacked out to avoid being seen by enemy planes. As the talk of war on Iraq increases she wonders what an Iraqi child's impressions might be. Once she was stunned, when peeking through the curtains, to see so clearly under full moonlight and wondered why they had to keep windows covered since the enemy planes would surely be able to see if she could: she was five years old! Around eight she realised that Santa was a myth and thought that Jesus was big people's Santa Claus! Kate was already questioning—and has not stopped.*

*From early on she was interested in science, sang in choirs, and went to art school, a broadening experience as she had attended an all-girl Catholic school. She was the only student in her high school to receive a national merit science scholarship: because the offers of scholarships came from non-Catholic universities, her school would not release her grade. After working part-time and studying education and philosophy in the evenings, she entered the convent where she stayed for four years and came out with the exodus of the 1960s. During the Vietnam War she worked Black activists on the war on poverty. Her first march was against discrimination in housing for Blacks in Detroit. She moved to California and studied anthropology and psychology before getting married and having two children. She was the first in her family to get a university degree.*

*Not wanting to raise "cannon fodder," they moved to Saltspring Island during the Vietnam War, started a parent coop nursery and an independent school. Later she was involved with the Victoria citizen counselling training centre. She heard the Raging Grannies on their second public appearance and knew she wanted to do that when she grew up! She joined a few years later. Being a Raging Granny made her "uppity" and her marriage did not survive. She took the bold step of moving to the country in her late fifties, a scary but wonderful move. She learned about chickens and sheep, donkeys and lambs, gardening, fencing, and composting. She experienced first hand what it meant to live in harmony with the earth. No longer a member of a Raging Grannies group, she remains an activist.*

*Figure 55. Kate Mortimer.*
*Source: Kate Mortimer Collection.*

In Toronto, Grannies put out a press release about their impending visit to the local army recruitment centre:

As senior citizens we believe we have a much greater responsibility for the policies of the Government of Canada than have the younger people who are required to lay their lives on the line during hostile confrontations such as the one which has recently developed in the Persian Gulf. We therefore insist on our right to join Canada's Armed Forces, and to woman such machines as the CF 18s currently in use in the region. We will demand that, during our training, we be permitted to conduct our low level flying over cities such as Ottawa and Washington where unusually large buildings such as External Affairs, the White House, and the Pentagon will offer us a challenge. It is our hope that, when we Grannies fly our CF 18s just inches from the office windows of Joe Clark and his accomplices, and let go some truly soul-searching sonic booms, we will be able to shock those boys into their senses.[12]

---

### There's No Business like War Business

Never mind the homeless and the hungry

Never mind the people without jobs

Nowhere can you get that special feeling

Like when you're piling up the bombs

...

Sixty seconds spending is a million bucks

...

So you bought yourself some Trident submarines, Goody Goody

With the power of several thousand Hiroshimas

Did you think that these would fix

The problems we must lick

Like the millions without food and homes

And water fit to drink?

...

Don't want to burn, da-da-da-da-da-da

Don't want to blow up, da-da-da-da-da-da

They're not going to spend my money

Like that no more

The bombs are now passé they must be put away

...

---

*Tune: Medley. McLaren and Maceharvey.*

When Toronto Granny Nest Pritchard was asked her age she answered, "Over 17!"

A recently formed group that includes women from both sides of the U.S.-Canada border in Windsor-Detroit, called Cross-Borders Raging Grannies, borrowed the idea and went to the Detroit army recruitment centre on December 21, 2002 as the U.S. was drumming up war plans against Iraq once again. Ideas are borrowed but often re-worked with creativity and flair to suit local situations.

## No Protection for Government Officials Either

 Like those little birds on hippos, Looking for fleas
If we elect' em, We inspect' em very publicly

*Tune: Meet Me in St Louis. Kingston Raging Grannies.*

Various government officials and commissions have also encountered the witty rage of the Grannies. One of the first actions by Montreal Grannies was to crash the Federal Environment Assessment Review hearings on a proposal by Atomic Energy of Canada Limited (AECL) to bury highly radioactive nuclear waste in the Canadian Shield. The Grannies' alternative was a Radioactive Road Resurfacing recipe, which Joan Hadrill outlines:

Take a pinch of plutonium (holding your breath because 1 microgram will give you lung cancer). Add half a cup of strontium (fast before the cup melts). Mix well and spread evenly on road surface. The formula, which only needs to be applied once a millennium…comes with the following guarantee: It will glow in the dark and is self defrosting for at least 1,000 years.[13]

     That Sinking Feeling

Women know somebody has to clean up
That's why we say stop producing this stuff!
...
With hills of mine tailings-Risks of radon daughters
Sinking nuclear junk down near the ground water,
Or the fuelling of bombs from Candu's nasty waste
They're incentives to close down- and do it with haste
They once said "Too cheap to meter-my son"
Now it's "Too safe to worry"- but we don't buy that one
Run 10,000 year trials- without toxic contents
Then we'll say, ok! we think that makes sense!
Deep disposal is like- deep denial you know
And what language- or pictograph- of risk could we show
Thousands of years in the future? Why, the idea is daft!
Again common sense is getting the shaft...
Don't buy this burial scenario from hell!

Out of sight, out of mind, this plan must be scrapped
We' d be out of our minds to accept such claptrap!
If they're planning to build a container leak tight
Be warned- waste did blow in the middle of the night
In Russia- at Khyshtym- long ago far away
Where it's still not inhabitable- to this very day
AECL says- if their plan's not approved
It's next generation's problem.
Hey folks, we've got news!
Seven thousand five hundred generations to come
Will be shafted with this stuff,
They don't know their sums...
We can't get insurance in case it goes wrong
This $13 billion boondoggle gets our warning gong!
...
We say- sinking nuke waste is a pain in the tax

*Tune: Sweet Betsy from Pike. Barbara Calvert Seifred Collection.*

Their "brief" is educational, with factual information buried in the humorous nature of their alternative. Is such an alternative any more farcical than burying the waste in the Canadian Shield? Barbara Calvert Seifred links a lack of recognition for consequences and a lack of willingness to clean up to gender.

Women are left to clean up but are not included in decision making. The Grannies' unannounced appearance is their attempt to include themselves in that decision-making process because the disposal of nuclear radioactive waste has grave consequences. But science deals in probability and cannot run 10,000 year trials, so the consequences for untold generations to come are not included in spite of AECL referring to future generations' energy production problems. For those who think it is safe, there is a reference to a nuclear accident that happened in Russia, a place where still no one can live. If we run out of planet Earth there is no other one to escape to. The language is poetic: "what language or pictograph of risk" reveals the impossibility to conceive of the horrible consequences where not even an image can be conjured. To their surprise, they were invited to submit their suggestions to the commission.

On June 3rd, 1994, the Joint Parliamentary Committee on Canada's Foreign Policy was in Montreal and although the Grannies were not on the agenda, they were allowed to present their "brief" at the end of the day.

Our eyes have seen the ravages
Inflicted by free trade / The factories are closing . . .

. . .

Maquiladora's calling, our / People are afraid
But we go marching on

Chorus: Mulroney signed the Trade Agreement
Liberals said they never would.
But once they got themselves elected,
They too caved in but good.

Textile mills are idle, and / Deserted is the loom.
Fine furniture and footwear, / Both silent as the tomb,
The Maritimes to the West Coast

Are feeding Yankee boon, / Should we go marching on?
The playing field's no level,

And all the decks are stacked. / Our publishers are hurting,
And Medicare's attacked.
Transnationals are coming / So let's retract this pact.
We won't go marching on!

*Tune: Battle Hymn of the Republic. Granny Grapevine, Spring, 1994.*

"The chairperson had no sense of humour whatsoever but at least our message is on the record. I wrote for a copy of the transcript to make sure," wrote Joan Hadrill. The Montreal Grannies also prepared a brief for the Joint Committee on Canada's Defence Policy but were not invited to present it. "So," says Joan, "we mailed a copy in to them and instructed them to sing it to the tune of MacNamara's Band. Of course they would miss a lot of a visual impact."[14] Even when not "allowed," they find a way to get their message across; their determination to put their views forward knows no bounds. They insist on being heard, and when they are not they find an alternative way to register their protest. They do not give up. They even generate humour by sending along the instructions for the "dignified" members of the Joint Committee on Canada's Defence Policy to sing the "brief."

Ottawa, official seat of the federal government, offers special opportunities for protests. The Ottawa Grannies had the most fun on

> …the day proclaimed by the Defence Department to search for the missing documents on the So-malia affair. We went down to the Defence Building to help them search. We were barred from the interior but, armed with worried songs, we chased personnel on their way to work, scrutinising their briefcases with magnifying glasses and pawing earnestly through waste containers.[15]

Calling themselves the Parliament Hill Mob, the Ottawa Grannies had another opportunity to put their search and rescue skills to work:

> Three of us went to the Human Resources Development of Canada (HRDC), the focus of scandal because they lost a billion dollars of taxpayers' money…In the food court (crowded at lunchtime) we hung the Raging Grannies sign at the bottom of an escalator and proceeded to offer our help, in songs, in the search for the money. When we sat down for our own lunch, several civil service types approached us to say, 'Good for you!' One even booked us for that very department's Women's Bureau, who wanted us on International Women's Day [IWD]. So we duly appeared, March 8th, and sang appropriate IWD songs, this time upstairs.[16]

To be invited back for IWD is an unlikely end for a protest. It shows that the Grannies create bridges; people could have seen their action as confrontational but instead wished to hear more. They take audiences by surprise but at times the audience also surprises them. The Grannies' spontaneity and humour call forth the same in others: when they cross into the domain of imagination there is licence for others to do the same. Humour conveys the Grannies' ability and willingness to engage with a wide range of people.

Victoria's elected officials were also deemed worthy of attention. When the Garden of Eden, a local sex shop, planned to add a twelve-booth pornography "Theatre," a "high-class peep show," the Grannies went into action:

> We wrote City Council, the BC Film Licensing officer and the media, warning that we would be out-side the Garden of Eden with cameras at the ready to photograph customers if they did succeed in opening the peep show. That set the cat among the pigeons, with Mr. Pash (!) the manager, phoning us up to complain, and dozens of citizens phoning city councillors to complain about Mr. Pash. We sat front row, in our finery, at the council hearing, hoping we looked sufficiently intimidating. Pash's lawyer, a Mr. Dicky (!) tried to make it sound as if the peep show would be akin to church, and the movies as innocent as flower-arranging. But Pash's application was turned down unanimously and

council is now planning to ban any similar peep shows. Lovely press coverage, and great fun to be pillars of morality for once.[17]

One can easily imagine the fun in it all as well as the pressure on councillors from the presence of these elderly women so eager to hear what they had to say on the subject. It also shows the Grannies' great minds for strategy, preceding their visit to city council with letters to all concerned, creating demands and expectations beforehand. In this case, their not-so-subtle pressure worked.

On March 28, 1996, Toronto Grannies created a stir at a meeting of the City Council Board of Health and Public Works Committee discussing the replacement of eroding Polyvinyl Chloride (PVC) pipes. Of the five Grannies in attendance, only Phyllis Creighton was left by the time the committee was ready for the Grannies, at 1:30 a.m. To the tune of "Silent Night" she sang:

*Figure 56. Cartoon by Trevor Bryden.*
*Victoria Raging Grannies take on the porn industry.*
*Published in the Esquimalt News. Source: Trevor Bryden.*

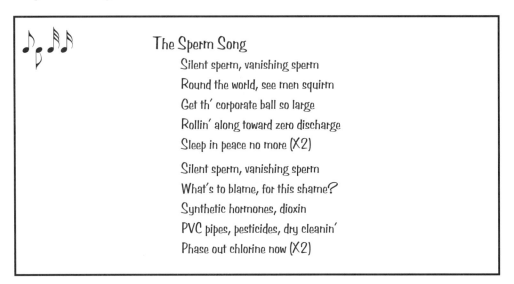

### The Sperm Song

Silent sperm, vanishing sperm
Round the world, see men squirm
Get th' corporate ball so large
Rollin' along toward zero discharge
Sleep in peace no more (X2)

Silent sperm, vanishing sperm
What's to blame, for this shame?
Synthetic hormones, dioxin
PVC pipes, pesticides, dry cleanin'
Phase out chlorine now (X2)

*Tune: Silent Night. Song by Colleen Cooney. Phyllis Creighton Collection.*

Laughter broke through the meeting! The three city councillors, clutching their sides, laughing, asked Phyllis, "Our first question is: Are you for hire?" People who stayed till the end of the meeting, at 6:30 a.m., told her that after her presentation there was a change in the character of the meeting, that "everything got very down to earth. There was no more baffle-gab. These long windy speeches…were gone." The songs had put a human face on the issue.

On May 30, 2002, Phyllis prepared a brief, mostly songs, for the public meeting of the Toronto Police Services Board at the Toronto Police headquarters. An article published the next day recounts the incident:

> It was an off-hand remark that sent more than one granny into a rage. Denied permission to sing part of their deputation to the police services board yesterday, Phyllis Creighton and her protest group of Raging Grannies were instead trying to explain their feelings on the police presence at demonstrations in verse. 'It sings better than it reads,' Creighton, dressed in regulation Granny gear—hat, shawl and protest buttons—told the board members. 'We've heard you sing before,' board chair Norm Gardner replied. 'Once is enough.' 'I didn't come here to be insulted, sir,' snapped Creighton, a historian and dictionary editor. 'Please mind your manners.' Gardner apologised, and the meeting—at which more than two hours were spent listening to police presentations and citizen deputations on the way the force handles protests and demonstrations—went on.[18]

The Grannies were concerned by the use of

> …Darth Vader helmets and shields, tear gas, and batons. As seniors, we have participated for years in demonstrations that have uniformly been peaceful protests. Weapons have, manifestly, a self-fulfilling character: they intimidate, foment mistrust and anxiety, and incite hostile response from citizens. As Raging Grannies, we resent the implication that citizens have to be threatened with violence, pepper-sprayed, tear-gassed, to prevent us running amok. We see no evidence that those joining us in demos are any different in their intent to express protest and opposition…The way in which police are armed and will act is a deterrent to our right to freedom of assembly and expression. We are alarmed. Citizens in any democracy worth the name *must* have freedom to dissent and to demonstrate…Preventive arbitrary arrest, on the assumption of terrorist intent and pending action, is permissible under the anti-terrorist legislation. The need to combat terrorism may be alleged to justify use of camera surveillance and undercover agents. We urge you to desist from that destructive route. If you don't, we won't have a democratic society—and the terrorists will have won by default. We know the risk of assumptions and labelling. Raging Grannies are labelled subversive by the RCMP and CSIS. So will this be our fate?…We urge you to take steps now to change the repeatedly intimidating—and potentially dangerous—police presence that effectively restricts demonstration. It is an exaggerated response that costs us taxpayers heavily, a response that limits our democratic rights to freedom of association and expression.[19]

Speaking truth to power, they put their credibility, respectability, and extensive networks at the service of their ideals.

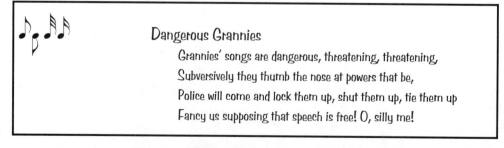

Tune: *Mama's Little Baby Loves. Betsy Carr Collection.*

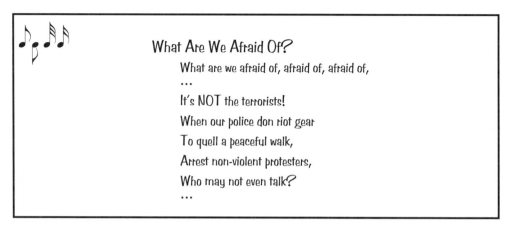

*Tune: Charlie Is My Darling. Betsy Carr Collection.*

They register their opposition but also educate the police on democratic rights.

## Democracy Is Not a Spectator Sport: Spirited Protests, Civil Disobedience, and the Sting of Tear Gas
### Spirited Protests: Proud to Be a Perennial Thorn

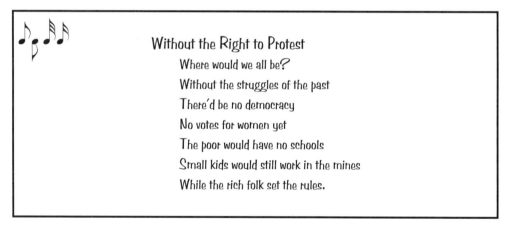

*Tune: John Brown's Body. Montreal Grannies.*

Being a Granny is the proud ministry of being a "perennial thorn" wrote a Granny. To be a Granny takes both, compassion and a willingness to take risks; it is not for the faint of heart or those wishing to avoid controversy. Daring is an important factor of the Grannies' effectiveness. It "took a while to come out of the closet," said Betty Brightwell who recalled their refusal to give their names to reporters in spite of promises to put their picture in the newspaper. Initially, they called themselves Daffidilly, Schemanny, Fifi, Millicent, Goodie Two Shoes, Nomimous and Mufee-free. While a later article by Leslie Campbell suggested Grannies sought anonymity because they wanted to emphasise the group and its message, not individuals, another article by Chris Banner suggested they "were embarrassed by the antics they had to perform to publicize their cause." But their nerve increased dramatically and quickly considering the types of actions they did:

When the Victoria Grannies roll across the stage, holding decidedly phallic versions of MX missiles while singing the old airforce ditty 'Roll Me Over,' even the most loquacious politician is reduced to aghast silence. 'My husband nearly flipped,' says Granny Betty Brightwell…But the Grannies weren't always this brash. 'It took us four tries to get out of the closet,' Brightwell admits.[20]

"It is this very serious issue that causes otherwise conventional women to be willing to make fools of themselves, to bring attention to the risks nuclear ships and subs bring into our lives and those of future generations," wrote Mary Rose. One element of their daring is a sense of togetherness: "We enjoy it when we are together. We could never do it alone," said Joyce Stewart. Together they crashed a variety of official events, hearings, and receptions. In Montpellier, Vermont, the Grannies politely announced their visit to the State House but were denied permission. Politeness did not work, so they showed up unannounced at mealtime in the cafeteria where legislators ate. Having warned the media, their protest of the lack of an adequate health care program was front page along with an article featuring them. Reappearing on Tax Day they got "an unprecedented three minutes on CBS news."[21] They sang:

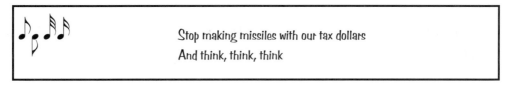

Stop making missiles with our tax dollars
And think, think, think

*Tune: Pack Up Your Trouble. Vermont Raging Grannies.*

Mary Rose grew up in a very capable all-women household and learned not to depend on men. They had to chop wood, mow the grass, whatever needed to be done: "Without a man you do all that stuff and it stood by me well having had all those abilities. I never felt fragile!" Initially, the Granny costume was a disguise for her: "I grew up in Victoria and I didn't want anybody to know that I was flaking around in these clothes and being funny."

An artist, she studied in Alberta and Ontario art schools. Politically involved with the Co-operative Commonwealth Federation (CCF), she recalls the founding meeting of the NDP. She joined Voice of Women during the Nevada nuclear tests and sent her youngest's baby teeth to the plutonium study.

Activism was in her genes: her mother was active in the community and her dad was much the rebel—he was part of the Wobblies, unemployed labour activists during the Depression who travelled across the country looking for work and protesting social conditions. Her husband's boss did not like that "communist wife of his!" She and her husband later ran a business in Victoria and she volunteered at the local peace office. She was later appointed to the Mayor's Advisory Council.

Now almost eighty, she lives alone on Gabriola Island, BC, is very busy, and spends summers gardening. Years of Tai Chi have kept her very agile. A few years ago she volunteered at an orphanage in India for four months.

*Figure 57. Mary Rose. Source: Carole Roy.*

The Grannies infiltrate all kinds of events. Five Montreal Grannies, including Barbara Calvert Seifred, joined Paul Martin—and a few hundred women—for a fun breakfast at a major hotel:

We walked in like real ladies with bags, and set the bags under the table. It was breakfast at the Ritz and it was $25. Well, we had a little money in our bank account so we subsidized to a certain degree. A friend said, 'Really eat your fill, you don't go to the Ritz for breakfast very often.' Well, never! Some had coffee; they passed a plate with some croissants and I thought, I won't have a croissant because it might spoil my breakfast. And I waited and waited, and people were chatting and suddenly I thought, that croissant *was* my breakfast! (laughs) I think I got two for my $25. I was so annoyed! Back to brunch with Paul Martin: So we finally reached down, pulled on our shawls and hats and sprang up and sang [about the Tobin Tax]. Well, some of the women were really pretty ticked off, but he really enjoyed it and said, 'I wish you'd come to Europe with me and persuade them.' …Afterwards I wanted to talk to him on the nuclear weapons issue and so when he turned to leave I said, 'Oh Mr. Martin I really wanted to talk to you.' Only afterwards did I realize that I was standing in a place where he couldn't leave the room until I moved. Got to remember that tactic!

Barbara also encountered another politician, this time on Parliament Hill:

To protest the second round of the Gulf War…I met up with two Grannies from Ottawa and we sang with the demonstration. It turned out to be budget day. One of the Ottawa Grannies was left and she says, 'gee, there are all the members of parliament going in that door over there, let's go over there.' The cops said, 'wait a minute, where do you think you're going?' We said, 'we're just going over by that door.' They said, 'you can't sing.' I said, 'what do you mean we can't sing?' 'No, no, you can't sing over there.' I said, 'what's the law about singing?' My friend said, 'we won't sing.' I don't think I said it, I don't know. If I did, I was lying…We started to walk and a limousine drove up quite near me, and Mitchell Sharp got out, who had been a minister but he was an 'éminence grise.' He got out and I just sidestepped and walked along with him and started singing:

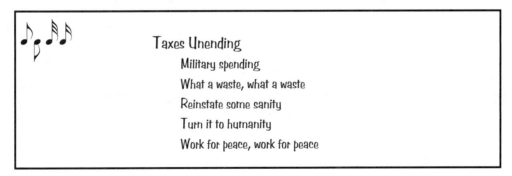

Tune: *Frère Jacques. Barbara Calvert Seifred Collection.*

He couldn't get away. The cops didn't arrest me because they wouldn't do that in front of him. When we came back from where the MPs were going in I was teasing the cops: 'What is it about the sight of feathers and ruffles that makes you so afraid? Are you jealous of our uniforms?'

*Barbara Calvert Seifred is a member of the Canadian Coalition for Nuclear Responsibility (CCNR) and went to the United Nations Conference for the Nuclear Non-Proliferation Treaty and Preparation Commission in New York in 2002. But she was not always an activist: "When I was married I was just running...I could barely keep up with my life. When that ended I thought, now it's time for me." She heard about a peace demonstration and went alone, as she knew no one else who was going. From the U.S. to the Soviet consulates, they "spread out in this long line and made the connection. It was kind of this lovely electric moment. I was very excited by the whole concept." She became active in the peace movement immediately and joined the West Islanders for Nuclear Disarmament (WIND).*

*They launched the Montreal Grannies at the WIND Annual General Meeting in late 1989—"And we were pathetic!" said Barbara. "We came in, in our hats and costumes and singing with these timid little voices to the tape that Ottawa had lent us. Well, pretty soon we found our voice and got a little bolder!" She wishes she had started an activist life much earlier: "I would have had a lifetime of this kind of fun! Because I've been a very shy person before, I never would have dreamed that I'd go out looking like we do and singing into microphones and singing in people's faces, challenging politicians. I've just made the most interesting connections of my life. I mean, this is the most interesting time of my life."*

*"There's an obligation to not let things just slide into ruins...I don't think you can exaggerate the seriousness of the situation and I think in the...nuclear weapons age, there are no more exaggerations, they are the exaggeration of power and destruction and horror beyond exaggeration, so it's just time to do something...When they argue for deterrence my answer to that is, 'where is the credibility in a lunatic act?'"*

*Figure 58. Barbara Calvert Seifred at the Un-convention in Kingston. Source: Carole Roy.*

## Civil Disobedience

Although a minority, some Grannies have been arrested for non-violent civil disobedience. In August 1988, Victoria Grannies Lois Marcoux, Doran Doyle and Anne Pask were part of the Grandmother Peace Action, an attempt to symbolically reclaim Winchelsea Island for peaceful purposes. Winchelsea Island is the nerve center of the Canadian Forces Maritime Experimental Test Range (CFMETR) at Nanoose Bay where the U.S. military tests its underwater weapons, which can later be fitted with nuclear warheads, and which bring nuclear powered and/or nuclear weapons-capable U.S. warships and submarines into the surrounding waters. They were arrested for trespassing on Department of National Defence property, a criminal offence with a penalty of $1,000 fine or one year in jail if found guilty. "I felt very strange getting arrested. I'd never been arrested before. When we came back to Victoria I felt…like I crossed out of the range of respectability," said Doran Doyle. In *Free Women of Spain,* Martha Ackelsberg says that when "those who cross the boundaries of what is considered appropriate behavior do so in the context of a supportive group, they can become empowered and come to question the appropriateness of those boundaries in the first place" (1991: 165).

For Lois Marcoux, "Winchelsea Island, that was a risk" but being part of a group made it possible. Lois, "a bit of a risk taker even though you'd never know it," also sees herself as a follower. Yet when looking back she sees a thread. She always made up her own mind, marrying a Catholic against her parents' wishes (they were from a different religion): "Maybe the fact that I could do that meant I could also get myself arrested." After the arrest, she was ostracised by the leaders of the Girl Guides group she and her daughter belonged to: she had broken the law. Even though she "felt rejected or pushed down or cast aside," she was never sorry that they crossed the line. Their action was in the news and civil disobedience was controversial: "I'm against nuclear subs, too, but I'm not about to invade territory that is off limits to the public," said Gorde Hunter, a Victoria columnist. To a lesser degree, the controversy also existed in the peace movement: the concept of property is very deeply ingrained.

*Figure 59. Saltspring Island Raging Grannies in Calgary to protest the G-8 meeting in Kananaskis, June 26, 2002. Many police officers came from across the country. Source: Marg Simons Collection.*

*Figure 60. Saltspring Island Raging Grannies at the Knit-In during the G-8 protest in Calgary June 26, 2002. They brought along their very topical banner—Knitting the World Together. Although Marg Simons designed and created the banner only intending to depict the world coming together, it is difficult not to see the military-looking helmet in it as well. Source: Marg Simons Collection.*

*Figure 61. Victoria Raging Grannies with banner during the Snake March at the G-8 protest in Calgary June 26, 2001. Source: Carole Roy.*

Other Grannies have since been involved in civil disobedience. Cori Howard, a journalist with *The Vancouver Sun*, sees the Grannies' involvement in civil disobedience as dispelling the idea that radicalism is synonymous only with youth. Alison Acker and Ria Bos were arrested for protesting logging at Clayoquot Sound, the biggest mass arrests in BC, and spent time in jail. Alison, a retired university professor, sat in the road, knitting, until the policeman arrested her and carefully took away her knitting. "He was so nice about it that afterwards I knitted him a pair of socks," said Alison who spent two weeks in jail with two other Grannies—and around 800 other protesters. "It was really important to show that it's not just young people who are concerned about the future of the planet. Us old birds care too," says Acker. In an article by Simon Birch, Acker adds that it is important that the Grannies "break the stereotyped image that all environmental activists are trouble-seeking youngsters. As Grannies, we were concerned that the press was making it look like only a load of crazy young kids was protesting about the logging." "We're so proud of our illustrious ex-convicts," says one of the Victoria Grannies in an article by Karyn Woodland.

Halifax Granny Betty Peterson, recipient of an Honorary Doctorate in Humane Letters from Mount St Vincent University, "an eighty-one-year-old fireball"

> …has been in and out of jail for protesting since the 1960's. 'I believe in putting your body on the line and witnessing what you believe in for peace, racial equality and social justice.' That life philosophy has landed her handcuffed and carted off by angry RCMP officers repeatedly. As recently as 1994 she's sacrificed her body and rooted it in front of charging oil trucks.[22]

Eva Munro jokes that 93-year-old Muriel Duckworth "hasn't been in the clink, but there's lot of time yet!"

Jean McLaren has been arrested for civil disobedience numerous times, a few of those at the Nanoose Bay Military Base against the testing of U.S. underwater weapons, but each time charges were dropped.

> They have a hard time arresting older women, especially when you're nice to them and you say, 'I don't want to be dragged because it hurts my shoulders,' so I walk…Anne Pask was with me the first time. It was our first arrest at Nanoose. One of the officers said to Anne, 'Oh you're just like my grandmother, I don't want to arrest you.' And she said, 'It's okay'…It was quite an experience, but you know it's not the worst thing in the world.

Dressed as Mother Earth she joined anti-logging protesters at Clayoquot Sound:

> They didn't want to arrest me. They said, 'Are you sure you want to get arrested?' They were so nice to me. They took my fingerprints and said, 'Now, don't get your dress dirty!' (laughs) I was definitely arrested that time and they didn't drop the charges. So we had to go to court.

She was arrested at the Nevada nuclear test site. Upon return from Nevada, Victoria Grannies agreed to be contacts for draft evaders who could say they were visiting their grandmas! This ability of the Grannies to see the potential humour and turn any occasion into a catchy, yet meaningful line, makes them good news. Jean was also arrested in Israel:

> I was arrested three or four times, walking for peace. The second time we had permission to walk in the West Bank and then they stopped it. There were 200 of us, 113 got arrested. They put us in jail for 48 hours. That was not fun. There were 48 women in that one jail. Fifteen people in our room and our room was fifteen by twenty. There were all these bunks in there, all crowded. We had one toilet in the corner, four people had diarrhea and were sick, and there was no door on the washroom. We had no towel. They actually gave us fifteen bars of soap, and we juggled with them. And we sang. We had a workshop on self-defence and we decided we were not going to have political discussions. We just played and sang and we made it! 48 hours. They have to let you go or take you before a judge after 48 hours, so they let us go because we said, 'the whole world is watching.' We had all these film crews with us and they had filmed it all.

One group took such risks as a group. On February 13, 2000, headlines in London read, "Raging Grannies Take a Swipe at Squeegee Law." To mess with squeegee kids in that Ontario town is to mess with the Grannies:

> That's the lesson London motorists learned…as eight Raging Grannies staged an act of civil disobedience on a busy street corner to protest homelessness and raise money for London's food bank. The guerrilla action took place just after 10 a.m.…where the rabble-rousers sang, squeegeed, distributed pamphlets and asked for donations from stopped motorists. After an hour of panhandling, the Grannies…had already raised $158, which they celebrated by singing in front of the closed office of MPP Bob Wood (PC London West). 'People have to become more aware of the homeless,' said 86-year-old Florence Boyd-Graham, who blasted the province's crack-down on squeegee kids and noted that at her age, she doesn't 'give a hell' about what people think of her politics. A police officer did stop to question a Grannie after the action, but no charges were laid under a new law banning soliciting on public roadways that went into effect Jan. 31. 'We thought we were going to get locked up,' said Boyd-Graham, laughing. Michelle LeBoutillier…said the Grannies were 'concerned' they might get charged, but were compelled to disobey the law because they 'felt so strongly that poverty isn't being addressed in the way it should be.'[23]

In defying the new law they offered opposition to the government and support to young squeegeers. The visible protest of older women gives credibility to the struggle of youth, and others, against poverty. What does it say about society when women in their eighties have to risk arrest to raise awareness?

## The Sting of Tear Gas

One of the most courageous actions the Grannies took part in was the Free Trade Agreement of the Americas (FTAA) protest in Quebec City in the Spring of 2001. The media referred to the Grannies in order to give a sense of the range and diversity of protesters: "*Even* [my emphasis] the Raging Grannies showed up for a protest" in Fredericton in support of FTAA protests, wrote Shannon Hagerman. The Grannies are seen as one end in a continuum: "Thousands upon thousands of union representatives headed the parade, followed by an array of other activist groups that ran the gamut from communists and hardline Quebec separatists to the Raging Grannies," wrote Allan Thompson. A vice-president of a public employees union was reported as saying: "What was heart-warming for me was to see the diversity of the people in the march. To look around and see groups ranging from the Raging Grannies to young children." A certain comfort is felt in seeing the Grannies in the crowd. Joan Hadrill was there:

> I felt very privileged as a Montreal Raging Granny to be invited to be part of the Teach-In at the People's Summit of the Americas in Quebec City with people like David Suzuki, Naomi Klein, Alexa McDonough and many from South and Central America who talked about the negative impact of NAFTA on their lives. It was very empowering to be marching with over 30,000 people there because of their opposition to Free Trade, people representing many religions, social justice, environment and human rights…Two of our older Grannies rode in wheelchairs in the march and were photographed by people impressed by their determination and stamina. At times, we felt the sting of tear gas as the people who went to the fence were gassed a few blocks away.[24]

It was courageous to go in the vulnerability of a wheelchair given the worrisome preparations of authorities to rely on force. "Even if they weren't banging on the wall, they still had the effects of the tear gas," which makes it "living a little closer to the edge than many people our age would put themselves in," said Angela Silver. A Granny in her 90s who went in a wheelchair told the Un-convention the following year how she had defied her family to go to Quebec City: it was that important to her to be there. Seeing her frailty, I was filled with awe and respect at her moral strength and determination. Those who made it to Quebec City

...sang songs composed just for this event with great gusto and were often cheered and hugged along the way. In our outlandish colourful hats and shawls, we were happy to put a face to those of 'mature' age who felt just as outraged as the younger protesters at what was being cooked up.[25]

### The FTAA Hokey-Pokey

They put the rich folk in / They put the poor folk out,

They put their ideas in / And they hide them all about.

They spin the information

Chorus: And they twist it all around

That's what it's all about!!!

They have the corporations in / They have the little guys out

The NGO's are nowhere really / They're neither in nor out.

They do some hocus pocus /

They let the media in / If the media are good

They let the media in / If they spin it as they should.

They spin the information / And they twist it all around

Do you know what it's all about?

They want the big money in / And the ones with the power

The corporations make the rules / While the countries are devoured

They do some hocus pocus / To convince us all is fine /

And that's what it's all about

*Tune: Hokey Pokey. Vernon Raging Grannies.*

### FTAA Don't Fence Me Out!

Just let loose, no excuse for the secrecy and lies

Please don't install a Berlin wall

Where the sense of freedom dies

So I must fight for what's right while the talk commences

Face police violence, 'til I lose my senses

I can't stand tyrants an'

I can't stand fences, don't fence me out!

*Tune: Don't Fence Me In. Victoria Raging Grannies.*

On the day of the big march, most Grannies followed the safe route away from where rows of police were guarding "The Wall." Most, but not all:

> When clouds of tear gas were seen rising from the fenced-off areas above us, some decided to go and show solidarity with the younger folks. They headed up the steps towards the freshly tear-gassed area. They were warned by fleeing protesters to turn back but continued on.[26]

Alma Norman recalls the decision-making process about going to the wall:

> Now some of us, and I was one, said, 'I came to Quebec City to go to the wall because that wall is an abomination and I'm here to accept my right as a citizen to do that. So I would like to go to the wall.' Well, some of the other members of the group said there was tear gas all over the place and there might be very unpleasant consequences. And…other members said, no, I didn't want to do it, I have asthma I can't take a chance on that. Others said, no, I just don't feel that's what I want to do. And I said, 'I won't go alone because I came with a group and I don't feel I can just walk away from the group and do this thing. And yet, it is very important to me. If I don't go to the wall, I will feel as if I have in some sense failed in my purpose in coming here.' Two of the other Grannies and two people, who were not Grannies then but have since joined us, decided to come with me.

A small group left the safety of numbers and ventured down another road: "We were somewhat nervous about being tear-gassed but felt that possibility had to be faced. We were lucky. There had been gassing before we arrived," said Alma.

They came across a group of heavily armed police in full combat gear. The police were unaccountably preventing the peaceful progress of a small group of protestors trying to make their way down a street: 'The police looked more like armadillos,' according to the small Granny's band fearless leader Alma, aged 78. One 'armadillo' stepped forward, fingering his rubber-bullet gun. Undeterred, the Granny group linked arms and put themselves between the small group of protesters and the police. First they sang 'Hysteria.'

Then [they] took small steps towards the police. Then it was, 'We Shall Overcome,' and a few more steps forward, voices cracking a little, according to the youngest, an apprentice Granny. Finally, Alma, the 78-year-old Granny leader, explained to the police that the Grannies could indeed be their mothers or their grandmothers, but that they were simply there for peaceful purposes and posed no danger. Amazingly, the police then retreated a few steps. The Granny group blew them a few kisses, and turned and made their way back down the hill… Grannies' actions definitely have their place in the world![27]

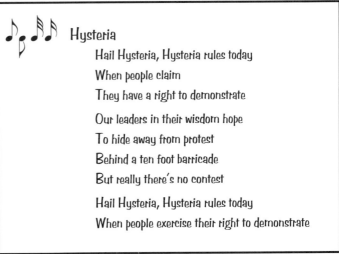

Hysteria

Hail Hysteria, Hysteria rules today
When people claim
They have a right to demonstrate

Our leaders in their wisdom hope
To hide away from protest
Behind a ten foot barricade
But really there's no contest

Hail Hysteria, Hysteria rules today
When people exercise their right to demonstrate

*Tune-Chorus: Rule Britannia; Verse: In Days of Old.*
*Ottawa Raging Grannies.*

Their way back from The Wall was eventful for another reason, says Alma Norman:

What was very moving was that, as we were going down the hill, all these young people who had been standing down the hill came up to us and hugged us and said, 'thank you, thank you, thank you so much, thank you for being with us, thank you for coming, thank you for supporting us.'

Youth "even came up for hugs. It was a tremendous moment of solidarity," wrote Alma. Grannies were happy to contribute their maturity and stop critics from making easy generalisations about protesters being young and ignorant, wrote Peggy Land. On that hill an intergenerational web of resistance was woven, which extends into the future. Courage is inspiring, at times contagious. When we witness others' courage we have a chance to grow in our perception of possibilities, an opportunity to aspire to "becoming." In going to the wall, Alma was called a "fearless leader." Leadership is important in situations like Quebec City, leadership that can express itself with determination in spontaneous ways while also respecting limits, one's own and those of others. In this case, the Grannies were assertive with police without being aggressive. Alma has much experience of protest, which gave her perspective and courage. At a demonstration in Montreal a few years ago she saw cameramen taking pictures of everybody for the first time so she went up to them and asked who they were taking pictures for? Not happy with the lack of response, she

…went to the police and asked, who are those guys taking pictures? 'Oh you know, that's press.' I said, that's not press. They were all dressed alike…So I said to them, 'you're hoping to take pictures of every person in this crowd? You'll run out of film.' But they reminded me of Jamaica. I was in something like that at the time of the Soweto riots in the 60s and police were on the rooftops.

Having prior experiences and a sense of her rights help her keep things in perspective, judge new situations, and defy the fear that the level of "security" at Quebec City was meant to inspire. Courage is also a question of practice. Alma is clear about citizens' rights and is determined to voice her views even when they are not welcomed. Confronting intimidating forces when one can is necessary, otherwise rights will erode from disuse. Linda Slavin wrote about not going to the wall:

I went to Quebec City because my planet is under siege. The environment is threatened, people I know are hungry, homeless, and without the most basic rights. When politicians meet behind barricades to promote the text of a commercial agreement allowing corporations to make money while threatening education, health, social services and nature, I have to be counted…Saturday's parade for the People's Summit of the Americas was glorious. Walking peacefully with the Peterborough Raging Grannies and 50,000 others down the streets of Quebec City was an energizing experience…But, at a crucial point in the march, we were told to turn right. Traces of tear gas had us reaching for scarves soaked in lemon juice to cover our faces and, before we could assess the situation, we walked away from the barricades instead of towards them. At the steel fence were thousands of others equally concerned about our world. A few were unnecessarily violent but the state violence in Quebec City was far worse: plastic bullets, tear gas, and pepper spray linked the Canadian government to the systemic human rights abuses in many of the countries represented at the summit. Most protesters were determined to confront this insult to democracy creatively. These young people were prepared and disciplined…They rocked the fence and the politicians while the rest of the parade walked the other way…The state, the police, the media, and indeed some of the leaders of the People's Summit divided us. I realize now that we should have been all together…at the fence.[28]

Quebec City was a confrontation with forces of globalisation perceived by Grannies and others to erode democracy, increase inequities, and hasten ecological destruction. In spite of the government's effort to scare people from going to Quebec City, Grannies were there in wheelchairs and on foot, singing with the crowd, or risking tear gas and rubber bullets on a path of expression and solidarity at the wall.

The following fall, a meeting of the G-20 took place in Ottawa. The Ottawa Grannies started at Le Bretton Flats by singing their own version of "O Canada":

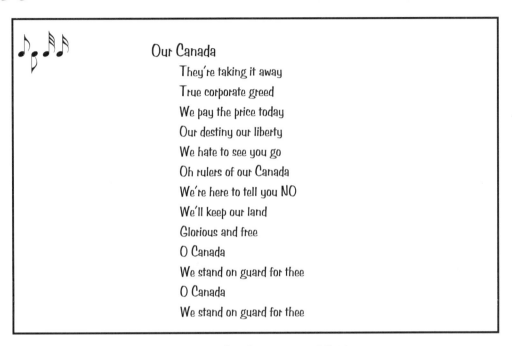

Tune: O Canada. Alma Norman Collection.

This brought much cheer. Then they were on their way with the crowd: "That's where we saw police-instigated violence," said Alma Norman. Ava Louwe recalled the scene:

> The police were really, really threatening…whole phalanx of plastic shields and black helmeted, you know the Darth Vaders, and the storm troopers with their truncheons and…rifles and dogs and whole lines of them on both sides of the road…They were looking for troublemakers, they were looking to incite trouble, and they did. [But] the crowd was amazingly restrained…The police came into the crowd…And hauled out one or two reporters with cameras.

"And knocked them about," added Alma. Many Grannies have long been activists but for new activists like Ava the experience was a real eye-opener.

> I was just shocked. You could feel the energy of the police and the animosity. And the fear in the crowd you could feel it, you could put your hand out and touch it. It was palpable. And the crowd was amazingly restrained. They grabbed a young man dressed in black and a young woman and they were roughhousing her off to the side…And the crowd said, 'let her go, let her go, let her go.' The crowd stopped and I think they did let her go and then the crowd continued. But for a while I thought, Oh my God what are we gonna see here? It felt to me that the crowd at the demonstration

would have been completely peaceable but the police were determined to create an incident. Like they were there to make the crowd look as if we were all a bunch of rabble rousers, there with no purpose. They create trouble so we will lose credibility. It was shocking for me. It was almost as though the police had been set up to hate the crowd. The crowd was the enemy and they were there to make sure that peace prevailed.

Ava continues, reflecting on the contradiction she became aware of during the march:

I'm just getting my eyes open as to what is really happening. I find it very distressing. What I find so unsettling is that when I read letters to the editor, of course, they always put in letters that are provocative, they want to get the readers' reactions, but some of these people who wrote letters were saying, 'What's with these demonstrators? What are they doing?' And I think, bless you people, don't you realise that our civil rights are being taken away and one day…you'll wake up and you'll realise you have no rights. And the people who are demonstrating are there now fighting for your rights. It's shocking and, to be honest, I have to work very hard to keep my optimism up because there are times when I feel that the ones in authority are doing a pretty good job of hiding the real undermining of our civil rights. And I have lost complete faith in what our government is doing. I think that they're all very underhanded and they do not honour the people's rights. It's shocking. We are in a democracy. That's Canada. And our rights are being taken away.

Unlike Alma who has a lifetime of protest and dissent, Ava finds herself demystifying authority, seeing the brute power police sometimes use to intimidate. Being present has a radicalising influence on her because it disturbs assumptions about what happens in Canada. She has seen the contradictions between what happened and what is written in the media about protesters out of control: in this case, she has seen for herself that it was not true. She kept saying how shocking it was. It is doubtful that Ava would have joined the march had she not been with a group she trusted, respected and felt safe with. Otherwise, she would have read about it but the contradictions would not have come to the surface so starkly. Involvement often radicalises understanding and helps well-meaning, sincere people demystify the use of power in society. The beauty of the Grannies is that women with such different backgrounds and experiences can engage and stand together.

Alma, on the other hand, went to the citizens' panel on police (over) reaction:

One of the points we made was that what Grannies can do at demonstrations is simply to be there as witnesses. But also, if we see a confrontation building up, to interpose ourselves between the confronting parties and perhaps begin to sing, so that the song itself begins to defuse the situation.

Alma's idea of "interference" in situations of potential violence found an echo in Jean McLaren's experience at the same protest. Jean had joined the Wiccan Living River Cluster, another group she belongs to, and had an experience she will never forget:

We were walking along in a peaceful parade…All of a sudden the police just came up from a side street and started grabbing young people who were dressed in black and had their faces covered. They [Black Bloc] were walking alongside of us. It was very frightening, as they [police] started beating them…They were beating anybody that went near them even, so we sort of surrounded them and we were standing aside and saying, 'leave them alone, leave them alone, don't touch them.' And then, we sat down on the road and wouldn't move. Finally, they let us go. And we're walking along and one of the young people was right next to me and I said to him, 'in all the years that I've been an activist, over 50 years, I've never covered my face or hidden or refused to say who I was.' About a block later he said to us, 'will you people surround us for a few minutes because we want to take off our black clothes and put them in our packsacks!' That was just amazing!

She adds:

I asked them if they needed fairy wings and they laughed. We chanted, 'Pagans support the Bloc,' and they chanted back, 'Bloc supports the Pagans.' When we got there, we asked them if they would come over and tell us a bit more about why they were doing what they did and why they wear black…They didn't want to have any one person as a leader, they wanted to be all together, they're anarchists. So we said, 'that may be okay, but when you cover your face, you're being targeted by the police obviously…Is that what you want, to be beaten up?' For the rest of that rally they didn't wear black, didn't cover their faces. It may have been an eye-opener to them. And they danced the spiral dance with us.

Jean spent the summer of Clayoquot massive civil disobedience at the Peace Camp,

…with all the young people. Working with them for three and a half months gave me a lot of insights into what it is they want, what they need, and I think it is the role of older women to try and move the energy.

Alma and Jean believe Grannies can help to decrease potentially violent situations. Their ability to be effective is partly due to their credibility as peaceful activists, their maturity and wisdom, their sincerity, and their appeal to youth. They are a living example of the determination to participate and be heard. As Eva Munro says: "No, we're not worried about being gagged. We'll say anything, can't shut us up."

*Figure 62. Millie Ryerson holds her ground in front of riot police during a demonstration outside the G-20 finance summit. Montreal, October 24, 2000. Source: CP PHOTO/Tom Hanson.*

Millie Ryerson had been involved in peace groups, activism, and arts all her life. While in her 80's, she had been part of Raging Grannies for 10 years. Millie, a recipient of the Order of Canada, died last year.

*Jean McLaren joined the Communist Party 53 years ago because they were the only people she knew who were working against nuclear weapons. At the time, getting a petition signed required her to stand on a corner in downtown Vancouver and expect to get one signature in an hour. She worked for women's rights and belonged to the Congress of Canadian Women. She lost friends when she joined the Communist Party and lost her Communist friends when she left the Party in 1968 because of the invasion of Czechoslovakia.*

*Having spent a lifetime in meetings, she did not want "to go to any more meetings with grouchy people fighting with each other," or not being heard as a woman. Things were fine if she did office work, envelopes stuffing, and looked after the books, but as soon as she spoke out she was dismissed. So she thought: "I don't need that anymore, the heck with that! I don't do things any more that don't bring me joy, I just don't. Things in the world are hard and I do a lot in my community." She ran the food bank and organised many events and actions. Ten years ago she became Wiccan, a step that helped her integrate spirituality with politics and move anger into positive action.*

*She has been arrested nine times for civil disobedience, including being jailed for two days on a peace walk in Israel and arrested during a march at the Nevada nuclear test site. Trained in conflict resolution and non-violent protest, she offered to educate RCMP officers in how to handle civil disobedience more effectively as part of the 75 hours of community service she had to serve for her conviction when protesting forestry practices on the BC coast. She lives on Gabriola Island, BC. A weaver and artist, she started painting five years ago and now exhibits and sells her art.*

*Figure 63. Jean McLaren. Source: Carole Roy.*

*Alma Norman was first invited by a friend to join the protest of the Ottawa Raging Grannies at ARMX [bazaar of military products]. She was not new to street theatre: she came across an article on street theatre while teaching English and history to high school students in Montreal in the 1960s. Thrilled and intrigued, she put together a plan for a course in street theatre at McGill Summer Open University. She perceived it as a potential tool for political action and believes the encouragement she got that summer made it possible to go out in the streets and experiment. "And then I was off and flying. I did it in Montreal and in Ottawa," where she moved twenty-five years ago.*

*She thinks people need "a situation in which they can do these things." Always a leader, she guided many all-women canoe trips. Although a member of the Voice of Women in 1962 when it started, she lived in*

*Figure 64. Alma Norman in her colourful Granny clothes at the G-20 demonstration in Ottawa. Source: Jacques Lacroix.*

*Jamaica then. Now at seventy-nine she remains dynamic and active. A doer rather than an observer, she now thinks it is important to hold back at times and "just be with people who move more slowly and feel more restricted...It's easy to feel—not superior—but invincible."*

*In December 2001 she wrote to Prime Minister Chrétien: "As women we have lived through at least two major wars. We cannot accept that waging war is the proper means of solving this problem...Although a nation may use its military power to destroy an enemy militarily, armed forces cannot destroy the factors which lead to terrorist activity...Billions of dollars used to destroy would be better spent in helping countries deal with their on-going needs in the fields of health, education, housing and infrastructure, which help to fuel the anger and frustration which can make terrorism seem the only option. Therefore, support for military action against Iraq or other chosen targets is both morally wrong and politically unwise."*

## Notes

1."Raging Grannies Sing," *The Esquimalt Star*, 7(29) June 19, 1988: 2.

2. *Granny Grapevine*, Spring 2001: 2.

3. Alison Acker, *Granny Grapevine*, Winter 2000: 10.

4. Toronto Raging Grannies. Poster. September 1997. Dorothy Fletcher Collection.

5. Catherine Dunphy, "Grannies' mock nuclear plant." *Toronto Star*, September 21, 1997.

6. *Ibid.*

7. Lyle Stewart, "Peaceniks 'an embarrassment' at local trade show." *Monday Magazine* (Victoria), October 26, 1989: 4.

8. Jean McLaren and Heide Brown, eds., *The Raging Grannies Songbook*, Gabriola Island, BC: New Society Publishers, 1993: 7.

9. Dirk Meissner, "Recruiters calling back 2 Grannies." *Times-Colonist* (Victoria), November 3, 1990: D1.

10. A. C. Tassie, "Grannies: Ship 'em out." Letter to the editor. *Times-Colonist* (Victoria), November 10, 1990: A4.

11. G. A. Rodger, "Anti-Saddam weapon." Letter to the editor. *Times-Colonist* (Victoria), January 30, 1991: A4.

12. Joanne Young, Press release, November 21, 1990. Dorothy Fletcher Collection.

13. "Raging Grannies propose solution for nuclear waste," *The Montreal Downtowner*, November 21, 1990: 1-2.

14. *Granny Grapevine*, Saltspring Island Raging Grannies, Spring 1994: 12.

15. *Granny Grapevine*, Fall 1996: 13.

16. Pat Howard, "Report from the Parliament Hill Mob," *Granny Grapevine* (Victoria), May 2000: 24.

17. Alison Acker, *Granny Grapevine*, Spring 1996: 9.

18. Jennifer Quinn, "Police presence criticized." *The Toronto Star*, May 31, 2002. Betsy Carr Collection.

19. Phyllis Creighton, personal communication, June 7, 2002.

20. Lynne Van Luven, "Times not changing fast enough for the Raging Grannies." *The Edmonton Journal*, August 21, 1989: A10.

21. Lucy Nichols, "The Raging Grannies: Singing out on social issues." *Peace and Freedom*, 55(4) 1995: 16.

22. Jeremy Greenberg, "These Grannies are raging." *Excalibur*, October 1999: 5.

23. Brodie Fenlon, "Raging Grannies take a swipe at squeegee law," *The London Free Press*, February 13, 2000: A1.

24. Joan Hadrill, "Grannies march, rage in song," *Senior Times*, May 2001, reprinted in *Granny Grapevine*, Spring 2001: 6.

25. Peggy Land, "Moments of faith at the wall," *Peace and Environment News*, May/June 16, 2001: 2.

26. *Ibid.*

27. *Ibid.*

28. Linda Slavin, "Should have gone to the fence." Letter to the editor. *The Peterborough Examiner*, April 24, 2001: A4.

# Chapter Five

# GRANNY GORILLA WITH LOTTA 'TUDE
## Fun, Caring, and the Gang

*Figure 65. Cartoon by Gamboli. The spirit of the Raging Grannies could revitalise the country. Illustration for "Spunky Grandmothers' Feel for Canada Sorely Needed." The Gazette (Montreal). Source: Anthony Gamboli Harpes.*

In "Spunky Grandmother," written by Mike O'Connell, (*The Gazette* May 5, 1991) the Raging Grannies are seen as "the custodians of one kind of cultural memory—notions of gumption, principle, integrity, courage, ethics" which is good news at a time "when political morality is not…receiving even a semblance of palliative care."

## In Times of Trouble

Ribbit, ribbit Get on the bus
Ya gonna mess with our kids— ya gonna mess with us!

We're Granny Gorillas with a lotta 'tude
BIG granny gorillas and we're in the mood
So we've taken our stand— at the head of the line
Doin' it for our grandkids— yours and mine

There's the water and the air and the earth to clean
So much to do— we gotta make a scene...

Those granny gorillas gave us wisdom to trust
You gotta get on out, get out in front protect those kids
from you know what, and you know what, and you know what
see that yellow school bus with the red stop sign?
full of granny gorillas sayin' Get in Line! Get in Line! Get in Line!

*Connie Goodfellow, Granny Grapevine, May 1998. (Some Grannies wear baseball caps backward for this rap inspired by Germaine Greer's suggestion about grandmother gorilla protecting mothers and kids in times of trouble.)*

## "My Planet Is Under Siege": An Ethic of Care Counters Cynicism

Caring is empowering for Raging Grannies. They "don't give a darn" if they look like fools because they really care, says Joan Hadrill, and they share "an overriding philosophy of community and concern" for people adds Kathleen Dunphy. In *The Cost of Living*, Arundhati Roy passionately calls for people to "take it personally," which rang like a bell for Barbara Calvert Seifred, who takes peace very seriously and very personally. Echoes of "I care! I care!" are heard from Joan Harvey. While denying maternal instincts, Joan talks fondly of those with "fur or feathers" as her children and vows to do her utmost to protect them: there is no assurance that there will be a next time so it's time for passion. Joan's compassion for animals started early as she helped her veterinarian uncle. She translates compassion into action:

> I would get so upset and so angry, not at the things that can happen to pets but at the things that were done to them. I couldn't sleep at night and I cried. I couldn't put the distance, just a little space between me and that animal that was being abused or whatever was done to them, that was so cruel. Then I became an activist instead; then I could deal with it. I just felt so strongly, so strongly.

Joan's caring leads to vulnerability and is at the source of her anger, rage and courage: "If people all through history didn't stick their necks out to help other people, where would we be?" One must keep caring, no matter what. It "gives you the energy and the commitment to keep at it": without a sense of connection "you wouldn't put your neck out and you wouldn't put yourself on the line and you wouldn't open yourself" to verbal abuse and ridicule. "Caring is the heart of freedom" but freedom is not just a feeling, says Ian Rudkin. "Humour is our first inkling of this, our recognition that freedom to live has been done, given, accepted, and is now being used."

Joan Harvey lives in Toronto. A lifelong activist, she grew up during the depression when they "couldn't even afford a bicycle." For twenty years, she travelled from Jamaica to Britain, Australia, New Zealand, South Africa and beyond, mostly hitchhiking and often getting rides on ships. She has freelanced for consulting engineers, has done secretarial work, accounting and bookkeeping, and has taught ballroom dance and wordprocessing for IBM.

A passionate animal rights activist, she is also a dedicated union member and delegate on women, health, safety, and environment committees. She is "rambunctious and mouthy but would never hurt anything." She loves classical music and started a community orchestra while a university student getting a BA in English.

"The Raging Granny is sort of the culmination of all the things that I've stood for and done all my life, and the things I've learned and the way I've learned to put things in perspective and cut the fallacious and untrue and malarkey, putting it nicely! Well, it's who we are and who we've become. Each one of us is completely different from the others, completely different. But our understanding and our compassion and our rage at some of the things that are going on, such as putting nuclear weapons and bombing back on the table south of the border…it is so horrific, even the concept of considering such a thing!"

Figure 66. Joan Harvey visiting with residents of a seniors' centre. Source: Joan Harvey Collection.

Her rebellious streak showed early. At seven, told at Sunday school that only humans, not animals, had souls, she decided never to return. Single, she has many "children." "All animals are my own, because that's my family, we're all animals."

*Louise Swift has long been involved with the Canadian Campaign for Nuclear Disarmament and the Voice of Women. Starting in the 1960s, she remembers:*

*"We used to march down Jasper Avenue [Edmonton] with our kids in baby buggies. It was a Mother's Day march and we protested the war in Vietnam. In the 70s, the environmental movement sprung up and that was the beginning of STOP [Save Tomorrow Oppose Pollution]…it went for 25 years…There is still an environmental resource center in Edmonton, sort of an offshoot of the original STOP."*

*In an article by Scott McKeen, Louise, the founder of STOP, was called "the mother of the environmental movement in Edmonton" (E5). She talked about her involvement:*

*"All of us have gone to governments, and stood up before committees and boards and made pleas, and read off briefs, and talked till we were blue in the face and written letters and we feel that those kinds of things have had no effect. And maybe what we are doing now has no effect on those same people, but we are reaching ordinary Albertans with a message and I think that the more people we can convince, the better off the community will be."*

*Louise is empowered by memories of other struggles: "In the Voice of Women days, when we were reeling against above-ground nuclear testing, we did the baby teeth campaign and…we were proven right. What we were saying in those days was, 'what we are doing is dangerous,' and we were right. And I think that those kinds of successes help us to know that what we are saying is the correct thing to say, even though we shouldn't have to do those kinds of things. I don't think we've said, 'I told you so' very many times but I think that a lot of the population realises that what we're saying is true too. They might not be convinced but hearing our message is the first step."*

*Figure 67. Louise Swift singing against the Alberta Government's controversial health care bill, April 16, 2000. Source: Photo by Charlene Ball.*

*Louise Swift*

Elinor Egar Reynolds' willingness to take an unconventional stand comes out of a long, and at times, painful journey trying to understand what was happening:

> It's in the truth sort of penetrating slowly: 'This isn't right.' It's painful and hard because it takes a long time and you sort of go through a fog. And you say, am I right? Am I right? And then, after many years, many times of things happening, my gut says, 'yes, I'm right.' And you know then, you're right. You know something that comes from within. It's like being brought up Roman Catholic and I'm from southern Ireland…very rigid and…totally dominated by the priests…Years later you begin to realise that this is totally wrong, there is no such thing as love or compassion, not even truth. You begin to separate them: 'This is right and that's not right.' For me it's a painful process, something I hadn't thought of in years. But I remember going through it.

Phyllis Creighton has known the privilege of wealth, formidable intellectual powers and is very articulate. She has written countless briefs and papers, made submissions to hearings and commissions, sat on numerous boards and been recognised for her contributions in many ways. Yet it was moving to hear her talk of love as the basis for her involvement:

> I wrestled with the issues of the commandment 'You Shall Not Kill'…That led me to the conclusion that the under girding force in reality, in life, whether you want to name it God or not, is love. I used to say to people who said we'll never get rid of war because there's this aggressive instinct, I would say, no, war is a human institution. What you're not going to get rid of is this thing that human beings have, this desire to give themselves without counting the cost. You can say that because they create dependent life and then they nurture it and they bond with it…It is the outstretched arms on the cross; it is what makes most people feel fully alive when they give of themselves in generosity and in caring, whether to animals, to earth, to people, or to the feeling of spirit and love, to awe. This is the deepest reality. Once you know that, you can understand the truth of Ursula Franklin's most profound statement that the moral is practical because things that are based on greed, injustice and callousness, grind against the basic reality of life.

While the Grannies sincerely and profoundly care, which people often expect of mothers, Phyllis says:

> You don't need to be a mother, you don't need to be a grandmother, you do have to be a woman, you have to be willing to wear silly hats, you have to sing, you have to have 'attitude!' Attitude means the ability to be critical, to use the right side of the brain, to take an off-beat angle and find ways to defy authority when necessary.

It is thinking outside the box, as others might say. Attitude is to deeply love but not be sentimental. Attitude is the ability to be compassionate, yet hard as rock when standing one's ground in defence of people, principles, or the earth. It is about integrity, about managing paradoxes. It's a refusal to let bureaucracies dictate, as they tend to atrophy the spirit or ossify life into meaningless patterns. It is the willingness to compromise for peace but never for the appeasement of conscience. It is a willingness to be spontaneous and trust oneself and others to figure things out when time is taken to reflect and discuss. 'Attitude' is about acting as if it matters how we act, because it does. It is the willingness to engage with a great variety of people with respect and honesty. It is recognising limits yet persisting in having a voice and not giving in to what may appear as overwhelming odds. "Even if one cannot do much, one can still bear witness," says Angela Silver. And it matters that one does so because the stakes are high. As Shirley Morrison, a Seattle Granny, explained after their participation in the WTO protests in Seattle in 1999: "Our most valuable possession all over the world is our children, we've got to make the world a better place for them" (*Grapevine*, Winter 2000). Barbara Calvert Seifred recalls the early days of her activism at a time when her daughter was talking about having children, a frightening prospect given how the world is such a dangerous place. But caring, once again, is a source of hope and courage for her:

> Of course we have to carry on and we have to have hope and we have to work for change and work to give hope to young people, because I think they must be bloody well pissed off, if I may say so, with what we've done with this world…There's an obligation…to speak up whenever I can and rattle the bars, rattle the cage…practice democracy…It's…our obligation as citizens.

Barbara links caring with democracy and citizens' obligations.

The Grannies' aim is to increase awareness and action, not trigger fear. Although Grannies are often seen and heard as protesters, their perception of possibilities for grassroots empowerment, community building and community development speaks of an educational outlook rooted in an ethic of care. According to Muriel Duckworth, one important aspect of their work is their support of other groups:

> The thing we're best at right now is showing support for people who need to know that they have support. I'm not sure we're converting anybody, but we are helping in a difficult time to support the spirit of people who are trying to say something to the public and trying to change the world…We're not good singers, nobody listens to us for our music, but I think it's a question of conviction and commitment.

Writing songs and singing gives visibility, recognition and legitimacy to issues and the people struggling with them; it is important to be part of a larger movement. For Muriel, there can be tension between the popularity and visibility of the Grannies, and their desire to be in solidarity and collaboration with others:

> If we're gonna get attention, we've got to get it for something worth doing…You don't want to take the attention away from what others are doing, but if what you can do adds to the tension of the total effect, well, that's all for the good. But you don't want to be like a child who gets into the picture and the media focuses it all on the child rather than on the issue. So we don't want to do that, to take people's attention away.

There is much wisdom and insight in a perceptiveness honed over a half century of activism and struggles. She was absolutely clear that the Raging Grannies in Halifax seek to support, empower, and validate groups struggling to voice their particular issues. Rose DeShaw also sees their role as buoying and encouraging others, especially youth:

> You fight, you fight, and you fight, and then, all of a sudden, you lose somebody [to burnout]…I want them to step back. I think laughter is important…You just need to say, 'we can't rush all the bridges.'

The French speaking group in Montreal, Les Mémés Déchaînées, orient themselves towards community development and have undertaken different activities. They invite community members to a monthly Sunday brunch for discussion and a sing along. They plan to share individual Grannies' "small histories" as a way to discover the larger, collective history. They do not want to tell people what to do but want to be among people, of the people. They want to go beyond the intellectual and make closer bonds with others. Coming from organisations involved in community development, they see the Raging Grannies not only as a protesting and educational tool, but also as a vehicle for community development. While many women may not feel ready to demonstrate or perform, they could be involved in other ways like fundraising or outreach. They made Christmas fruitcakes, "cerises-à-l'eau-de-vie" (cherries in brandy first made by settlers in Quebec), home-made cookies, and "sucre-à-la-crème" (traditional fudge), pies, and jams for sale under a label showing the Grannies at their pots, cooking up a storm. They made buttons that show them "knitting the future of the earth," a play on the stereotype of knitting associated with older women. They plan to have a regular column in a newspaper to analyse specific issues. They could keep many battalions of Grannies busy. What is interesting in their approach is that activism is integrated within a larger context of community building.

## Taking Togetherness to Heart: "When Spider Webs Unite They Can Tie Up a Lion"[1]

The Raging Grannies are a collective venture; only exceptionally do they act alone. In fact, most groups require a minimum of Grannies before they accept a gig. Hilda Marczak points to the importance of "knowing you are not alone." In an article by Karyn Woodland (*Focus on Women* October 1998), Anita Bundy admits: "It was exhausting—all those years of trying to fix the world by myself…Protesting with the Raging Grannies is more effective." Rose DeShaw is also clear: "It's so much easier to do it as a group. It gives you a lot of confidence and courage." People "often want to do something but can't do it alone and what the Grannies meet is a need to be very active and outrageous," says Alma Norman. Fran Thoburn has done actions with only one other Granny and says it is possible "because we're not alone, it's SO important." For some, joining the Raging Grannies provided a group of friends in a new environment. Eva Munro moved back to Halifax after many years in Toronto:

> When I came back here, I didn't have any friends. I'd left all my friends in Toronto. I didn't know anybody. To move when you're my age, start all over again—if it hadn't been for the Grannies, I wouldn't have any friends. I can't imagine life without some friends to talk to, to share things with.

Lanie Melamed spoke of how great it is "to have friends finally at this stage of one's life and not feel that everything has to be so untruthfully worked at in order to be successful." For others, finding women to be politically active with was very satisfying. For Hilda Marczak, it felt good "to be part of the women…have the strength to stand up and do whatever needed to be done to get a message [across]." Pearl Rice has been active on various issues most of her life:

> I have been aware of most of the issues that we cover and have done something about it one way or the other…I know women who agree with our thoughts and are supportive but they would be unwilling to come out and make public statements, you know, go public about it. That's one thing I really like about the group—that we basically support the same things so far and it's good to know that there are people who are willing to stand up for what we believe in.

Getting together for discussion is educational, even healthy for individuals to know they are not alone, says Betty Mardiros:

> One tends to think nothing can be done, like…globalisation [being] too big to comprehend. That is very disturbing…It's very healthy for individuals [to know] there are other people who share your feelings…because it's awfully easy to get depressed, cynical and just negative…so many awful things happen all the time to people and societies. But it is very good to get rid of those feelings. It stops you from being cynical if you do something to express them.

The healthy benefits of activism are not often extolled. Yet being actively involved with others in issues that one deeply cares about contributes to living life with meaning and having a stake in how the future unfolds. The future remains a horizon to reach for. A recent British study by psychologists at the University of Sussex, and referred to by Reuters on December 23, 2003, suggests that "positive experiences and feeling part of a group can have beneficial effects on health." According to the researchers, "people who get involved in campaigns, strikes and political demonstrations experience an improvement in psychological well-being that can help them overcome stress, pain, anxiety and depression." Dr. John Drury, one of the researchers, suggests that "feelings of encouragement and confidence" emerge "from experiences of collective action" because participants feel they have "a collective identity with fellow protesters" and "derive a sense of unity and mutual support" ("Protesting may be good for your health"). For Lois Marcoux, the camaraderie, the travel and sense of purpose were very stimulating as she was exposed to other peace and social justice organisations to which she has since devoted time and energy.

Collective enterprise offers wonderful opportunities as well as challenges. Fran Thoburn finds the "creative hodgepodge, that creative dissonance…just marvellous," although it apparently leads to very noisy and loud meetings. She adds that when they meet they talk about themselves "in very personal ways before we start talking about the horrors of the world and exchanging information…That is so important, it moulds the group. We're friends." Eva Munro found a group of friends when she joined the Grannies, but points to the usual challenges of group dynamics:

> We're all different. Mind you, keeping track of them in a meeting is like keeping track of a bunch of cats! We all have different ideas and different ideas of what the group should do. We like to work by consensus but sometimes it's hard to get consensus.

The image of independent cats is a strong one, and I suspect from the comments I heard from other groups, quite realistic. Grannies are of strong minds and passionate voices. Alma Norman is surprised that with all these strong women they don't have more clashes because "we're strong women but we are also prepared to step back and respect others." The Ottawa Grannies never use confrontational language and if there are people who for whatever reason seem to require attention, some Grannies "seem to have a natural peacemaking" ability so there has not been any "unpleasantness or nastiness." In spite of the usual challenges of group ventures, there is respect and a willingness to find ways that allow everyone her place.

*Eva Munro grew up in Halifax but spent many years in Toronto before returning to the East Coast in 1995. New to town, she did not have many friends. When she got a call from Muriel Duckworth, "I hear you are a bit of a social activist. I thought you'd fit in with the Grannies," Eva jumped at the opportunity and "met wonderful women and have done very exciting things with them."*

*She was always involved with the creative movements of skating and dancing, and worked at the YMCA in fitness and exercise programs. She describes the mentality of her early years as a time when 'real' women were encouraged to kind of 'wrap-yourself-in-saran wrap-when-your-husband-comes-home-he'll-love-you-forever'—all that crazy stuff!...I'm 77 but I'm still going, I like to move; I walk quite a lot. I wish there was more modern dance here" as she finds that most dance classes are " 'Simon says, Simon does' for older people but there isn't a lot of creative things."*

*The Grannies was her first taste of political activism. An idealistic youth, she was determined to enjoy her life but "didn't want to leave the world without having done a little something. I didn't have any idea that all this was going to happen, the environment was gonna be trashed, the United States would want to buy our water, use our lumber...To see that we've destroyed the earth without even looking at what we're doing...Now it's just slash it all down and plant it full of Christmas trees...I feel so sorry for the kids growing up now."*

*She describes her view of the world with a metaphor consistent with her love of movement: "We're walking on holy ground and they just walk on it like, you know, they can do what they like with it, no reverence for the ground or for the growing things." Eva feels she is just beginning to fight. A turning point was the birth of her granddaughter.*

*Figure 68. Eva Munro.*
*Source: Eva Munro Collection.*

For some, the attraction is to be part of a group which does not follow Robert Rules of Order or collect membership fees, has no bureaucracy, no office, little formality, no minutes or attendance-taking. To be part of a group yet retain a sense of freedom is always a challenge, a negotiation between the social and the individual. By appealing to freedom and to a desire for meaningful and fun-filled actions, the Raging Grannies create a group that, while not utopian, allows much space for individuals to be authentically themselves. There is an ability to recognise individual gifts that contribute to the whole, be it creativity with costumes or songs, or the skills to analyse technical information, or develop an understanding of political issues and processes. Some bring their ability to listen during conflicts, while others have the courage to honestly put forward dissenting views and provide new opportunities for education. Some are very creative and daring and would walk naked down the street for something they really care about while others are attuned to the community and how to best reach out. Some are quiet and shy and articulate their ideas better in smaller groups while others thrive in the light of media and can confront a row of microphones, with a spark in the eye and their tongue sharply connected to their brain, under pressure. What makes it rich and possible are a commonality of purpose and the diversity of talents and experiences.

Joyce Stewart connects group process to creativity: "All those ideas would come up just talking with one another." For Ava Louwe, the creative process of the group is a source pleasure:

> How the songs come together is always amazing to me. It's amazing because nobody really tries to manoeuvre it to work a specific way and it just kind of evolves. There is quite a general sense of going with the flow.

Doran Doyle also emphasises the collective dimension of creativity:

> I would be cooking or sweeping the floor or something, and if I knew I had somebody who would be…like in communion, or somebody who would say, 'yeah!' then I could phone them and say, 'let's do this,' and quite often things happen that way.

For Doran, relationship is intrinsic to creativity: "Being able to play together as a group" made the Raging Grannies capable of tapping into a creative spring. Lois Marcoux called Doran the spark. Doran recognises her creative temperament and identifies the encouragement and support received from others for seeing "the humour and the mischief in things." Yet the same collective process can also make it hard on those who "carry a spark" when faced with resistance to unconventional ideas. While success with creative ideas can spur more daring, it can also spur more competition, at times an antidote to group creativity. Given that women have had to contend with invisibility, the original Grannies' success brought to the fore a greed for individual visibility and recognition that ran counter to the collective magic that led to success in the first place. Doran, who felt that notoriety and fame might lead to a loss of their abrasiveness thinks "integrity means biting into something." She also saw the danger of taking themselves seriously in a way that endangered spontaneity and playfulness.

Grannies face other dilemmas. One is the balance between energy devoted to the functioning of the group versus energy spent in actions. One group in Vancouver made the choice to splinter: "We're less interested in being cohesive as a group than we are in being effective as activists…We want to be an active part of any rally rather than being the 'star' of it. There is a difference," wrote Joanna Nagel (*Granny Grapevine*, Winter 2002). Others struggle with values: "We had a winter with too few gigs and too much struggle over what beliefs qualify one to be a "real" Raging Granny" (Zawallsky, *Granny Grapevine*, Spring 2001). In Ottawa

Alma Norman recognises the wide range of views and experience in the group. She recalled one woman saying:

> We have to be very very clear about how far we'll go or what we'll do because there may be mem-
> bers who don't want to be associated with a group which might be on police records or might be
> confronted by the police…might not want their name associated with it.

Alma continues:

> I guess the decision we will have to make is what is the group? An all-encompassing one that any-
> body can fit in, or if you're not comfortable with it maybe you need a more conventional type of
> group…There might be some that are frightened. I remember when we talked about the
> criminalising of dissent…one of the Grannies said very seriously, 'Why don't we invite the police
> here to tell us what is okay for us to do and what is illegal?' One or two of the others said: 'No, that's
> not what we are about. It's how do we feel about doing these things. It's not a question of only do-
> ing what we're allowed to do.' But here is a very, very, lovely committed woman, very active in a lot
> of social justice things, whose first thought was, 'Let's find out what's the law so we can obey it.'

Alma Norman herself is not overly concerned about being obedient! While she refers to "a couple of things
that went on with a little edge" she acknowledges the range of experiences among Grannies:

> I have been in riots that police have started, it doesn't intimidate me…The first time it happens
> you're terrified and then you realise what it is. But if you've never been in that sort of thing, your atti-
> tude is different. And if you haven't for a long time thought, 'I have to stand my ground against au-
> thority,' if this is a new thought to you, then it's already a great leap of consciousness.

For some Grannies who are still employed, considerations can involve not participating in some protests because of the possibility of reprisals from employers.

*Figure 69. Raging Grannies conga line playfully weaves its way at the Un-convention in Kingston,
June 2002, on its way to the Dandelion Festival. Source: Carole Roy.*

*Bonnie Doyle lives in Regina. Her grandparents immigrated to Canada from Scotland/Ireland and Germany/Poland. She loves to sing, comes from a musical family, and sang in choirs at school and church. She is still employed full time and works in a stressful job in a traditionally male domain but would rather not mention her employer.*

*While she has not been involved in organisations, she was always interested in women's issues and says: "I used to go to meetings for various groups for the rights of women when I was quite young. I have two daughters and I always wanted to do things to…make it better for them when they had children, when they got into the work force…The other thing that really attracted me was that we were making statements on things. I am really interested in the quality of our food and our environment. I've had some health challenges over the years and some of that had to do with toxins in our food, maybe pesticides and various things in our water…to keep our earth a good place for our children and our grandchildren. Plus I like having fun, and we have fun singing together."*

*Figure 70. Bonnie Doyle.*
*Source: Bonnie Doyle Collection.*

*Facing a strong-willed and controlling father made her strong and capable of fighting for what she believes in. She found a mentor in her strong and independent grandmother who worked until she was 65, had her own pension, drove her own car until she was 90, and did not shy away from going to city council to make her views known when she deemed it necessary. Interestingly, Bonnie mentioned her granddaughter: "I have a two-year-old granddaughter and I'm always singing the songs to her and she comes out to watch once in a while and my son-in-law said if he sees his daughter out protesting he'll know which Granny to blame!"*

*Louise Edith Hébert-Ferron is a French-speaking Mémé in Montreal and grew up the only child of a loving family. Her father was a pianist and she was encouraged early to study the piano. But an accident when she was a teenager forced her onto a different path.*

*Dance, painting, music, creativity in general have always been part of her life. She worked as a fashion designer and was the first in Montreal to have models dance during fashion shows. She has since been involved in art therapy and gives workshops on creativity for high school students.*

*Principled, she believes in the importance of focus and discipline. As a young woman she wanted to save the world and sensed a vocation as a missionary or a contemplative but decided to "not give her life for a cause, but live it." Her sense of duty and responsibility is as developed as her creativity. Ambitious and enthusiastic, she sits as a director on numerous boards of community organizations. She enjoys challenges and trusts herself to realize her goals*

*Figure 71. Louise Edith Hébert-Ferron.*
*Source: Louise Edith Hébert-Ferron Collection.*

## Lots of Fun: Sustaining Openness of Spirit

Fun is an important element of the Grannies' approach. For Lois Marcoux, it is "closest to the most fun I ever had in my life." Many said that if it is not fun we do not do it, as did Lorna Drew:

> Why would you do it? Why would you go out and sing wearing stupid hats with flowers hanging from them and birds sitting on them and dark stockings? You have to want to dress up in costumes and kind of enjoy yourself and make other people laugh…You wouldn't want to do it if you were totally serious.

"So many things in life are serious…We have enough gloom and doom" thinks Angela Silver. Jean Watson from Minnesota suggests that "fun is the bottom line" and Fran Thoburn insists that "the adventure is fun but it's got to have a point, it's got to have a really good reason to do it." Other women have also identified fun as a sustaining element of struggle. The Shibokusha (elderly) women of Mount Fuji, rural Japan, have been resisting the encroachment of the military over their lands since the end of WWII and have faced harassment, stones, and fire. In small groups they

> …make their way into the exercise area, crawling around the undergrowth and popping up in the middle of the firing. They plant scarecrows to decoy the troops. Sometimes they'll build a fire and sit around it singing and clapping…totally ignoring officials who try to move them.[2]

They refuse to give their names when arrested: they are too old to remember when they were born or who they are! Police do not want to provoke them: they hate it when the women scream and "realise that though we are physically easier to arrest than men, we're more trouble afterward!…It's fun to make a nuisance of ourselves and embarrass those men" (Caldecott). Their struggle moved from recovery of land to anti-militarism, which they see as violence against the land. They insist: "It's quite fun and everyone is cheerful. If it weren't for that, we wouldn't keep it up for so many years," said Amano Yoshie (in "We Will Grow Back"). By then it was a twenty-eight year struggle. Having fun may be important to resistance. Louise Edith Hébert-Ferron, a French-speaking Granny, does art therapy and says that through play we learn to relativize, to share, and to support each other. Spontaneity and collective actions provide excitement as they court the unexpected.

## Notes

1. Ethiopian proverb.
2. Leonie Caldecott, "At the foot of the mountain: The Shibokusa women of Kita Fuji." In Lynne Jones, ed., *Keeping the Peace: A Women's Peace Handbook*. 98-107. London: The Women's Press, 1983: 104.

# Chapter Six

# "WASTING THEIR SWEETNESS IN THE DESERT AIR" OR "COOKING UP A STORM?"

## The Raging Grannies' Impact on Issues, Ideas, and Media

It would be nice to think that it really has some impact, and the people are listening. Do you think they are?
—Elinor Egar Reynolds

*Figure 72. Cooking up a storm that is coming "Any Minute Now."*
*Raging Grannies at the Un-convention in Kingston, June 2002. Source: Carole Roy.*

## Squawking Gets Some Success

> No matter who is in power, they often find it wise
> to take this sorority of silly singing sisters seriously.          —David Ferman

Are they "wasting [their] sweetness in the desert air?" asks Elinor Egar Reynolds whose mother used the expression to convey futility. Elinor wonders at the growing popularity of the Grannies:

> Is it because these words need to be said? Is it because of the older women or ancient women who totter around the stage and may not be in tune sometimes, and funny? But we're not funny, we're not entertainers, and this is one of the things we try to make sure that we're not. [But there] certainly seems to be a respect out there for the Grannies.

Others also raised the issue: "Sometimes we wonder if we've achieved anything, if we just went as entertainment or if it was amusing and maybe our humour titillated a little bit," said Joan Harvey. "We just don't know. It's casting your bread upon the waters," says Betsy Carr who, at times, needs the reassurance of knowing that what they are doing is worthwhile. Lorna Drew also shares some of the questioning that goes on in the Fredericton group:

> Sometimes we talk about this in the group…We don't know if we are making a difference or not… Probably the biggest impact we have is turning age on its head. I doubt if we change anybody's mind out on the streets…Hearing the Grannies is not going to change their minds about whether or not we should have bombed Afghanistan, or should be bombing Iraq if they're already decided.

The Grannies' concern for a wide variety of issues, some of them global and international in scope, makes it impossible for this research to evaluate their impact on all the issues that they espouse. Their goal is a more peaceful and just world, no small matter. To a plea for ideas to combat the neo-liberal agenda, Phyllis Creighton wishes she "could offer a magic wand," and adds that their singing at protests

> …has helped buoy up people. Keeping spirits up is vital in such dreadful, depressing times when we feel powerless. Your songs can help others know why they are standing up against the government and to feel new energy in knowing they are not alone. Speak the truth to power…laughter has a rock bottom strength, it gives you hope and perspective…Hope for tomorrow and work like hell today. But let's hang together because there are more of us…and we will weather this storm.[1]

Yet it is clear the Grannies have had a meaningful impact, on some issues, on stereotypes, on the media, and on individuals. You never know where "that little idea you've tossed into play into the air will land and how it will grow. You can't measure that," says Angela Silver. The fact that the first group has grown to more than fifty groups across Canada, the U.S. and as far as Greece and Australia means they have touched a nerve amongst older women—and some younger ones—who want to have a voice. The creation of the Raging Granny persona provides a public forum where they can air their views.

The Raging Grannies have received recognition in a variety of ways. "Their act attracts a full house," said Charlie Fidelman in *The Gazette* (December 5, 1996) when the Montreal Grannies sang at the food bank Café Dépot. Some groups of Grannies are recipients of awards. Project Ploughshares Edmonton presented the 1998 Salvos Prelorentzos Peace Award to the Edmonton Raging Grannies, an award that was established as

> …a tribute to a man who was a soldier during the Second World War and who never forgot the horrors of those events. It is awarded annually by Project Ploughshares Edmonton to individuals or

groups who have made a significant contribution to peace and disarmament issues in the Edmonton area.[2]

Granny groups in both Halifax and Montreal received the YMCA Peace Medal-Award for their work on peace issues in their respective city. An article in the *Edmonton Senior* praises volunteers:

> Several ad hoc groups are deserving of mention. Foremost among these are the Raging Grannies. These hardy senior ladies have braved rain, wind and storm to convey to everyone, in rhyme and song, their message about injustice.[3]

Sometimes there is success as a result of Grannies' efforts or as a result of collaborative efforts with other groups. The Ottawa Grannies appeared before the city's hearings on a pesticide law, sang "Ode to a Lawn," and suggested that Ottawa's Tulip Festival become the dandelion festival. The committee voted to ban pesticides on city public property. But success for Grannies is not defined in conventional terms. In spite of their efforts to make a suitably impressive protest against workfare, the Kingston Grannies were not expecting the reaction, says Rose DeShaw:

> Over our shoulder is the spectre of the BC Grannies who got arrested for their stand. Well, we've tried. Believe me, it isn't that easy to get arrested these days. We did go down to City Hall when council was deciding on workfare, fully prepared to sing outside till we were carted off, but instead council welcomed us warmly, put us on the agenda and sang along when we passed out our lyrics.[4]

The Halifax group protested French nuclear testing by boycotting French wine in front of the Liquor Commission store, which

> …was sufficiently threatening to have the store manager bring in the police to keep the group under control. For the second time the Raging Grannies made it into the newspaper and had radio and TV interviews aired about French nuclear testing.[5]

The Sunshine Coast Grannies in BC were "assigned" victory by the rumour mill. Apparently they had been protesting:

> Once again the act of a 'boat blow-up' as part of the annual Gibson' Sea Calvacade, considering it to be detrimental to the environment as well as being a stupid example to youngsters, when any attempt at emulation on their part would brand them trouble-makers. However, this year the blow-up was a fizzle, and word went around that the Raging Grannies had put a hex on the whole spectacle. Hooray! Meanwhile we'll try to think of a good alternative for next year, which might be acceptable to the reigning powers-that-be.[6]

As for political effectiveness, the Grannies agree that they have not solved all the problems tackled, but they help create awareness. They have become a name to people in positions of authority, locally, provincially, and nationally. They create a new space for politics. Warren Magnusson, professor of political sciences at the University of Victoria, sees them as an example of lateral politics where hierarchies are done away with. Unlike mainstream organisations with centralised, democratic but hierarchical structures, like Greenpeace and Amnesty who accommodate ordinary people as foot soldiers, the Grannies rely on consensus, not hierarchy, and allow a high degree of creativity to individual members (1990: 536). They turn their identity, usually considered a liability, into a resource. Magnusson allows the Grannies a marginal impact on the political scene, but readily concedes that compared to opportunities open to ordinary people in other organisations the

Grannies have created a space best suited to their talents and interests. The Grannies' way is influenced by feminism, according to Magnusson: based on localised concerns, they rely on lateral and non-hierarchical relations, and are oriented towards dialogue to raise consciousness through the stimulation of political debate and to influence the grassroots. The Grannies share with other social movements, the peace movement, the environmental movement, and the global human rights movement, the assumption that, "what ordinary people think and do is actually more crucial for the movement's success than what the states do" (1990: 536). In a 1981 March issue of the *Sierra*, Dennis Pottenger reports that an American woman member of Grandmothers for Peace, Barbara Wiedner, believes grassroots organisations can influence global policy and refers to a conversation she had with Eduard Shevardnadze, then Soviet Foreign Minister, at the Moscow Summit [1988]: "The summits and the INF [Intermediate-Range Nuclear Forces] treaty wouldn't have happened if it hadn't been for the pressure that groups like ours put on. We are getting through."

Betty Brightwell sees some tangible results at the base in Esquimalt (Victoria):

> They have a continuing radiation monitoring now and, thanks to us I think…they monitor a ship 24 hours when it's in, and they've got equipment, which they never had before. And in addition they activate a crew of twenty-four, I think, Nuclear Emergency Response Team, every time a ship comes out, nuclear warship and nuclear submarine. And the Base Commander has himself admitted that he is not allowed out of Victoria when they're in. So despite the fact that they say there is no risk, they've been doing these things and I think that is public pressure.

There have been other victories. In Kingston, they helped stop a casino from being built and helped stop plutonium from coming over the Thousand Island Bridge from the U.S., and taught their songs to some young men from Greenpeace in the process.

The Fredericton Grannies' initiative in solidarity with the gay and lesbian community received praise in a letter to the editor:

> I am writing to express my disgust and frustration at the letters written to the editor recently regarding the gay pride issue. I was…unaware of the misanthropy and blatant bigotry that exists in the city where I was born and raised. I am shocked and disturbed that so many of my fellow citizens appear to be consumed by hatred and ignorance…I would like to congratulate the group known as the Raging Grannies on their compassion and goodwill as well as their willingness to speak up for what they believe in. There are many people who could learn a valuable lesson from this group of ladies. Kudos to you Raging Grannies. I hope that more and more people will begin to speak up on behalf of the gay community of Fredericton.[7]

Even a longtime MP for Fundy-Royal and a former chairman of the Canadian Human Rights Commission publicly supported the Fredericton gays and lesbians and offered recognition for the work of the Raging Grannies:

> In Fredericton, it is to the Raging Grannies who were protesting in front of the city hall that we look for courage. By their action these women make real the inclusiveness of the community. By their brave act, Raging Grannies are demonstrating the broadest meaning of equality for all people. Gay-bashing, like other forms of bigotry, is the coward's way of registering their fear of the unknown. Gay-bashing has no place in the plural society that is modern Canada. It may be that the Grannies' use of wit to advance their cause is the key to success. Perhaps their funny costumes and comical songs may in the end break through the barriers of stubbornness that now prevail in this

stand-off between the mayor and the gay community. The Grannies present a formidable challenge to the mayor because their protest draws attention to what should be an issue that can be resolved by the stroke of the pen.[8]

In Kelowna, the Grannies tackled homelessness. When six "tent people" camping on city property were "rudely and roughly evicted" and arrested, a young man ran to Grannies for help, three of whom went to the police station. Pat Grinsteed writes:

> Most had been released, two were still in holding cells…The four released camp members arrived in smoke signal fashion, having heard that they had some community support but knowing a fig about Raging Grannies…The remaining two members were released…one without his shoes. The weather was cold…All their gear and belongings had been taken to the city yard, too far…to walk…[We]…offered our vehicles to…collect their stuff…The five men and a woman were frustrated and angry…We learned a lot about the Kelowna homeless…Our community contact for the homeless invited us to a council meeting…Someone informed the press that WE had managed to get into it [city council agenda]…We walked out into the media, all that is available to us in Kelowna, outnumbering us five. We just had to smile…It all turned out remarkably well…Daily paper…radio and TV were there…We got a lot of positive feedback on this TV segment. Since then the media have done just about all it can in interviewing…the NGOs who feed the homeless, researching the facilities offered and the roadblocks to helping the street people. Some churches are considering uniting with each other to provide overnight shelter with no strings attached. We learned that some organized hostels for men used methods of persuasion to convert them to their faith. There are NO overnight facilities for homeless women. Of the 100 or so out on the streets, at least 50 are very ill in one way or another…Now one month later, the subject is still in the headlines.[9]

Some evidence of their impact comes from unexpected sources:

> If the Raging Grannies had any doubts about whether their good-natured social activism was being heard in the halls of power, their doubts were allayed last fall when the RCMP Public Complaint Commission released to the APEC [Asia Pacific Economic Conference] inquiry secret documents containing defence department 'threat assessment' reports.[10]

During the enquiry into the RCMP handling of protesters at APEC in Vancouver in November 1997, secret military documents revealed the RCMP had an eye on the Grannies as a potential threat ("Are the Raging Grannies 'anti-Canadian' " *The Unitarian*, 1999). Another article by Allan Thompson, "Are Raging Grannies a public enemy?" said:

> Military documents marked 'secret' and 'Canadian eyes only' contain assessments of the threat posed during the last year's APEC summit by a host of terrorist groups—as well as the Anglican Church and the singing group, the Raging Grannies. Documents made public by the RCMP Public Complaint Commission [say]…'the Raging Grannies, while considered a low risk, were assessed as 'anti-Canadian forces' in the military documents.'[11]

Betsy Carr lives in Toronto and is a determined and energetic former social worker who worked with Children's Aid and in a mental health clinic. She was always "prepared to see what was reprehensible" around her and speak up as she wanted to help make the world a better place, make life more bearable. So being a Raging Granny does not seem such a big step because she has always believed in justice and, she says, "of course I'm a feminist." A proud mother and grandmother, she has no intention of meddling "in anything there, they're doing just fine." So she needed something worthwhile to do.

"A Granny isn't a grandmother, a Granny is a frame of mind. Attitude! You don't have to be a wife, a mother or a grandmother to have it. What you need is fervour, vehemence and commitment," she says categorically. Although much remains to be done for women, she has seen positive changes and feels women in Canada have come a long way in the last 30 or 40 years. She acknowledges that there are plenty of women in the world that have not had these opportunities, including women in the United States. Betsy praises the "first leaders in the women's movement in Canada."

Figure 73. Betsy Carr. Source: Eva Munro Collection.

Add Amnesty International and the International Centre for Human Rights and Democratic Development to the list. "Of course political cartoonists and humorists grabbed the knitting ball and ran with it" (S. Mardiros), not to mention the Raging Grannies. Joan Hadrill reacted swiftly and humorously:

You asked…'are Raging Grannies a public enemy? The Military listed the group as a slow-risk threat, secret papers show' (front page, Oct. 11). Obviously, you haven't been following our career as ragers for the past 10 or 11 years or you wouldn't be asking that question…Our mission statement says…that we believe in resolving conflicts in a non-violent manner. If that can be interpreted as 'anti-Canadian forces,' I'll eat my flowered hat and my feather boa. Really, how paranoid can you get! However, we are very happy to be lumped together with such distinguished groups as Amnesty International and the Anglican Church. We'd rather be on their side than Suharto's.[12]

Moira Dunphy, a Granny's daughter, inherited a gene for humour and wrote a letter to the editor, "That's my mother, sir—second terrorist on the left," in response to the article wondering if Grannies are a "public enemy":

Regarding the photograph that accompanied your Oct. 11 front-page article on APEC security, 'Raging Grannies a public enemy?' I feel it my civic duty to identify one of the 'anti-Canadians.' Second from the left, with the blue and white shawl, is my 72-year-old mother, Kathleen Dunphy. I sympathize with the military, for I also have felt threatened—since my teens—by her singing in public. Just say the word and I'll get the other senior terrorists identified by putting the thumbscrews to her.[13]

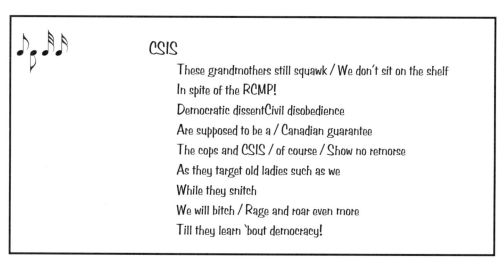

CSIS

These grandmothers still squawk / We don't sit on the shelf
In spite of the RCMP!
Democratic dissent Civil disobedience
Are supposed to be a / Canadian guarantee
The cops and CSIS / of course / Show no remorse
As they target old ladies such as we
While they snitch
We will bitch / Rage and roar even more
Till they learn 'bout democracy!

*Tune: Grandfather's Clock. Barbara Calvert Seifred Collection.*

Barbara Seifred kept notes:

As reported in…*NOW Magazine*: Colonel Peter MacLaren, in 1993 head of military police, asked for a list of what he called 'extremist and activist groups, membership in which could possibly be grounds for subsequent action by the Canadian forces'…or to which 'military personnel should not belong'…This was at the request of Robert Fowler, then (1993) Assistant Deputy Minister of National Defence, and now Canada's Ambassador to U.N. The Raging Grannies made the list. Thanks guys!

This may become a HIT SONG! Among others on the list: Project Ploughshares, Canadian Coalition for Nuclear responsibility, B'nai Brith, Roman Catholics, Sikhs, Baptists, United Church, Mennonites, the Hell's Angels and fourteen other motorcycle gangs, fourteen Asian Triads, white supremacist groups, left-wing groups, right-wing groups…AND THE DANGEROUS RAGING GRANNIES!

Songs convey the defiant and vibrant spirit of the Raging Grannies:

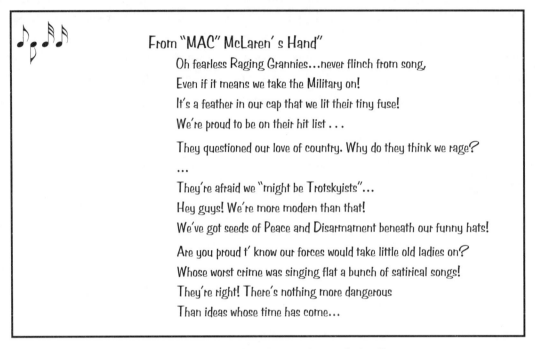

### From "MAC" McLaren's Hand"

Oh fearless Raging Grannies…never flinch from song,
Even if it means we take the Military on!
It's a feather in our cap that we lit their tiny fuse!
We're proud to be on their hit list . . .

They questioned our love of country. Why do they think we rage?
…
They're afraid we "might be Trotskyists"…
Hey guys! We're more modern than that!
We've got seeds of Peace and Disarmament beneath our funny hats!

Are you proud t' know our forces would take little old ladies on?
Whose worst crime was singing flat a bunch of satirical songs!
They're right! There's nothing more dangerous
Than ideas whose time has come…

*Tune: McNamara's Band. Barbara Calvert Seifred Collection.*

The fun continued. In "Silly Spy Files Aren't Limited to the U.S.," Allan Fotheringham compared these "revelations" to similar futile U.S. missions:

It comes as no surprise…that the FBI kept a file for 27 years on that dangerous terrorist known as Groucho Marx. A University of California professor, Jon Wiener, under the U.S. Freedom of Information Act, has obtained 27 pages of Marx's Federal Bureau of Information files. The file frequently misspells Groucho and 14 of its pages are still blacked out. We are not surprised because such nonsense, it is discovered, is going on to this day, on our own turf. Buried deep in the Ottawa documents uncovered over this APEC farce-inquiry going on in Vancouver, there has been found evidence that the RCMP—frightened to death, apparently—had fingerpointed the Ragin' Grannies as one of the threats to be watched at that summit conference last year. The documents show that the Ragin' Grannies—an amateurish blue-rinse group that plays at charities—are listed by the RCMP as 'anti-Canada.' This ranks right up there with the gumshoes of the FBI filling their notebooks with Groucho jokes that made fun of mum, apple pie and the flag…These dangerous youthful demonstrators who were not allowed to criticize the dictator Suharto were arrested but never charged with a single offence. This is Canada? In a more famous swoop, under Pierre Trudeau's War Measures Act, some 400 Quebecers—including prominent singers, poets and journalists—were jailed and not a one charged. At least some politicians thought the country was at peril then. Now we have a Key-stone Kops episode unfolding, with the revelations that Suharto thugs had hired beefy professional wrestlers to guard the Hotel Vancouver quarters where the now-deposed dictator stayed…It is not a good time for the horsemen, who may wish they were back in the Rockies with Nelson Eddy and Jeanette MacDonald. They have never really recovered their reputation since, asleep at the switch, they allowed a drunk to stumble his way into 24 Sussex Drive, leaving the confused and sleepy Prime Minister to defend himself with an Inuit carving. Now they're keeping files on a troupe of pensioners, who dress like something out of Ma and Pa Kettle and whose only weapons are canes and knitting needles. When the fuzz busy themselves being showbiz critics, we know the nation is really in trouble.[14]

While funny, Fotheringham brings up the seriousness of the RCMP arresting 400 people without charge during the 1970 October Crisis. Dissent is fundamental to democracy. The criminalising of dissent is a dangerous and slippery slope that must be checked. While being labelled "anti-Canadian" or "subversive" did not silence Grannies, one of them took it seriously and was afraid. After September 11, one Granny's husband also took it serious and wrote to their MP about the bill that would increase CSIS' powers asking if his wife was running any danger of being held incommunicado in jail for 72 hours since she was a member of two groups apparently on a list of "low-level security" upgraded to "subversive": the Raging Grannies and the Anglican Church.

Joan Harvey also reacted to being named subversive: "At first I was taken aback…[but] then I thought, God, we're being effective." French-speaking Montreal Grannies see it as a reflection of their effectiveness, a sign that it matters what they do, that they count. To be on the same list as the Anglican Church or Amnesty International is a form of recognition for this small group who "nickel and dime" their way. Another article raises that issue again:

Raging Granny Elinor Egar Reynolds isn't sure whether Mounties are infiltrating her organization. Just the same, there's a part of her that wants to believe the RCMP cares enough to listen in. 'We're invited to certain places,' Egar Reynolds deadpans. 'Sometimes, we turn up uninvited.' According to a report by Southam News and the *Ottawa Citizen*, the Grannies—who 'sing' about social justice on the protest circuit—have crashed enough events to make it onto an offbeat list of mild mannered subversives targeted by the RCMP. 'We all joke about that,' says Egar Reynolds…'The youngest in our group would be fifty-something. The eldest is 93. We pretty well know everybody, so it would be very difficult [to infiltrate]. I mean, I don't see a Granny coming in, joining and then running off to the RCMP and tattling. My feeling is that we've been considered by the RCMP a minor risk. That's damn good. With that in mind, we are probably down as, 'keep an eye on them. I don't know why, but keep an eye on them'.' The RCMP, meanwhile, denies reports that it is investigating or infiltrating the Grannies…Decked-out in pop bottle glasses, vintage hats, serious shawls and big purses, the Raging Grannies prepare for the demonstration fray with lyrics such as 'Oh, give me a home/where rivers don't foam/and the squirrels and chipmunks can play.' With groups in the U.S. basing local chapters on the Canadian Raging Grannies, they have gone international. More recently, they were credited with saving a throng of Quebec City protestors by getting in front of police and breaking into a song, which is probably why Egar Reynolds can't be sure about potential infiltration. 'It wouldn't surprise me,' she says. 'But it's so silly.'[15]

Underneath the fun, there is an underlying current of seriousness due to the consequences such labelling can have, especially since September 11, 2001. The Grannies' refusal to let this report intimidate them is reminiscent of Women Strike for Peace, a group of active U.S. housewives for peace who refused to be intimidated when fourteen members were subpoenaed to appear in front of the dreaded House of Un-American Activities Committee (HUAC) in 1962. Instead, Amy Swerdlow writes, women from all over the U.S. flooded the HUAC with requests to be subpoenaed so they too could appear in front of the notorious committee to share the wonderful things they were doing for their country! "For the first time HUAC was belittled with humour" and dealt a setback (1993: 117). Political theorist Jean Bethke Elstain suggests that Women Strike for Peace "showed the grand deconstructive power of a politics of humour, irony, evasion and ridicule" (in Swerdlow, 1993: 119). The Grannies are also exploring the possibilities of humour for political and social transformation. Their indomitable spirit of irreverence refused to be silenced; instead they memorialised this moment in song while the RCMP was creating a new unit, the Public Order Program (POP), after the APEC report.

**POP Goes Our Freedom– Democracy– Country**

Every time the Grannies go out / To sing a song of protest
Sargent Pepper starts to shout / POP goes the Mounties!
Round and round the summit site / The Mounties chase the people
"We don't want to see your signs" / POP goes our freedom

Threats to National Security
From COC [Council of Canadians] and the churches
Demand political purity / POP goes democracy,
They won't hear the COC / Nor unions, nor the Grannies
Rubber bullets in their guns / POP goes our fannies

To stop the appeals off Amnesty / For all political prisoners
They're putting POP in the RCMP / POP goes our community
Half a ton of pepper spray / A hose full of water
Blast the people off their feet / POP goes our balance

We are telling you in this song / Of the public order programme
The threat it presents is a serious wrong / POP goes our privacy
We love our country Democracy too
We want freedom for me and for you
And the Right to protest we had hitherto (slowly last three words)
OR– POP goes the country

*Tune: Pop Goes the Weasel. Granny Grapevine, Fall 2001.*

Unwittingly, the powers-that-be provide their own share of humour! The Grannies' name on the list of anti-Canadian groups generated humour, disbelief, but also concern: how can the authorities be taken seriously? What does it say about democracy and the right to dissent peacefully in our society? In a way, it is a measure of the effectiveness of the Raging Grannies that in fifteen years and with such a relatively small number, they managed to be a presence across the country. Being visible, they also become a symbol; how they are treated, or mistreated, is a measure of the depth of democracy in our society. They act out our democratic freedom and let us see how far it extends. In an editorial, "Hassling the Grannies," *The Gazette* (Montreal) "uses" the fact that Grannies are considered worthy of surveillance as a gage of our public freedom:

*Figure 74. Cartoon by Graham Harrop pokes fun at the RCMP or being suspicious of the Raging Grannies as anti-Canadian. Published in The Vancouver Sun, this cartoon was named the best editorial cartoon at the 11th BC Newspaper Awards. Source: Graham Harrop.*

> Freedom of expression is a precious and perishable thing. It can easily be whittled away by the kind of activity Canadian police and intelligence forces have engaged in recently. A Southam News series in *The Gazette* has detailed how the Royal Canadian Mounted Police and the Canadian Security Intelligence Service routinely spy on citizens or groups whose only 'crime' seems to be that they hold dissenting views on globalization, free trade or Canadian foreign policy. Groups subject to spying or infiltration have included the Canadian Labour Congress, the Council of Canadians, the satirical Raging Grannies, the Anglican Church and Amnesty International…There's a world of difference between monitoring a violent, anarchistic group like the Black Bloc and harassing a church group. This kind of Cold War mentality sends out a chilling message to those who hold dissenting views. It has no place in a liberal democracy. A properly functioning democracy should be a riot of competing voices clamouring to be heard. A society that can't accommodate free-wheeling debate or that won't make room for the vigorous expression of dissent can't really be called democratic [freedom of expression]…It's a freedom guaranteed by law, subject to reasonable restraints…We may find the protesters' point of view wrong-headed, even ridiculous. But we should defend their freedom to express it as if it were our own. That means being vigilant and demanding that Ottawa back off on its zeal to silence legitimate dissent.[16]

The message is clear: watch out, not for the Grannies, but for those who would like nothing better than a silenced, cowed population. In the mean time, Grannies keep their eye on things.

*Elinor Egar Reynolds lives in Halifax and heard about the Raging Grannies when her daughter sent her the Raging Grannies Songbook from British Columbia. When she saw the Halifax Grannies singing for International Women's Day she went up and said, "Can I join you?" "I was an activist but in a very small way. A youngster growing up in the south of Ireland, I used to be angry about things like the church and the facts of poor people...I belonged to the Irish Country Women Association [but was] always getting into trouble—minor, minor of course—sitting there thinking about injustice." After marriage and a move to Ottawa, she got involved in the community association, got a community center and a magazine going, which are still going on thirty years later. Moving to Prince Edward Island, she found few opportunities for activism but organized self-defense courses for women. She wonders why women are not more angry with all the violence and abuse that goes on.*

*She loves being a Granny: "In another life, I must have been a fool because just being so silly and dressing up makes so much sense. I did a little bit as a child...One time I dressed up as a cleaning woman and...I had a bucket of water, a scrubbing brush and a cloth. Well, the havoc I created with that bucket of water! I spilled it on people's shoes and I loved every minute of it. I thought, oh, I'd loved to keep doing this kind of stuff [but] you could be murdered, somebody might shoot you because you ruined [things]—putting water in people's boots and things like that. I love to do things like that."*

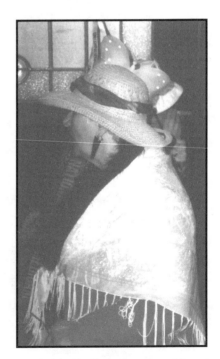

Figure 75. Elinor Egar Reynolds.
Source: Carole Roy.

*Elinor volunteered with community organizations until recently and although the other volunteers were "wonderful women, wonderful women," she did not tell them she was a Raging Granny "because they were either widows or wives of wealthy men and they wouldn't understand." Grannies "sing stuff that isn't being spoken about generally in public...We can say what we want and we can do what we want and...We don't give a damn."*

## Chipping Away at Stereotypes of Aging

We tried growing old gracefully but it was too damn boring!    —Betsy Carr

Call me "senior," call me "oldster"

Call me "Nanna" or "Gram"

Call me "elderly person"

That's not all I am

Inside I am young, maybe younger than you

Becoming somebody

Still finding out WHO!

…

*Tune: Moonshine / I'm a Rambler. Raging Grannies "Carry On" Songbook.*

Grannies challenge stereotypes of grannyhood and "the elderly, feeble female" (Woodland) "who shuffles onto a TV ad looking for Geritol," adds Moira Walker.

### Wrinkle, Wrinkle Aging Star

Wrinkle, wrinkle aging star,

Who cares just how old you are?

Your hair is grey, your dentures click

Your bosom sags, your ankle's thick

Your joints all creak, your arthritis plagues

You've got all the symptoms of Raging Age

…

Hurrah for Age, Age, now's the time to rage

…

Hurrah for Age, Age, to Hell with being beige

We won't stay cooped up in a cage

Our eyes are dim but our tongues are sharp

We go out on a limb, our wits are sharp

Yes we've got years, years and you'd better get it clear

A raging gran's a force to fear

*Tune: Twinkle, Twinkle Little Star. Parliament Hill Mob (Ottawa Raging Grannies).*

Overlooked by men or younger women in mainstream organisations, older women became the norm within the Raging Grannies and could find their own voices, says John Burns. Lorna Drew adds:

> What we're about is more power and visibility for older women. That might change some people's minds…To see a bunch of old ladies out there looking funny and singing about it, you have to wonder what's going on…I don't know that it changes minds politically but maybe if you get people thinking…And once you make an inroad, who knows what is going to filter through.

They "may look like a group of kind, little old ladies. But looks can be deceiving," says Heather Bell, acknowledging the Grannies do not behave as expected. So if you "tend to equate grey hairs with seriousness and meekness, think again. The Raging Grannies have proven that it's not only wisdom that comes with age—humour, courage and outrage do too," wrote Anna Quon. "They've managed to remind me that elderly people are capable of many things," said a sociology student at Vanier College in Montreal. The Grannies make aging more attractive. Betty Mardiros' granddaughter wants to be a Raging Granny when she grows up and one student told a Granny, "Gee, I can't wait to get old so I can join the Grannies!" Such comments are not unusual, says Angela Silver. Loretta Biasutti, a Calgary Granny, explained that their power comes from playing on stereotypes of their granny image and their subversive ways. Their challenge transforms older women into people capable of a lot of playful energy, said Doran Doyle. Sarah Ellis, who wrote a review of children's literature in *Quill & Quire,* agrees:

> We have a splendid regiment of young women in our books…I expect these girls to weather the storm of adolescence, to tackle whatever adult life presents with zeal and humour, and to join the Raging Grannies when they retire. This is also my confident hope for the readers of great books for girls.[17]

Social activism can not be identified with any one generation. "Women can feel good that they have a place when they get older, and they could be considered write-offs you know," said Doran Doyle. The figure of the Raging Granny provides a dynamic group identity for older women, an identity that allows them a public voice. At times, the media use Raging Granny as a generic term to denote persistence and humour and, occasionally, silliness. The image of the Raging Granny stuck in the media and people's minds, which supports Doran Doyle's assertion that "imagination is power." Their approach allows women a wider range of emotions and turns rage into a positive transformative energy. There is a role for older women's power and the Raging Granny figure is one way to gain access to power, wrote Rose DeShaw:

> Underneath the humour in the songs and costumes there is a nod to the wisdom of older women. Walt Whitman calls it 'the divine maternity.' He talks about a woman of 80 called 'The Peacemaker'…'who was tacitly agreed on as…a settler of difficulties and a reconciler in the land.' That's my granny model. If ever a country needed reconciling, it is Canada at the end of the nineties. Governmental dumbness has spread so fast it could keep an entire platoon of grannies singing our lungs out. Some buffoon wants to turn the 300-year old fort in our town into a casino. Abused women are now allowed to stay only two days in shelters in Ontario. And they're trying to privatize fire departments.[18]

"The world needs more Raging Grannies," says a letter to the editor in response to criticism of the Grannies' stand against the U.S. war in Afghanistan:

It has been said that women's pattern of activism, culturally, is often different from men's. Women become more radical with age, men become more conservative. Perhaps that is why we have the Raging Grannies singing their pleas for 'justice, not revenge' and why their critics are male. No, I don't believe the Grannies are naïve. By the time they became Grannies they had, no doubt, memories of…the First World War and had heard the stories of those who had not returned or returned shattered. These women are of an age that has seen brothers, friends or husbands serve in the Second World War or Korea. They remember the casualty lists and they are determined that the children they bore or the grandchildren they have seen come into this world are here for some other purpose than as sacrifices to war. Generation after generation is told, 'This is the war to end all wars,' but wars are never really over and history is written by the victors…According to the United Nations Food and Agriculture Organization (FAO), approximately 35,600 children died from conditions of starvation on September 11. There must be hundreds of potential Raging Grannies in Brantford. I only wish I could carry a tune.[19]

## Media Magnets: Not Only a Protest, an Event!

"Sure, plenty of other groups protest against clear-cutting, unfair taxation and nuclear arms, but only the Grannies can turn a protest into an *event*," wrote David Ferman. The Grannies enliven laborious meetings, like the one on amalgamation that took place in Ottawa:

> Just as journalists were ready to write off the whole exercise as exceedingly, mind-numbingly dull after five hours of torturous bureaucratese, along came the Raging Grannies. The senior citizen protest group, often spotted at events with their trademark bonnets, knitted shawls and tambourines, stood before the board and put their concerns to song…The sextet was like a breath of fresh—some might say frivolous—air after five, straight, sleep-inducing hours of presentations from interest group after interest group who politely objected to everything from privatizing public health programs to library cuts. After it was recommended last week that 800 to 900 full-time jobs be eliminated and at least $60 million be cut from 24 merged departments, we were expecting fireworks… Instead, we were faint with boredom. 'The opportunity to create a department of planning, which is the best of its kind, is remarkable,' was just one hotly inspiring statement heard throughout the day, from Ottawa Construction Association president…But, wait, there's more—And then there were the life-saving Raging Grannies, delivering their message to the tune of 'Glory, Glory, Hallelujah.' Previously numb board members suddenly came alive, grinning from ear to ear, not really caring what the seniors' message was, just delighted that they were jarred out of their stupor.[20]

The mood in a Toronto amalgamation meeting was similar:

> In the lightest moment of often angry anti-amalgamation arguments…the Raging Grannies donned their floral bonnets and drew giggles from committee members with a protest song, 'Say good bye to megacity,' waving gleefully to the…Legislature general committee…The singing grannies weren't officially named as a group on the list of 41 deputations…But the packed room instantly lit up with laughter, smiles and applause.[21]

In Guelph, they drew giggles during the provincial election campaign:

Humour wasn't on the agenda, but it was a big part of [the] Ontario's provincial election meeting in Guelph where everyone, from candidates to moderator to audience, were cracking jokes. Perhaps the Raging Grannies, a group known for their songs of protest and sense of humour, set the stage. They stood up, pulled out their tambourines and began to sing about five minutes before the meeting got under way.[22]

The Raging Grannies rarely go unnoticed. While some thought that board members did not really care what the Grannies' message was, board members were not listening to any other message either. But the media noticed.

## Making Media Headlines or Landing on the Cutting Room Floor?

Are you landing on the cutting room floor asked *Granny Grapevine* (May 1993)? Which media would not like colourful and witty actions? The media generally responds well to the Grannies' ability to capture the attention and deliver a message. The Raging Grannies are newsworthy and for some that is a sign of their effectiveness. In her article about the Greenham Common peace camp, Shelly Romalis (1987) reports that the media was "caustic in its labelling of the Greenham women as freaky, lesbian, dirty, noisy, causing tumult" and "capitalized on the sensational aspects of the camp rather than on the continual, solid acts of resistance that characterize everyday activities" (91).

The media use the colourful and innovative presence of the Grannies, but rarely in a vicious way. Kathleen Dunphy believes that their value and relevance are in catching people's attention; theoretically, anyone can stand up for what they believe, but the Grannies just found a way to make sure they get a platform, and sometimes it works.

Lorna Drew wrote to the local newspaper and acknowledged its help:

Thank you for the excellent coverage you gave the Raging Grannies when we demonstrated at the Atlantic Breast Health conference at the Delta Brunswick. Since the Delta Brunswick ejected us (it's amazing how a few singing seniors armed only with clothespins and a wooden spoon can raise the anxiety level of officials), it's good that the *Times Globe* was able to bring the issue of breast cancer and the environment to public notice.[23]

Their experience with a mostly favourable press resembles the experience of the Love Canal's protesters where reporters became part of the scene. Both groups presented themselves as outraged mothers or grandmothers, making it interesting for media but difficult for authorities to deal with: they used stereotypes in their favour while challenging other aspects of the same stereotypes.

At first glance, it is difficult to take the Grannies seriously. Three of the 13 members, women dressed in flamboyant hats and aprons and waving wooden spoons, are engaged in a passionate discussion about the hot water they could get into today. It may not sound like the workings of a growing social action group, but a few moments spent listening to their voices mingling on issues of social justice soon persuades the doubtful of their commitment to the issues.[24]

The Raging Grannies provoke the imagination of the media. They were called a "kazoo-playing troupe [who] would rather needle politicians than knit," a play on the stereotype of older women as knitters. They are "Grannies who combat war with comedy" or are "about as subtle as a chainsaw at a church social," which convey their irreverence. Raging Grannies are referred to in military terms, "elite squadron of activists" or

"Grey power platoon." They are said to be unstoppable, outraged, outrageous and fun-loving cartoon Grannies, a rag tag group of grandmothers or a gaggle of Grannies, crooners, or social activists in sensible shoes. They "terrorize" the stage or "warble against war toys." "Don't Mess with these Nice Old Ladies" because Grannies are "Mad as hell!" "Not Older Women—BOLDER Women!" who are "Rebels With Parasols" or "Thorns in the side of the establishment." In the early days, it was said that there was "not a hairnet, knitting needle or bottle of blue rinse" in sight and that they were the "liveliest social rights group to hit the scene" (Reffes 12). They have been called "grandmas of dissent" with "feisty attitudes [that] have gotten the Grannies kicked out of malls, and into all sorts of mischief for the greater good of humanity" (Hausknecht 19). They "cause a ruckus everywhere they go." One article expands:

> The Edmonton Raging Grannies might look like a clique of cookie bakers when they're in costume, but believe me, they are not…These are kind, caring women. But they should never be taken lightly, or painted with some kind of tired stereotype. Nor should their movement be shrugged off as a quaint hobby for the old folks, like lawn bowling or macrame.[25]

Someone even suggested the Raging Grannies have become so familiar across Canada that they might be an entry in the next edition of the Canadian Encyclopedia. They are "veteran warriors" or "off-beat Grannies" singing "songs of cheeky irreverence." In Saint John, New Brunswick, an article puts the city on notice of the arrival of the Raging Grannies:

> If Saint John businesses put profits before people, they had better listen for the shuffling footsteps. If corporations spray herbicides, they'd better be ready to face raucous music. If anybody in this region does anything that might hurt the future of our world's grandchildren, they ought to be prepared. Prepared for bright purple. Prepared for clamorous singing. Prepared for the Raging Grannies. They've arrived in Saint John.[26]

In Peterborough, they are also descriptive:

> They're grannies and they're rocking, but not on their front verandahs…[They] like to kick up their heels, raise their voices and everyone else's social consciousness at the same time…There's little doubt the Raging Grannies like to take a kick at the can any chance they get. Ageism is one social issue they tackle with particular joie de vivre. The clunky shoes and sagging nylons worn by some members in performance gives the group the chance to collectively thumb its nose at anyone who thinks that's what being over 50 is about, says member Joan Smith…Smith heartily debunks the myth that youth and rebellion are synonymous. In her mind, a seasoned mind and body can also make a fine bedfellow when social change is on the agenda.[27]

The Calgary Raging Grannies "don't have a lot of time for knitting and sewing…It's just that swimming against the Conservative Calgary mainstream takes up all the spare time" wrote Shelley Mardiros. They have become a common presence at peace and environmental rallies. The media obviously enjoy coming up with humorous images and descriptions of the Grannies, keeping in tune with the Grannies' own style of doing things. It does make for lively articles.

A few images had negative connotations: they "rant all day" conveys mindless prattle, which limits discussion of the issues they espoused. Another article reports that the then Minister of National Defence, William McKnight, was no admirer of Victoria's Raging Grannies. In a speech to business people, McKnight suggested that they should raise their fees if the Grannies were part of the community. He was reportedly quite irritated with the Grannies. Irritation means the former minister's sense of control was affected: had he been feeling in control he would have been dismissive or condescending, not irritated. Irritation is certainly part of the response some people have to the Grannies. Remember the Victoria Grannies trotting off to the Armed Forces Recruitment Centre to volunteer for service in the Gulf and there were letters to editors by people angry at their antics. Peter C. Newman also used the Grannies in his advice for Kevin Benson, then CEO of Canadian Airlines who saw his whole board of directors resigned:

> The Buzz Hargrove corporate courage under fire award to the ten directors of Canadian Airlines who, at the most critical moment of the company's struggle to stay aloft, resigned to protect themselves against law suits—while at the same time endorsing a ten per cent wage cut for employees. Memo to Kevin Benson: next time hire a troop of Victoria's Raging Grannies to sit around your boardroom table. They'll rant all day, and they never quit.[28]

While the writer obviously has a different opinion, the Grannies are a symbol of persistence that he expects the mainstream audience to understand. This shows how successfully the Grannies have penetrated the Canadian culture.

Humorous expressions of dissent generate an atmosphere where opposite views can be aired. Instead of fist fights or analytical debates, which often narrow options, humour expands possibilities by encouraging new connections that allow opponents to engage in some, if limited, exchange. The Grannies can use humour because they are "extremely well informed about complex social and environmental issues," said Murray Thompson of Peacefund Canada (Semenak 1991). They are often referred to in media reports as a measuring rod, "even the Raging Grannies," which is meant to convey the non-violent, good-natured aspect of the event. Some may interpret the playful, humorous tone media often use with the Grannies as a put-down. In the early days the Grannies expressed no ambiguity towards the media but felt it was a positive experience. Over time, though, some Grannies are more critical.

Aside from their outlandishness and humour, one writer believes that:

> Their success lies in the fact that people suffer from media 'fatigue' when bombarded with globally grave issues such as the greenhouse effect and world poverty. With their canny self-deprecation and humour, the Grannies get their message across to an otherwise unreceptive audience.[29]

Ralph Nader has a view of the media that is of interest:

> It is a sign of a closing media pattern when jokes, humor and laughter have to be the principal means of conveying concerns over injustices and abuses that affect many innocent people. In the U.S., as serious public discourse over television and radio dwindles to a trickle, Politically Incorrect, Saturday Night Live and Larry King become occasional sound-bite outlets for a serious point or two. As the mass media expands the entertainment and advertising worlds, the serious world begs for some little attention in between.[30]

Nader's idea strangely echoes backwards to a 1989 letter to the editor of a Victoria newspaper which reveals how the Grannies were, at times, successful in spreading the news of incoming U.S. nuclear vessels in Victoria's waters:

> I noticed that on June 12 [1989], you covered the 'Raging Grannies' response to a U.S. nuclear-armed submarine visiting our harbour—but your own Marine Watch column did not include this informa-

tion. Does this mean that the *Times-Colonist* has now relegated the visits of nuclear warships to the world of fantasy and humour rather than the world of fact? With all due respect to the Raging Grannies, they do have a way of making light of serious matters, as a way of surviving in this nuclear age. But I am not sure that a newspaper should devote itself exclusively to a granny-view of things…I would like to see our harbour declared a nuclear-free zone as a small first step. And until that happens, I would love to see the visits of nuclear warships made front-page news. At the very least, they should be in the Marine Watch.[31]

By their antics, the Grannies provided the newspaper with colourful news, which publicised the coming of these ships, and this reader demands higher quality journalism because of what the Grannies highlighted and what the newspaper ignored, except as theatrical antics. In this light, the Grannies had a positive impact on the dissemination of information by being newsworthy. They found a crevice in the media world, which they managed to fill at that time. But they are aware that humour can backfire, as Granny Helen Budd Hannah said: "There is a difference between being viewed as 'humorous' and being trivialized. Freedom of press means that we will not be part of the editing and production decisions unless invited."

In spite of the coverage Grannies' actions get, at times it is without much substance, especially on TV, as the reasons for their protests are quickly brushed aside. Muriel Duckworth agrees: "The media likes to take the pictures but the caption does not say much about what the issue is. It always annoys me. It says the Raging Grannies sang but it doesn't always say what the issue was." Muriel feels the attention they get must be "for something worth doing." She continues:

I just can't believe that people aren't so outraged about what's going on that it overflows in the media. And the media's coverage is so bad. They're just taking what the government is giving out… That's another thing that we have to do…try to get out what's really happening. There's some e-mail that's doing the job that the regular media should be doing. What people have to be paying attention to now is the alternative press because we're not getting it very often from the regular media.

In such a vacuum of real reporting, activists like the Grannies almost become a form of alternative media themselves as they highlight the media's "sin of omission." Fran Thoburn adds:

Our media is so strongly controlled by the conservative right wing…that we no longer have that protection against criticism. People who are flamboyantly angry about critics get a lot of air time and a lot of newspaper time now…Before, they'd be mentioned and then go on to something else, but now letters are written explicitly criticizing what we do without another letter saying, 'Yeah, the Grannies are blah, blah, blah.' A supporting letter, small, might appear three days later rather than together. There used to be much more balanced coverage of some of our outlandish stuff.

Yet Fran says TV is often their best friend and recalls the visit of Stockwell Day, then leader of the Alliance Party, during a federal election:

I was pulled over backwards. I was holding a banner and they pulled the banner, grabbed it the minute it went up and I was pulled over backwards and then they started to grab me and push me and the TV camera came on and everybody was hands off…Well, they know they don't want Stockwell Day supporters looking like they're beating up an old lady.

So the image of Grannies as older women acts as a protection. Again, Fran says:

Our older image is important to us and it makes us kind of untouchable in a way, used to anyway. We didn't used to get arrested but now we get tossed around a bit. I've never been arrested but I've done a lot of civil disobedience. I've been carried bodily out of places but they didn't use to dare touch us, manhandle us. But now they don't seem to care so much. The last three years it's got worse. [Since the interview Fran has been arrested at the BC Legislature protesting cuts to healthcare.]

It is also true that the Grannies get things reported by being such a visible and persistent "pesky" non-violent presence, and not only because of humour. Their humour and unpredictability keep them worthy of attention—a foot in the door of the media so to speak. At times, a reference to the Grannies' presence is used to reveal ill-thought plans or overreactions by authorities:

The Premier had just announced his resignation and jelly doughnut dust had the potential to incite near panic, and there, in a downtown Toronto park, a couple hundred of police officers—clad in body armour and sporting the very latest in crowd control weaponry—were closing in on a few old ladies. A scene from a very odd day, during very strange times. The ladies were handbag-toting, shawl-wearing members of the Raging Grannies protest group, and all that was left of an innocuous rally held Tuesday at Simcoe Park, following a morning of wider protest in the financial core that saw major traffic disruption, heated exchanges between activists and motorists, and petty vandalism. Organizers of the 'snake march' have faced harsh words for holding such a protest at a time when people are still in shock…over the September 11 terrorist attacks. Toronto Mel Lastman called the 2,000 protesters 'animals.' Police Chief Julian Fantino labelled them 'organized criminals.' A judge presiding over a bail hearing for some…protesters…weighed in, calling them 'potential terrorists.'[32]

The article suggests that organisers considered scrapping the protest given it was so soon after the events of September 11, but after consultations with various groups decided the need to speak out was greater than ever. They were very careful about tactics so as not to upset the public mood. The Grannies were courageous enough to show up in such "strange times" and refused to be silenced. In contrast, we see the overreaction of the police and the raw nerves of authorities who display little understanding of the fundamental role of dissent in democracy. By their presence, the Grannies, who unquestionably represent a non-violent approach, highlight the contradictions between the pretence of democratic rights and the lack of understanding of the fundamentals of our society. Non-violence seeks to highlight such contradictions in a system that makes legal claims yet disregards them in practice.

The Grannies attract international attention. Margaret Horsfield, who interviewed the Saltspring Grannies for *The Guardian,* played some of the interviews on BBC, which resulted in "all kinds of enquiries about starting Grannie groups in England," wrote Lou Rumsey (*Granny Grapevine,* May 1993). In the summer of 1995, a Japanese film crew working on a film about environmental issues filmed them (*Granny Grapevine,* Summer 1995). Faith Petric, a San Fransisco writer, wrote a column, "The Folk Process," in *Sing Out!* magazine and used Raging Grannies' songs (*Granny Grapevine,* February 1997). A reporter for the medical press asked for a copy of a song that "packed a punch" at the Romanow commission on health care in Montreal. Their participation in the WTO protests in Seattle attracted much media attention: *Times, USA Today, The New York Times, The Wall Street Journal, International Herald Tribune.* Since the WTO, the Seattle Grannies "have become even more in demand," been interviewed by a magazine in Paris, and appeared in an Australian newspaper, to name just a few. The Grannies hope such reports will spark "the birth of Raging Grannies groups in cities all across the U.S. just as now exist across Canada" (*Granny Grapevine*, Winter 2000). Simon Birch begins his article in a travel magazine published in the UK (*Saga* September 2001), with "meet the Raging Grannies, one of Canada's best-loved and most celebrated environmental and activist group." Doris McNab wrote since then,

> …the response has been amazing. Letters asking how to start a Raging Grannies group keep pouring in. I have sent off 15 packets to the UK…Then they write back with news clippings about marches of 100,000 in London that we never see on TV…A visitor to our church told us about a Seattle march of 15,000 and Vancouver had a peace walk of 5000. Nothing on radio or TV or in the papers. But when 3000 Canadians organized a demonstration to support the U.S. in New York [after September 11], there was loud and long coverage.[33]

Such networking fills a void left by the media's omissions. In another international venue, this time at the Hague Appeal for Peace, three Raging Grannies from Toronto were invited to perform in front of illustrious and internationally known politicians and activists working for peace; their picture was published in the Hague Appeal for Peace Newsletter. Interestingly, the Grannies' presentation was featured in one of the seventeen minutes of *The Hague Appeal for Peace* video, which is intended to accompany the booklet with the Agenda for the 21st Century fifty points for activists.

*Figure 76. Toronto Raging Grannies Betsy Carr, Philippa Jecchinis, and Phyllis Creighton sing for an international audience, a program that included a speech by Kofi Annan, at the Hague Appeal for Peace Conference, May 26, 1999. Source: Phyllis Creighton Collection.*

## Notes

1. *Granny Grapevine*, Winter 2002: 5.

2. Project Ploughshares Invitation, October 15, 1998, Louise Swift Collection.

3. *Granny Grapevine*, Fall 1997: 3.

4. Rose DeShaw, 1997, "Goofy-hatted reconcilers in the land," *The Globe and Mail*, April 10: A20.

5. *Granny Grapevine*, Spring 1996: 14.

6. *Granny Grapevine*, Spring 1994: 8.

7. Leanne Smith, "Hatred seething just below surface in gay pride controversy," Letter to the editor, *The Fredericton Daily Gleaner*, August 27, 1998: A6.

8. Fairweather, "Woodside must protect the rights of this minority," *The Saint John Telegraph-Journal*, July 21, 1998 [np]. Lorna Drew Collection.

9. *Granny Grapevine*, Winter 2002: 20.

10. Shelley Mardiros, "Raging gracefully," *Alberta Views*, 3(1) 2000: 30.

11. Allan Thompson, "Are Raging Grannies a public enemy?" *The Toronto Star*, October 11, 1998: A1.

12. Joan Hadrill, "Grannies rage peacefully," *The Toronto Star*, October 21, 1998: A21.

13. Moira Dunphy, "That's my mother, sir—second terrorist on the left," *The Toronto Star*, October 21, 1998: A21.

14. Allan Fotheringham, "Silly spy files aren't limited to U.S," *The Kitchener-Waterloo Record*, October 17, 1998: A19.

15. Vern Smith, "RCMP targets Raging Grannies," *Eye News* (Toronto), October 11, 2001: 12, 14.

16. "Hassling the Grannies," *The Gazette* (Montreal), August 24, 2001: B2.

17. Sarah Ellis, "Great Canadian books for girls," Book review, *Quill & Quire* 63(7) 2002: 51.

18. Rose DeShaw, "Goofy-hatted reconcilers in the land," *The Globe and Mail*, April 10, 1997: A20.

19. Doris Marcellus, "The world needs more Raging Grannies," Letter to the editor, *Brantford Expositor*, November 21, 2001: A4.

20. Jacki Leroux, "Pain without passion: Megacity talk a snoozefest: From the painfully boring to the playfully bizarre," *The Ottawa Sun*, August 2, 2000: 4.

21. Lisa Wright and Paul Moloney, Four Raging Grannies spark mega-giggles. *The Toronto Star*, February 7, 1997: A8.

22. Janet Baine, "Election meeting a real hoot: All-candidates debate features, Raging Grannies' laughter," *The Kitchener-Waterloo Record*, May 27, 1999: B5.

23. Lorna Drew, "Raging Grannies appreciate coverage," Letter to the editor, *The Saint John Telegraph-Journal*, May 15, 2000: C4.

24. Stephenie Campbell, "Onward Raging Grannies," *The New Brunswick Telegraph Journal*, July 8, 1998: [np], Lorna Drew Collection.

25. Scott McKeen, "Raging gracefully: Edmonton Raging Grannies raise their voices to save the planet," *The Edmonton Journal*, October 11, 1992: E5.

26. John Mazerolle, "All the rage," *The Saint John Telegraph-Journal*, April 16, 2001: A3.

27. Cindy Nuttall, "These Grannies debunk myths," *The Examiner* (Peterborough), August 17, 1996: D4.

28. Peter C. Newman, "Most memorable 1996 absurdities," *Macleans'*, 109 (53) 1996: 96.

29. Simon Birch, "Where middle age is all the rage," *SAGA* (Britain), September 2001: 108.

30. Ralph Nader, "Raging Grannies: An instrument of protest," *Briarpatch*, July/August: 3, 1998.

31. Hubert Meeker, "Watching for nukes," Letter to the editor, *Times-Colonist* (Victoria), June 24, 1989: A4.

32. Jim Rankin, Sonia Verma, and Tony Bock, "Staging protests in strange times," *Toronto Star*, October 21, 2001: A7.

33. *Granny Grapevine*, Winter 2002: 3.

Chapter Seven

# NO MOVEMENT WITHOUT PEOPLE, NO JUSTICE WITHOUT CHANGE
## The Raging Grannies' Impact on People, Themselves Included

If you do not specify and confront real issues, what you do will surely obscure them. *If you do not alarm anyone morally* you will yourself remain morally asleep. If you do not embody controversy, what you say will be an acceptance of the drift to the coming human hell.
—C. Wright Mills

*Figure 77. Victoria Raging Grannies share their songs with young students.
Source: Hilda Marzcak Collection.*

## Can You Be This Outrageous and Not Meet Opposition? Not Only Admirers

Given the controversial issues the Grannies deal with, they have their opponents. While the tone of most of the articles I read was curiosity or appreciation, a few were negative. Early on, the University of Victoria Progressive Conservative (PC) Youth Club was critical of the Grannies who planned to attend, and no doubt disrupt, a meeting their club had organised with the Defence Minister:

> Unfortunately your enlightenment has come years too late. The problems of our generation such as the National Debt and environmental decay were caused by your generation. By obstructing an attempt to discuss today's problems with your cheap public stunts, you may ease your conscience and provide filler for the TV cameras but you do nothing to alleviate these problems. Any fool can criticize but hard work and a positive attitude is needed to build for the future.[1]

The Grannies "put some people off, turn others on…When you say raging, it's usually *against* something," says Betty Mardiros who feels it may come across as negative. Elinor Egar Reynolds met with dismissal from a friend who thinks the Grannies are just a laugh, doing basically nothing, and having no impact. While Elinor was dismayed by her friend's view she does not "give a damn" about what people think. Phyllis Creighton recalled the curt and obstinate reply to her letter of explanation from a well-known columnist who took a dim view of the Grannies in his published column. When the Vancouver Grannies sang in support of the Concerned Citizens Against the Casino (CCAC) presenting a brief to the Vancouver Parks Board, the casino developers were definitely not amused, but the clapping of CCAC members made up for the hostility. When the *Times-Colonist* (Victoria) music reviewer listed "never having to hear the Raging Grannies sing again" as one of his New Year's wishes, Fran Thoburn emphasised her love for "the atonal quality" of their singing.

There have been times when opposition is vocal and very public. One protest drew fury. When soldiers were leaving the military base in Esquimalt for the 1991 Gulf War, six members of the Greater Victoria Disarmament Group (GVDG) and a few individual Grannies "wrapped themselves in green garbage bags…and rolled down the sidewalk" to the entrance of the base. This protest was viewed by many as a "distasteful, insensitive" body bag protest although, according to Jeff Morrow's article, the protesters' press release stated their wish "to dramatize the real possibility of our children being killed in the Middle East." The *Times-Colonist* (Victoria) editorial was very critical:

> Symbols can be positive and inspirational but they can also be deeply offensive and frightening…In selecting such powerful symbols to dramatize their protest and embarrass the Canadian government, did the anti-war protesters consider the possibility that they would exacerbate the sorrow and anxiety for scores of local families?…The peace groups should have…directed their pitch to Ottawa in less offensive ways. By tactics such as these they simply alienate public support for their cause.[2]

One distinguishing feature of this protest was the lack of the Grannies' usual humour. Betty Brightwell, married to a retired military officer, did not agree with the action but wrote this letter, "Shock Tactics," to a local newspaper:

> In the case of the Persian Gulf affair, there is no justification for going to war. Our young men and women are being told to restore a filthy-rich dictatorship in Kuwait, to die for a guaranteed world oil supply and to fight for the state of Israel if a war escalates. I regret that the street theatre performed by an ad hoc group of peace activists offended some people. That is the nature of truth. Sometimes when truth is exposed, it is offensive and shocking. In this case, by rolling body bags down the hill to the gates of CFB Esquimalt, it was intended to be just that.[3]

Lorna Drew, one of the Grannies who took part in the Closets Are For Brooms protest in support of gays and lesbians in Fredericton, got "some pretty nasty and vicious comments." Lorna even got a letter in her university mailbox chastising the Grannies saying: "Who are you anyway?"

> It was really quite weird. It was cranky. He signed his name but I didn't know who it was. Just somebody who didn't like what we were doing. We had people on the streets making obscene gestures and shouting, not a lot, not [enough] to disrupt.

Being vulnerable to criticism has led some Grannies away. Lorna remembers:

> Somebody who was with us is no longer a Granny because she was threatened in terms of losing her government job…You can't take sides if you're working for the government. She is one of the younger Grannies and she's got a few years to go. The minute she gets her walking papers she's gonna be a Granny again, but that was pretty scary. We hadn't realised that kind of thing could happen. And of course with the political climate now, we're all on a hit list somewhere, I'm sure that we are. We were declared [subversive].

Muriel Duckworth wishes for more contact with opponents: "It's all to the good that people are paying attention. I wish that the people who don't agree with us on something would ask us to sing for them! They don't. We've never been asked by the military to sing for them." Edmonton Grannies sang for the Liberals and the NDP, but the Conservatives and the Reform (then Alliance, now Conservative) have not yet asked them; still, they suggest that they "often sing *to* the Tories [in power in Alberta]" but not by invitation! On one occasion they were invited to a Legion and got a polite but frosty reception from the veterans. For her part, Fran Thoburn is more afraid of police and security guards overreactions since September 11, 2001, yet a few months later she and four Victoria Grannies "shouted down provincial politicians" in protest of cuts to health care, "temporarily halting proceedings in the legislature while security officials scrambled to usher them out of the chamber…The five women were banned from the legislature," wrote Jim Beatty. Fear, as Audre Lorde said, need not stop us.

At times, support comes in the midst of opposition. A Saskatoon Korean War veteran wrote a letter to the editor because he felt he

> …must apologize to the representatives of various peace organizations, including The Raging Grannies, Veterans Against Nuclear Arms, Ploughshares…and Food Not Bombs, who were evicted from the property just outside the main entrance to the Canada Remembers International Air Show…These groups had been granted permission to set up an information/entertainment site but were later told to clear out, after several veterans had complained to managers of the Air Show. It seems we veterans love to prattle about how we saved the world for democracy and the Four Freedoms, but we have no scruples about denying these fine groups their right to exercise free speech. I kind of wish the groups hadn't left when ordered. It would have been a real hoot to see octogenarians maced, manacled and led away.[4]

He points to the superficial understanding of democracy shown by this incident and perceives the power of seniors standing up for their convictions. To generate public discussion on various issues, Grannies risk rejection and ridicule which requires conviction and humility, and is easier done with the solidarity of a group. The Grannies like to say that they do not take themselves seriously, a healthy approach for people courting controversy.

Angela Silver was invited by members of her church to join the Raging Grannies. Born and raised in French-speaking Montreal by Russian Ukrainian parents, who were immigrants, she is sensitive to the plight of new immigrants. She worked for a union before retiring, discovered the uses of humour, and always had a love of theatre and singing. Although always very active, she did not think of herself as an activist until CBC phoned her saying, "we have you on a list of activists." "Oh my goodness, I'm on a list!" said Angela. She is curious, gregarious, and a great believer in coalitions.

She is inspired by Archbishop Oscar Romero of El Salvador who politicians thought was "safe to promote because…he was sickly, and he was conservative. He wouldn't stir the pot. But he became interested in the poor and…became much too radical and they got rid of him." She says, "Christianity can be hazardous to your health. It was certainly hazardous to Jesus' health, it's hazardous to many who take a stand…When our church was battling with whether to let gay ministers be ordained…I was very proud of our church in that moment. It was a very heated debate…Leaders in the church…discussed their positions. Some of these positions were quite remarkable. But then an ordinary little man would get up, no great theologian, not a minister, just a man, and he took…just a simple position of compassion and sympathy and human rights. There is a hero, not one of those people you expect to say great things…but just an ordinary man. I said, can the church do less than human rights?"

She likes to be inclusive. Her message to the church (or others) is: "Keep the door open…You don't have to finger-print everybody who comes in the building or make them sign their lives away. Let them come in and participate…they can be here and look and see and hear, and if it's fine with them, fine; and if not, it's not a failure, that's part of the process. Different views are very important and it's healthy to question, whether in politics or in the church. I never accept wholeheartedly what I am told, which has often put me into trouble."

Figure 78. Angela Silver.
Source: Angela Silver Collection.

## Reaching Out, Touching People

Overwhelmingly, reactions to the Raging Grannies are positive. Not only do the Grannies offer alternative images of wit, wisdom and energy for older women and help demystify negative stereotypes of aging, they touch people often favourably. Like Ian Rudkin, they understand that "truth is shared, not taught." Recall the phone call Lorna Drew received from an anonymous woman who was afraid but wanted to thank the Raging Grannies for their support of gays and lesbians. Angela Silver of the Montreal Grannies recounts one of her encounters with feedback during their yearly anti-war-toys protest:

> We were singing, 'GI Joe, please don't go.' There was one fellow, he was leaning against the wall and he looked so sad and I wondered did he understand the songs? I went over and spoke to him. And he said, 'I'm from El Salvador. My little brother, he was only three years old, he was killed. You know the violence there. It's good what you're doing, guns are bad.' It struck him very deeply.

By being out there, they sometimes hear stories and provide comfort to people who are concerned with the same issues. This time, their presence provided a moment of painful memories for that man but also the comfort of knowing someone cared enough to bother doing something about it. For people who put their views forward like the Grannies do, feedback is energising and encourages them to continue.

While not all feedback is of such profound or dramatic nature, over the years a wide range of people have expressed their appreciation directly, by letters, or through comments reported in the media. "We can always count on the Grannies when there is an important issue—thank you," said an elderly man fighting the cuts to a stepout program that allowed Vancouver house-bound seniors two hours a month for an outing (*Granny Grapevine*, Spring 1994). Dorothy Fletcher told of a low-income community group who appreciated the Grannies' dedication to come out on a very cold night to share their songs. She also remembers a group of citizens for democracy who wrote of their profound admiration for the Grannies' enduring commitment to improve society, something fundamental to democracy. Another group invited the Toronto Grannies to their Annual General Meeting because several members had enjoyed their thoughtfulness and comedy at various events. A secular progressive Jewish group wrote:

> In this time of so much conflict and injustice around the world, it is refreshing to hear your voices singing loud and clear for peace, justice, political accountability and human dignity—and 'raging' against violence, brutality and degradation of the environment…issues which have preoccupied our members for more than seventy years. In a sense, you were singing to the converted. However, we all need to hear these messages positively affirmed and that's one of the very special contributions the Raging Grannies make to us all! Until that day comes when we have achieved a world in which justice has bred peace, we hope you will keep accepting our invitations…You…inspire and strengthen us in our efforts.[5]

The effect of the Grannies' presence is often immediate and at times they sing to indulgent applause, wrote Betty Brightwell. "The audience laughs, tension eases, they can discuss the upcoming catastrophe…with lighter hearts," wrote Rose DeShaw (A20). The French-speaking Grannies find that people smile as soon as they hear their name, Mémés Déchainées. Muriel Duckworth says that people often sing along with the chorus and look as though it lifts their spirits. Victoria Grannies have been repeatedly invited to the Seattle Folkfest, a big yearly event of folk music:

Once again we were gratified…to note that there was standing room only in the theatre we were given for our 45-minute 'production'—and we got a standing ovation again…When we were doing our stuff in downtown Victoria a couple of Seattle visitors insisted on having their picture taken with us! Yes, they had seen us at Seattle's Folkfest.[6]

The Grannies received accolades and praise from public figures. In the foreword of McLaren and Brown's book, *The Raging Grannies Songbook,* Pete Seeger wrote about the Grannies' "bold and original approach to social change and protest" and added, "they are a generation that most people do not take seriously, but their effectiveness is truly inspiring." Bill Phipps, the outspoken former moderator of the United Church wrote:

Why don't the media bring us inspiring stories of peace-building, such as the Women-in-Black…the Raging Grannies, Project Ploughshares, numerous interfaith gatherings, the Coalition of Women for Peace in Jerusalem? True security and democracy requires knowledge of alternatives, vigorous debate and ethical analysis. Real courage demands honesty, probing complexities and genuine collective commitment to address a whole range of issues to which we continually turn a blind eye. What democracy and civilization are we fighting for when real debate in Parliament is perfunctory at best and consumers (oops, I mean 'citizens') are encouraged to act like lemmings?…It seems to be that our society, most visibly reflected in our political leaders and much of the media, is suffering from an arrested imagination…Why do we check imagination at the door of decision-making?[7]

Coming from someone flamboyantly direct himself, to be on such a list is recognition of the Grannies' integrity and courage. As for imagination, the Grannies constantly demonstrate it by their ability to renew their protest to fit the needs of the moment. Ralph Nader, prominent U.S. consumers' advocate and presidential candidate, was the keynote speaker at the 1998 Edmonton Parkland Institute Conference on public healthcare. He called the Raging Grannies "an astounding instrument of social protest" and said they "found a way to break through, without ever losing their dignity [and] make good, visual media" (Nader, 1998: 3). Lanie Melamed reportedly heard that Nader considered the Grannies "one of Canada's best exports to the States."

Victoria and Vancouver Grannies joined the Seattle gaggle during the now famous Seattle protests of the World Trade Organization (WTO). They walked and sang, wrote Anna Johnson,

…pausing only for the many people who wanted to take our photograph. The attention we received was heartwarming. We learned that young activists see us as role models and hold us in a sort of reverence.[8]

In a short article, Jocelyn Dow, President of WEDO [Women's Environment and Development Organization] and founding member of Red Thread in Guyana, mentioned the Raging Grannies twice as part of the vibrant force of women she experienced in Seattle. An item in the *World Trade Observer,* published during the meetings of the Ministers at the World Trade Organization in Seattle in 1999 said:

Proving that the walking cane may be mightier than the sword, a group known as the Raging Grannies of Seattle [BC Grannies were also there] took to the streets…to add their voices to the chorus of anti-WTO protesters. Urging fellow demonstrators to, 'get off their fannies,' the singing group proved that activism 'knows no age limits.'[9]

Anne Moon adds:

They loved us six Grannies at the hostel—lectured us for breaking curfew, allowed us extra blankets and pillows and were just terrific. We were six in a dorm, with three intrepid Grannies using the upper bunk. Many of us ventured out after curfew and spoke to police, National Guard and even a couple of Secret Service men, detailed to guard the President. We met two Direct Action Network volunteers, collecting evidence for a lawsuit against the police. Their gas masks were hidden under their scarves. The Seattle Mayor had ruled that possession of a gas mask was a criminal act. When we left, over 500 people, mostly peaceful protesters, were in jail. Grannies were mentioned in major media all across the continent. Am I glad I went? You bet. I saw democracy as she should be served…I think we all had a little role in making the WTO more accountable and we helped forge a unique link (at least in the U.S.) between labour, environment and social justice advocates.[10]

Seattle was not without risks, and for Granny Alison Acker who "witnessed police confrontation in Chile, Guatemala and El Salvador," Seattle "looked like (George Orwell's) *1984*." The willingness and determination of Grannies to go into such uncertain situations is inspiring to young activists.

## Super Cool Recycled Teenagers Appeal to Youth

The youth in the streets of Seattle are not the only ones inspired by the Grannies. The connection with youth is a strong one, suggests Barbara Calvert Seifred:

Kids, they really connect with us…The year before Seattle there was a big demonstration in Montreal at…a big economic world conference. I was involved in some planning meetings…and it was mostly students. They were asking which groups were going to participate and people got up and mentioned their group. I said, 'I'm with the Raging Grannies and I'm hoping to have the Grannies there on the day.' Oh! They were just thrilled. That got more reaction than any announcement!

The Grannies' spunky approach makes grannydom more attractive to youth. "I hope I'm doing that kind of stuff when I'm older," said a high school student witnessing the Grannies' anti-war toys protest (in R. Munro). Another young woman did not want to wait: "Today I want to be a granny," wrote Emily Worts shortly after September 11, 2001. Looking for hope, as everyone was at the time, she found some with the Grannies:

With more stories of groups like the Raging Grannies we might all come to embrace what years of wisdom has taught them: 'We hold peace, forgiveness and love in our hearts and we will not be caught up in fear.'[11]

Such a statement appeals to the idealism of youth that believes in tomorrow and in ideals. Refusal to let fear rule seems a natural connection between women fifty years apart. Maybe fear belongs to middle-age preoccupations with success. Youth still has ideals and experienced activists know what is truly important.

Educational institutions, from primary schools to universities, invite Grannies. A professor of nursing, who invited Raging Grannies to her class, wrote the following in a thank you letter: "It is important to hear about the specific issues that you address, but equally important is the opportunity for us to view the "medium" that you use to raise awareness of these issues." The Granny Gram Fall 1997 reported that a professor of gerontology also invited Grannies to her class because she saw them in action and found they made a difference. She wanted "students to have a chance to meet seniors that are motivated to do something about the problems in the world and give them a chance to ask questions." Other Grannies were invited to make students in "social work aware of certain problems." Joan Harvey recalls an occasion when a group of youth in a community centre paid scant attention to the Grannies' presentation until a song on homelessness:

> Then they listened and were riveted…Some of them had tears in their eyes and many of them came up to us, 'I have three friends like that.' 'I know somebody like that.' 'Somebody in my school is like that.' And the feedback you get! Even they were unsuspecting of these funny old biddies!

Early on, the Victoria Grannies often went to schools and received many letters of thanks. The following are some samples that were sent to them by junior high school students:

> …I personally am very afraid of nuclear war. I don't like living everyday wondering if disaster is going to strike. Watching you perform made me laugh but also made me think. If I had the guts I would get up and express my feelings to the world.

> …I'm very scared of nuclear war myself and I'm glad you're trying to make people aware of what's happening. Your presentation was entertaining and educational which is a great way to get an important message across.

> …I enjoyed your performance because it opened my eyes to what I was trying to ignore.

> …It was a great, happy/cheerful approach to raising the awareness of some of our defence problems. The performance was a nice, exciting change from the hum-drum everyday life of a young, nuclear-aged school kid.

> …I realised that I haven't really been thinking about nuclear arms and was surprised when you explained that we are going to be buying those submarines. I thought we were getting rid of our weapons not getting more! Well, you certainly opened my eyes to the real world.

> …When I first heard that you were coming I expected to see a bunch of radicals screaming about something. Your presentation gets a five star rating and I recommend it to other students.

> …I never really thought about our future but you certainly did help me…And I wouldn't mind seeing you 'gals' again.

While they provide inspiration for young people, connecting with youth is energising for the Grannies. Referring to a workshop they did at Ryerson on banning landmines Joan Harvey commented:

> The energy of the young people and the positive response, that is so gratifying…There seems to be a one- or even two-generation gap between us and the activists of today…We're some of the ones who were very active during the early times of the women's movement and a lot of them—I don't know how they lasted as long as they did because they worked, family and everything else. It is exhausting.

Joan is impressed by the commitment of young activists; it gives her "a high" that they are "not shouting into the wilderness." To see youth getting involved gives older activists a sense that their efforts have not been in vain. Joan feels youth recognise that the Grannies "sing out of a deep commitment" and do not identify them as entertainment. Being seen as entertainment is a downer, she says, but

> …when you get that solid positive enthusiastic feedback…I don't like to be pretentious and say inspire them, but help motivate them if they were perhaps thinking, 'I really wish there were some things I could do.' Maybe we press the on button, that means so much…At our age we are teachers

to a great extent. We don't profess to be teachers, not out of self-aggrandisement [but] the older generation has something of merit to say. We've been there and even though the times have changed, we've still been there…It's the same, perhaps framed slightly differently…And we're here now.

There is a willingness to share and a refusal to abdicate their place in the world: they have been there but they are here now! Kathleen Dunphy thinks that just being there

…may end up being our most important contribution, being there…Whenever I see young people supporting us, I like that. Because I think when they get older they may remember that. Not that we were significant but that they can keep on doing things. I also do think—there's no question about it—I hope if someone has a bad attitude about older women this will change it. [For] some I'm sure it reinforces it: everything they thought about older women going crazy! But many say, 'that's great, we can't believe you get out there and do it,' particularly women.

Not only young women are inspired by the Grannies. Kathleen Dunphy's sixteen-year-old grandson introduced her as a "super cool grandparent" on a national TV program. A young man approached the Montreal Grannies standing in line at an event with a message: "I think your group, you're really awesome." The following is an excerpt of a report by another young man who took part in a protest march against cuts and privatisation of health care in Montreal, and although the overall event was a disapointment—like attending a church tea party gone wrong—meeting the Grannies made up for it.

It isn't often that three scatter-brained male roommates wake up in the morning, grudgingly throw on wrinkled pants and end up dining with ten fabulous women they met walking down the street. Oddly enough, this was the reality of my Saturday past…A phalanx of older women, (aka Raging Grannies) were dressed in hideous layers of fabric and clownish shawls while they sang cheeky verses to common tunes…The Grannies were by far the highlight of a long march…Their enthusiasm and prominent performance was loved by all and the effort of four particular Grannies, who lugged along a stretcher bearing a fake corpse along the march route, was equally admired…There we were, living it large in Chinatown, surrounded by Raging Grannies. Having bumped into a group of Grannies on our way to the metro, we jumped at their invitation to go to a restaurant around the corner…They were fabulous. We talked, ate, and made quite a scene in a restaurant where the buffet's lacking variety was made up for by its colourful clientele. The ladies, who were in their 70's and 80's, were funny, polite and almost hardy enough to embarrass three not so impressionable young men in their early 20's, whose pride and machismo was put in jeopardy by the size of the plate that one particularly feisty Granny wolfed down. While the Grannies shared their political knowledge and concerns with us, they listened to what we had to say too. It was an enlightening exchange. Uncertain as to whether either of my roommates have grandmothers…it was refreshing to latch onto the ones we had met on the street, if only for an afternoon. I remember leaving the buffet feeling somewhat inspired. I had just met a group of extremely creative politically active older women who were trying to improve the lives of their fellow citizens in ways that could be effective. In parting, one of the Grannies mentioned that they might be attending the upcoming anti-globalization rallies in Quebec City next April. She said that if the Grannies were able to make the trip they would stand in the front line of the protest and stare down riot police, fluorescent shawls on shoulders, sun hats laden with protest pins, and song sheets firmly clasped in 80-year-old hands.[12]

The ease with which the Grannies make contact with youth is important in a society where inter-generational connections are fraying, often due to families separated by great distance. An inter-generational connection is especially important for activists as it helps keep alive the unofficial history of "ordinary people" and social movements, allows transfer of knowledge, and encourages youth. Real-life Grannies standing up to authorities, and for ideals, legitimises struggles for social justice and provides moral support to younger people probably more familiar with cyberspace than with the role of activists in our country's history.

## Braving the Storm of Change: Impact on Raging Grannies Themselves

And when there is a promise of a storm,
If you want change in your life,
> walk into it.

If you get on the other side,
> you will be different.

And if you want change in your life,
> and you are avoiding the trouble,
> you can forget it.

So Harriet Tubman would say,
> "Wade in the water,
> it's going to really be troubled water."[13]

Grannydom has given me a chance to dry my tears when the issues of child hunger, spousal abuse and decline of health care hit the papers. You can't sing and cry at the same time.     —Rose DeShaw

Hilda Marczak is unequivocal: being a Raging Granny gave meaning to her grannyhood. There is no doubt it has been a meaningful engagement. Being a Raging Granny is a vehicle for the expression of ideals but also an outlet for various feelings. Anger, depression and hopelessness are not surprising given ecological destruction, corporate greed, growing inequities, violence and talk of war. Being a Raging Granny, said Muriel Duckworth, is "a relief to us in that we could release some of our depression and various feelings about the war effort and the nuclear expansion that we were worried about." In an article by Lucinda Chodan, Inger Kronseth, who was involved with the Danish resistance during World War II, speaks of the Grannies' clowning as an antidote to being depressed and overwhelmed by pollution and war preparations. As discussed earlier, humour is effective in dealing with pain arising out of fear, anxiety or anger. Isolation can lead to frustrations and feelings of impotence. But active involvement while learning about social and political issues is a way to ward off cynicism. Awareness of problems

> …in isolation from active work for social transformation…can be paralyzing and the transformative power overlooked…In the context of work for social justice, the effect of these analyses can be quite different, sustaining a self-critical, even humorous sensibility.[14]

At times, "our knowing is in our action," says Donald Schon (in Berlak). Active participation with a group and in various activities that have meaning increases hope and self-worth. Rose DeShaw wrote eloquently about this:

What is it about grannying that makes it so great? Partly it's being able to have a voice in your times, to know you are fully living your life, taking the risks (and reaping the rewards from those risks)...Grannying forces you to stay on top of the political scene. Knowing where you stand in all this, seems to lead to personal growth...What about giving people with long-unused voices, the confidence to sing? Making people laugh at the right targets; the corrupt, the powerful, giving stupidity its proper place way, way down at the bottom of our consideration, broadcasting it as a means of bringing them down? To Granny means always working as a team with other stubborn, difficult women who won't shut up, running with our shared ideas, finding something genuinely funny in the bleakest moments. Grannying is the opposite of self-pity and depression. I love the opportunity to invent things to illustrate the latest political crime—costumes, props, dialogue, bits from history, songs, pictures, the wilder the better. The 'Will we be brave enough?' 'Will it change things?' The women who Granny have a toughness I don't find elsewhere...I love hearing from them, finding out how much I still don't know about our world, sharing the vision of hope up ahead in the young people that seem to gather round us.[15]

The Grannies' experience concurs with studies, Heather McGuffin's among them, indicating that being actively involved later in life is healthy; a sense of meaning and purpose have important physical and psychological benefits. A recent British study by psychologists at the University of Sussex suggests that those who participated in protests "felt they had a collective identity with fellow protestors...[And] derived a sense of unity and mutual support" from such collaboration.[16] Aside from a sense of purpose and meaning, there are other positive outcomes for individual Grannies in terms of their own educational interests, a sense of belonging, and feelings of empowerment.

*Figure 79. Kathleen Dunphy, Joan Harvey, Phyllis Creighton, and Inge Biskupsky, Members of the Toronto Raging Grannies demonstrate their readiness to take on the world. Source: Joan Harvey Collection.*

*Lanie Melamed, a lifelong activist, immigrated from the U.S. to Canada and was a professor at Concordia University where she taught group dynamics, conflict negotiation, and management. She linked being a Raging Granny to her earlier activism in the U.S. With her husband, she chose to live in an interracial, intentional community, in order to raise their children in a diverse neighbourhood. They were very active in their community. She taught international folk dancing and probably had the only integrated folk-dance school in the city of Philadelphia. They both were very affected by the Vietnam War and went on marches in Washington. They did not believe war was the way to solve problems, so took a big step and moved to Canada to protect their children.*

*Lanie believed that most Raging Grannies had been involved in the peace movement: women "don't join because we are cute." A member of the Voice of Women and an adult educator, she wrote a doctoral thesis on women and playfulness. Most recently, she was involved in the breast cancer advocacy movement and started HEAL—Health Environment Action Learning—a discussion and popular education group. Lanie poassed away in August of 2003.*

*Figure 80. Lanie Melamed's playfulness.*
*Un-convention in Kingston. Source: Carole Roy.*

*Lois Marcoux's activism is rooted in her mother's participation in the Co-operative Common-wealth Federation (CCF) in her native Saskatchewan. Her mother, "strong and fierce," came from Ontario to teach and seek freedom and was an early advocate of the legalisation of con-traception. Lois grew up during the "dirty thirties" and values her early hardships as they taught her patience and compassion. The disappearance of the roses and willow trees of her childhood makes her weep but also forces her to do something to save what is left.*

Lois sees herself as a listener and a follower, yet she showed her capacity for defiance early. An Anglican, she con-verted and married a Catholic against her parents' wishes. This is hardly the behav-iour of a follower! They had seven chil-dren and a happy marriage but she was widowed for many years before becomng a Raging Granny.

She is involved with Conscience Can-ada, which advocates holding back taxes going to military spending, as well as with the Catholic social justice committee of her parish. Between her concern for the envi-ronment, social justice, peace, and her at-tempt to live with integrity, she found herself in the Raging Grannies doing things and going places she never imag-ined. She walked for peace from Victoria to Nanoose Bay—and her determination was admirable during the five days it took to reach the destination. Later she was ar-rested as part of the Grandmotherpeace civil disobedience action at the Nanoose Bay military base.

*Figure 81. Lois Marcoux in "uniform."*
*Source: Doran Doyle Collection.*

## Still Learning, Always Learning

While the Grannies are involved in popular education, they are educating themselves at the same time. The group is a forum for exchanging views and information, a place where new knowledge is gained/created. Kathleen Dunphy says:

> I've learned a lot from the women. I learn every time we meet, and I learn from the people we associate with too…I love hearing…the different ways people do things, even if they don't agree. I love to hear why they don't agree and what their concerns are…It's a continuing learning experience being in the Grannies because of the people we meet up with. They're involved in things I care about. I can't think what damage I'd be inflicting on society if I wasn't doing this! Maybe I'm the least dangerous this way! (laughs)

Kathleen *needs* to be involved to satisfy a need for meaningful stimulation and to expend her energy in ways that are consistent with her values. Joan Harvey describes the impact of being a Raging Granny on her life as "considerable!" and adds:

> I've learned so much from the other Grannies, from their priorities. It's a constant education for me too. As long as you're alive you should be learning. Otherwise…I've always had a need to keep learning, not just an interest, because there's always new things, new circumstances. You go on seeing things that are…not right…but you can't do anything about it unless you know and understand about the subject and there's always new information coming up and there's always new spins.

Like Kathleen, for Joan learning is "not only an interest" but "a need." Being willing to learn is to be willing to challenge one's worldview and sense of self. Angela Silver recognises the on-going challenge that "never ends. Participation is important throughout your life" but she adds so is "the fellowship you get." For some, like Rheta Stephenson, the new knowledge is concrete:

> I came in knowing about inequality to women and victims and children but I've learned so much more…because other people have other causes. Now I find that I'm conserving paper. At work I used to throw out a lot of my scrap paper and now I save everything and I write on it. And I'm more careful with water than I used to be…So it has changed my life…Probably the main thing is that I am more conscious of some of the other issues that people have.

Rheta's interest in, and knowledge of, gender inequality led to her involvement, which in turn leads to new understandings and concerns about other issues, or new skills.

*Rheta Stephenson lives in Regina. A nurse, she returned to university later in life and is now a social worker for the provincial government. Professionally, she has always been close to the unprivileged and is especially sensitive to poverty and women's issues. She is herself the daughter of orphaned parents: her father came from England as one of the homeboys and worked hard to make his way up from nothing. Compassion is alive in her. "The main reason why I got into this [Grannies] was because of the inequality of women and also poverty and what it does to our children...I would just like in some way to make other people more aware...because I think that's the only way that we ever change anything, it's to make people aware."*

*Music is a big part of her life. While she did not have the opportunity to learn when she was young, she learned piano after she had children. She recalls the Regina Grannies' first gig being the entertainment for a volunteer group appreciation night. One of the songs they sang was:*

> *we are the women who do the work*
> *so men can get the credit*
> *we said leave it to us*
> *wish we'd never said it*

*"There are about five verses about changing diapers and everything else...To see the reactions of the women and the men, that was quite fun...Half way through the program...Bonnie's husband had to go to the bathroom and...this other fellow...said to [him], 'I wouldn't be in any hurry to get back in there because the entertainment sucks!' a comment that contrasted with the women's nods."*

*Figure 82. Rheta Stephenson.*
*Source: Bonnie Doyle Collection.*

Mary Rose, one of the original Grannies, offers her perspective on how far they have come in their level of comfort with public speaking:

> We weren't afraid. I wasn't afraid but we were nervous, at least I was. I don't know, maybe some of the others were much more self-assured than I was. At first, appearing at microphones and talking to the press and all that sort of stuff [was intimidating so we] had no names. But now, all the Grannies, if they see a microphone they turn on, and if you see a TV camera! So our attitude to the press and to public media certainly changed. I guess that self-assurance must rub off too on the rest of your life.

Mary's comment about changes in one aspect of self rubbing off in other parts of one's life is similar to Rheta's experience of getting involved because of one set of concerns, discovering new issues, and changing her behaviour with waste and resources. One key factor of the Grannies is that each woman is connected to a different network of groups and people with their own concerns, some shared, some unique. While networks and networking are "key practices of global civil society" they are also essential to community activism, writes Budd Hall (2000:10).

Belonging to a group is also a source of learning. Mary Rose wonders, "maybe I meet people much easier than I would have, I don't know. I don't know how I would have been meeting people if it wasn't for the Grannies." Elinor Egar Reynolds learned

> …not to be too much of an individual…To be more part of a group, give and take a little bit more, not do everything the way I want. Not a 'one-man band.' It's good, it made me a little more humble, respecting. I never really belonged to a group as such. It's been good. I like being part of this group.

For Rose DeShaw, who has a lot of initiative and creativity, "letting go" is a new learning experience:

> Oh heavens, I've certainly learned a lot about myself and about working with women and where I fit in almost any group of women, what's my role…About learning when to shut up. Lately I've been learning about how they [others] become connected and how you can let go of things…trying to get more involvement…You have to find a way to build the strength [of the group] so that everybody sees that their part is part of it…I have been there the longest…So I'm learning how to sit back.

Joan Harvey is learning "to have a better sense of humour. I'm still trying. I still have a lot to learn, very much more to learn, but I'm doing my best." Yet I found Joan's humour very lively. When discussing her twenty years of travel all over the world she said: "I have no natural sense of direction, which for someone who's travelled all over the world is ridiculous. You give me a map and I can take you to Mars and back!" Lorna Drew has learned that "you can put it out there, it's okay, doesn't have to be great poetry. Not everybody has to like it either. It can be changed, [it's] not written in the living rock."

The quest for perfection is over. Participation is what counts, to the best of one's abilities with the acceptance that one's knowledge or appeal is always partial. The Grannies can only be successful in their education of others if they themselves remain open to new information and to challenging their own views. The fundamental nature of their endeavour, education on current issues, requires that they keep moving and do not shy away from learning. They can educate because they are willing to learn and embrace change themselves. For some there is loss of political innocence as a process of analysis of power is triggered. Ava Louwe had always talked back to the TV but was not politically active. A series of articles on the criminalisation of dissent and her participation with the Raging Grannies really had an impact:

I knew that the Grannies had been under investigation by CSIS, which honestly, is a joke. But it made me realise how paranoid our so-called authorities are and how frightened the people in authority are of the average citizen standing up and being heard speaking his or her mind. Our authorities are terrified to hear us speaking the truth because they've got a veneer that they are trying to project onto us, or onto the world, and when we say, 'Hey! This is baloney, this is not the truth and we are going to sing the truth'…It was just a shock for me to see it in print, although I have heard rumours and comments and so on. But to see it there I find it a rather frightening prospect for us and citizens of our country. But not only our country, it's the world. It's happening everywhere!

For Ava, getting involved in the Raging Grannies

…has been an eye opener. I kind of had this rosy glow that I was gonna do good for society, I was gonna join the Grannies, picket or sing out for the homeless or for peace issues or for women or for-what-have-you and then when I realised that it's the very things that we stand for that seem to threaten people in authority so deeply, it was a shock, really it was a shock…It's making me think what degree of involvement do I want? Am I willing to stand up to this kind of a situation or that kind? At this time I don't know, but it's definitely making me think.

## Empowerment: Older and Bolder

One definite impact of being a Raging Granny is empowerment. There is a sense of achievement at living with integrity and zest. "Being a Raging Granny has made me a lot bolder" which "has fed into my willingness to throw in a prophetic and visionary view of things rather than stick to linear [thinking]," said Phyllis Creighton. The theme of boldness recurs. "I'm probably more outspoken…Oh, a lot more now. Being a Raging Granny helped me be outspoken," said Eva Munro. Barbara Calvert Seifred also suggests that it has had an impact on her life:

This is the most interesting time of my life…I would say it's my real work, it's important. And [it] keeps us going, replenishes us and recharges our batteries because when you really think of this, the problems that we're confronting, they're very depressing.

Dorothy Fletcher gets a sense of self-worth from being a Raging Granny which Barbara also experienced as she talked of being a Raging Granny in terms of her "vocation," her real work. Finding one's vocation and recognition from others are invigorating; lack of either can be limiting. Fran Thoburn acknowledged that the applause and recognition are:

Very ego-stroking…Applause can become addictive…I was a kid who grew up never thinking that people were listening to me enough…Being able to be heard, what a wonderful exhilarating [experience] for a kid that was always squashed, not listened to…Empowering is the word.

Empowerment has all kinds of consequences. Doran Doyle points to the fact that she, and a few other Grannies, are no longer married after thirty-five, even forty years of marriage: "I think the Grannies made us bold a bit." Marital break-ups are not unusual amongst women activists. Many women involved in the Love Canal struggle saw their marriages disintegrate. In her article, "From Trash to Treasure," Harriet Rosenberg suggests that in some households the tensions could not be resolved as husbands resented the new confidence of their activist wives and the result was separation and divorce. For Doran Doyle, being a Granny was a peak in her life as it affirmed her artistic side: married to a writer and a published poet, she had hoped she would not have to deal with that in herself. Between the Raging Grannies and feminism, she got in touch with it and her whole life turned upside down. She echoes Lois' sense of community: "I think most of us would say the experience of living like that was the most important thing for us and the experience of being in these social movements, there lies our community." Being a Raging Granny has made Doran's children very proud of her. She has a sense of journey: women have been "cast as hysterical and neurotic" but have learned "to burn with fury sometimes."

Betty Brightwell has also experienced change: "We are separated, my husband and I. It's partly a result of the Grannies, sure it is, sure it is…a certain empowerment that you get." She learned to use the Internet and e-mail to protest directly to MPs, the Prime Minister and the ambassadors from India and Pakistan when they exploded their own nuclear bombs, among others. Some years ago she made a presentation on nuclear emergency, as did the Commander of the local base, to the city council; she has since "been put on the…Emergency Measures Committee, so…although we initially started by writing to the Prime Minister and Minister of National Defence, when it comes right down to it you work in your backyard: my backyard is the CFB [Canadian Forces Base]…So we've done this," says Betty. Hers and other Grannies' journeys seem to validate Martha Ackelsberg's suggestion that "radicalization is born of action" and that developing a new sense of self by breaking with traditional models allows us to move in new directions (1991: 165). Ackelsberg also says that "participation in resistance often engenders a broader consciousness of both the nature and the dimension of social inequality and the power of people united to confront and change it" (1988: 307). It is a credit to Betty Brightwell's openness of mind that she could publicly challenge structures she had felt loyal to in her life. In an article for the *Times-Colonist*, entitled "Defending the difference," Betty wrote about her experience of when the Grannies met a group of transvestites and she ended up defending the transvestites when some young men verbally taunted and abused them. There is no doubt that Betty herself was surprised: she started the article by saying: "How did it happen? Me—publicly defending thirty transvestites" (1995: A5).

Some invitations carry more recognition for some individuals, depending on their life histories. For Dorothy Fletcher, who feels that being a Raging Granny is an expression of her spirituality, being invited by one's church to speak as a Raging Granny is a moment of pride. For Joan Harvey who worked with unions for a long time, to be invited with the Raging Grannies to a large gathering of unions and being warmly received, was a moment of pride and achievement as the different threads of her life came together, providing a greater sense of integration. At times recognition comes indirectly: Mary Rose smiled and was visibly delighted recalling her eleven-year-old grandson's essay, "My grandmother is a rock star!"

Being a Raging Granny has unexpected perks. Rose DeShaw discovered how much being a Raging Granny made her part of the community in a most unexpected way. While editor of the *Granny Grapevine* for two years, Rose had two operations and was waiting for a third one,

> …right in the middle of medicare cuts. I was lying in the emergency room…listening to nurses and doctors in the cubicles on either side asking the oldie occupants, 'What year is it? Who's the Prime Minister?' I knew my turn was coming and sure enough a doctor young enough to be my grandson came in. It was Thursday and I was frantically searching my mind for the date when he pointed a finger at me and said: '*I know you. You're famous. I've heard you sing!*' (at Hiroshima Day when Physicians for Peace often join us) So it was my Grannying that saved me from the fate of Oldies-In-Emergency, once again.[17]

*Ava Louwe was not in the Voice of Women: It took me a long time to get my voice." A "closet rabble rouser," she always talked back to the TV set! From Vancouver, she saw the Grannies on a five second clip in the late 1980s but only joined in the spring of 2001: "I saw these women singing and I thought, someday when my time is right, I'm going to join them. I'm going to do that because it just felt like the perfect way to get your point across, to take a stand on social issues and do it in a light-hearted, humorous but powerful way."*

*There was a lag of many years between the clip and joining the Ottawa group where she had moved. But as the birth of her first grandchild approached, she decided this was the time: "Now I'm a grandmother and I really do have an interest in what's happening to the next generation, a deep profound interest. Not that I didn't have an interest before, but this gives it a very powerful and meaningful one for me. I really have to make sure that there is a world for my granddaughter." Not knowing anyone in the social activist movement, and following her inner call, she found the Grannies through the Internet.*

*Figure 83. Ava Louwe.*
*Un-convention, Kingston. Source: Carole Roy.*

The Grannies create ripples, some not appreciated but most warmly welcomed. They touch people, especially youth. And being a Raging Granny has enriched their own lives. All dimensions of time are valued: the past, the present, and the future they are so ardently working to insure. They willingly engage with the uncertainty of social change, which requires a different kind of confidence—confidence that we matter, that our life matters, that we are capable of listening, creativity and sincerity. Their confidence allows them to engage and then their engagement pays them back in greater confidence to continue to take risks. They demonstrate the importance of action and reflection as they make research important to their form of activism. The Raging Grannies are willing to allow ambiguity and paradoxes rather than seeking to do away with complexity. It is that capacity to embrace complexities that permits them to create inventive and humorous ways of communicating their message.

## Notes

1. "Older generation blamed," *The Martlet* (University of Victoria), October 12, 1989: 4.

2. "This is 'God speed,' not a funeral," *Times-Colonist* (Victoria), January 4, 1991: A4.

3. Betty Brightwell, "Shock tactics," Letter to the editor, *Times-Colonist* (Victoria), January 11, 1991: A4.

4. M. Justice Murphy, "Peace advocates treated badly at air show," Letter to the editor, *The Star Phoenix* (Saskatoon), August 23, 2001: A 10.

5. Letter in Dorothy Fletcher Collection.

6. Victoria Raging Grannies, *Granny Grapevine*, Spring 1994: 8.

7. Bill Phipps, "Where is the voice of peace at this Christmas season? It is naïve to believe that waging endless war will result in quiet and security," *The Toronto Star*, December 24, 2001: A17.

8. *Granny Grapevine*, Winter 2000: 6.

9. Reprinted in *Granny Grapevine*, Winter 2000: 6.

10. Anne Moon, *Granny Grapevine*, Winter 2000: 8.

11. Emily Worts, "Grannies treasure songs of hope, songs of peace." *The Packet & Times* (Orillia), October 2001: 8.

12. Tom Fletcher, "Grandmothers making a difference." *The Concordian* (Concordia University), November 1, 2000: 4.

13. Introduction by Berniece Johnson Reagon to a song about Harriet Tubman in Sharon D. Welch, "Dreams of the good: From the analytics of oppression to the politics of transformation." In David Batstone, ed., *New Visions for the Americas Religious Engagement and Social Transformation*. Philadelphia: Fortress Press, 1993: 191.

14. Sharon D. Welch, "Dreams of the good: From the analytics of oppression to the politics of transformation." In David Batstone, ed., *New Visions for the Americas Religious Engagement and Social Transformation*. Philadelphia: Fortress Press, 1993: 173.

15. Rose DeShaw, *Granny Grapevine*, Spring 2002: 26.

16. "Protesting may be good for your health," http://story.news.yahoo. com/ news? tmpl =story2&u =/nm/20021223 /hl.nm /protest_ demonstrations_dc, December 23, 2002.

17. *Granny Grapevine*, Spring 2002: 2.

# Chapter Eight

# RAGING GRANNIES IN THE WIDE WEB OF LIFE
## Catching Historical Threads, Mending the Tear, Weaving New Patterns

We will weave a world web to entangle the powers that bury our children…
—The Spinsters[1]


…and our earth.


Never doubt that a small group of thoughtful committed citizens can change the world. Indeed it's the only thing that ever has.
—Margaret Mead

*Figure 84. Kelowna Raging Grannies Rage Against the Machine. Published in Showcase Capital News. Source: Desmond Murray.*

## Grannies: A Whole Lot of Trouble Because of Love

We learned that, at times, rage is the right response.                    —Doran Doyle

Faced with mega-billion-dollar expenditures on instruments of destruction and an environment tee-
tering on disaster, a passionate response is highly appropriate.          —Keith Howard

Resistance is rooted in care and awareness of vulnerability—of ourselves, of others, and of the environment.
Resistance requires an ethic of risk; the ethic of safety is for those with privilege. It is imperative to risk hope
given the corrosive effect cynicism has on individual and collective life. We must dare, be bold, and hope,
even (and especially) against the modern god of logic that justifies death, environmental destruction, and ob-
scene profits. Unlike denial of pain, which reflects powerlessness and helplessness, awareness and care often
lead to rage and anger at unnecessary suffering. But rage and anger in our society are portrayed as negative
emotions, often identified with blind and unrestrained lashing out, so they are frowned upon, especially for
women. Yet rage and anger that arise out of love, caring, and compassion are important fuel for change.

To focus on rage alone will exhaust our strength, forge our energy into a tool of the patriarchy's
death-lure, force us to concede allegiance to the path of violence and destruction…[but] Compassion without rage renders us impotent, seduces us into watered-down humanism, stifles our good
energy. Without rage we settle for slow change, feel thankful for tidbits of autonomy…It is with our
rage that we…find the courage to risk resistance.[2]

The Raging Grannies demonstrate a positive transformation of rage and anger. When outrage and anger are
used to fuel commitment and to promote change rather than being expressed violently they become a source
of energy. Such anger crosses boundaries of race, class, age, education, religion, and political beliefs. It also
gives courage to dare where one would not have before. Anger is an antidote to fear and despair (Garland
xviii). Anger is a source of energy and a mode of connectedness; its denial leads to boredom and low energy
(Harrison in Heyward 19). When we have no hope we become indifferent, not angry. Hope is not the avoid-
ance of pain and suffering. Rage can fuel creativity and risk-taking when faced with an apparently hopeless
situation. The power of anger combined with disciplined, focussed, and imaginative actions are a dynamic
mix. Women more easily challenge authority because they often have so little to lose. They also understand
the precautionary principle of the path of least harm, as well as the need to act in the face of uncertainty and
without definitive information, says Miriam Wyman. When they stepped out of line, the Grannies stepped
onto a political stage but also into a long line of women who have actively and publicly cared, even in the face
of great risks.

## Taking Their Place in a Long Unrecognized Line of Women Resisters

In other places and times women also stood up to new forms of oppression. While Japanese industrialisation
in the 1880s happened on the backs of Japanese women mill workers, mostly young illiterate girls, they were
the first to go on strike in Japan (Sievers). The English suffragettes fought for political representation with
courage and creativity a century ago. In the 1950s, the Cuban mothers of Santiago marched to defy the brutal
Batsista regime (Sharp). In the 1970s and 1980s, the Argentinean Mothers of the Plaza de Mayo and the Chilean Arpilleras makers also publicly demonstrated their defiance of brutal military regimes (Jayawardena).

Across the world, the Chipko women of India embraced trees to save them from logging, opposing governments, corporations, and at times their own husbands (Shiva 1988). Through the 1980s British women lived precariously on the edge of the Greenham Common military base, broke into the heavily guarded base countless times to dance on missile silos or paint evil planes in order to protest nuclear arms; women who had never been arrested willingly and consciously defied the state and went to prison in protest against the nuclear arms endangering their lives (Harford and Hopkins; Junor; Romalis). Like all these women who ventured on unbeaten paths before, many women around the world are courageously innovating resistance to environmental degradation. Facing environmental destruction, they protest to save the conditions for life to exist. It is remarkable how women, time after time, understand what is wrong and react to it. Women's resistance is a lesson in the pedagogy of persistence where joy and delight in life are held together with suffering and pain. Today industrial hearts have been so hardened by economic focus that they are almost impenetrable (Williams and Johnson). Native women point out the earth herself is an ally who has many lessons for us:

> No books…no videos…no overhead projectors…no media blitz…just profound simplicity…There are ways of seeing that have no vocabulary…qualities of the mind that all of us can re-learn and that can help us in our fight to protect the Earth Mother.[3]

Un-compromised activism is costly; to sustain struggles, collective action is of primary importance. Learning about oppression outside of active engagement is often overwhelming and discouraging. Personal power is not the goal of a feminist form of political action, "but collective power is sought because it is perceived as the only instrument of change," says Marjorie Agosin (14). Democracy demands citizens' involvement in public debates on a variety of issues.

---

## The G-8 Hokey Pokey

We ship the weapons in, We take their lumber out,
Liberians will suffer— they don't have any clout,
Accounts are fudged by Government— The people do without,
And that's what it's all about.

We send the big boys in, We take the diamonds out,
We link with eternal love, the locals do without,
The Government has turfed them off their plots for corporate mines
And that's what it's all about.

We send the big boys in, Tanzanian gold comes out,
The local miners are displaced, they don't have any clout,
The stakes are thirty times increased by companies, no doubt,
And that's what it's all about.

We send farm products in, Oil resources they come out,
Sudanese displacement left their miners with no clout,
Mining airstrips used, By gunships hold the pipeline route,
And that's what it's all about.

---

*Tune: Hokey Pokey. Regina Raging Grannies.*

To look at older women activists is an opportunity to contribute to scholarship on women's organising and social movements as well as offer recognition and learn from a group of women who have actively and publicly engaged with the issues of their time. To understand their motivations, their methods, and the results of their actions can contribute to the increased effectiveness of our own participation in a society facing challenges that will require continued involvement from a broad range of people, including an aging population. Elder women activists have a unique perspective to offer. As is obvious with the Raging Grannies, older women have much to contribute to society through their reflections and dissenting voices, the importance of which cannot be dismissed. In her book on the trial of Eichmann, a Nazi war criminal, Hannah Arendt suggests that "the most potent soothing of his conscience was the simple fact that he could see no one, no one at all, who actually was against the 'final solution' " (116). In this light, the Grannies' daring creativity and persistent outspokenness are necessary inheritances in a world desperate for new notions of political action. Their life experience, their continued engagement in social change for decades, and their present engagement, offer an opportunity to understand what learning takes place from active participation in social movements.

> As we engage in political action, we understand it better...Since the conditions are dynamic, there is much we cannot know until we try it. Only in the political process are certain kinds of insights generated for citizens.[4]

## Raging Because of Love: Environmentalism

> It is not books that politicizes people, and often not ideas either. It tends to be experience. I sometimes think that those people with the most political perceptions are those who have lived in the most multiple conflicts with the dominant culture. They are seldom power brokers.[5]

The impetus for the Raging Grannies was a sense of threat to the health of their families and to the environment from the visits of U.S. nuclear warships and submarines in the Victoria harbour, an action which evolved to include other environmental issues. Their sense of urgency in 1987 proved justified if we take a look at the global environmental picture we are now facing. While women have been involved in resistance and protests on a wide range of issues, one of the dominant themes in recent times has been the environment. Environmental degradation is worldwide and urgently requires attention. The World Health Organisation estimates that "each year 25 million people, primarily in the Southern Hemisphere, are poisoned through occupational exposure to pesticides; of those 220,000 die" (Wyman 1999: 21). China, with 20% of the world's population, is facing an environmental challenge greater than at any time before: of the ten worst cities in the world for air pollution, five are in China. Children in Beijing see blue skies with white clouds only in photographs; acid rain has fallen over 40% of the country. In the last decade, the mortality rate due to respiratory diseases has increased by 25 %, doubled for liver cancer, and tripled for lung cancer (Chen). In the state of Malacca, Malaysia, the rate of miscarriage has increased to 400% due to water shortage during severe disruption of local water systems, revealing the environmental hazards for women in urban settings (Kettel). Across the world in the Ukraine, the statistics are worse. Anna Golubovska Onisimova states that the population of Ukraine has decreased by 1.2 million in the past five years and that:

> Among those who remain, cancer of the thyroid has increased among children 40 to 50 times. Seventy percent of children born in Ukraine have birth disorders. Only 12% of school children can be considered healthy. Negative trends in fertility and increasing mortality rates are contributing to de-

population and the overall aging process in the country. Life expectancy has fallen to an unprecedented peacetime low. If the birth rate does not increase, in 2005 the population of Ukraine will
have decreased by 5 million. The number of disabled children has increased by 34.1% between
1992 and 1996. The main factors causing disabilities among children are poor working conditions
for mothers, high rates of maternal morbidity, a worsening of the ecological situation, absence of
preventive medicine and a lack of services to facilitate the medical and social rehabilitation of children. The role of genetic pathology among these factors is unclear because there are no data…
Ukraine may be subdivided into the following categories: conditionally clean areas, moderately contaminated areas, heavily contaminated areas, extremely contaminated areas, zones of environmental
hazards and zones of environmental disasters…Only one third of the territory of the country is safe
for the health of the population…An area twice that size is unfit for human habitation as a result of
thoughtless human activities…Hardly any of the drinking water in Ukraine corresponds to the sani-
tary, chemical and biological parameters laid down by the country's standards for potable water.[6]

To add insult to injury, the government did not inform Ukrainians of the Chernobyl accident in 1986, but revealed its awareness of the seriousness of danger as the children of top bureaucrats of the Communist Party
were quickly evacuated, something that has never been brought to court (Onisimova).

Closer to home the reality is also worrisome. Merryl Hammond reports that 16 million Americans are said
to be sensitive to pesticides; that there were 159 pesticide-related deaths in the U.S. between 1980 and 1985;
and that in 1988, 20,000 Americans were taken to emergency rooms in incidents related to pesticides; and finally, a recent study shows that 99% of Americans have detectable levels of pesticide in their blood! Nor is
Canada protected from such plight: childhood asthma is on the increase in the Montreal to Windsor corridor,
the worst area for air pollution in the country (Elston). According to Environment Canada, more than 500 active ingredients are registered for use in pesticides in Canada in about 5000 different pesticide formulations.
Only the "active ingredients" in a pesticide formulation have to be tested by law. Although many of the active
ingredients have been found to be toxic to humans, animals, and the environment, that is not the worst news.
Many of the so-called inert substances used as propellants, stickers, spreaders, emulsifiers, wetting agents,
penetrating agents and dispersants are even more toxic than the active ingredients. But these ingredients are
considered trade secrets and data about them are unavailable to the public. The Canadian Public Health Association estimates that we have adequate testing data on only 10 percent of the chemicals used in pesticide formulations, and testing involves only short-term tests of single chemicals. Who is monitoring the chronic effects
of the chemical soup we are exposed to everyday (Hammond, 1999)?

These statistics contradict the myth adopted by mainstream science that cancer is the result of individual
lifestyles or genetic traits (Brady). But women are not fooled: often responsible for the care of children, the elderly and the sick, they realise there is something wrong before other constituencies do. Many illnesses are
due to a damaged environment, a degradation that has arisen from capitalist exploitation of resources, making
illnesses the by-products of profits. Women's Environmental Network based in England asks why we keep fo-
cusing on the end point of the disease of cancer when prevention makes a lot more sense. Women's health,
they suggest, is "inextricably linked to their status in society" (Lynn 275, 277). Wyman agrees: "When disaster
strikes, women and the children they care for suffer most. Hunger and poverty are not impartial" (23). The environment is not subordinated to national borders: "Contaminants don't obey political boundaries," says
Wyman (20).

When we can see that the cancers from which we suffer have the same origins as the endometriosis suffered by millions of women in industrialized countries, as the birth defects among the children of workers in the maquiladoras of Mexico, as the thyroid cancers and leukemias among the people of Ukraine, as the sterility of banana workers in Ecuador and as the asthma that is paralyzing lungs across the globe—then, when we have identified ourselves as being victims of the same predators, we will have a basis for linking hands all around the world.[7]

The environment ties together ideology, economy, political power, and spirituality. It is one of the threads tightly woven across the world and across disciplines, the link between an individual and the process of life, the link also between economics and health. Environmental issues may be our best hope to challenge the present exploitative economic system since without a decent environment there will not be any life or profits for those obsessed by the bottom line! Many women's acts of resistance reveal the intolerable oppression of environmental degradation and its affront to human dignity, as well as the cracks in the prevalent system of the time. Women's resistance takes different historical shapes, and environmental resistance may be one of the distinctive features of resistance in this historical period.

> Only when the last tree has died
> And the last river been poisoned
> And the last fish been caught
> Will we realize that we cannot eat money.                    —Cree Indian saying

## Out of the Shadows, Sage Veteran Warriors in Sensible Shoes: A New Landscape of Aging

> What we grandmothers are doing with our lives, the problems we face now, the present true state of our relationships, the issues which we might raise as important—our priorities—are not considered interesting. These are never the subject of poems or political analysis by younger women. If they do break this rule, they are often punished by a rebuff from publishers who believe that 'old ladies don't sell.'[9]

In her address to the United Nations NGO Committee on Aging at the Secretariat in 1982, Rhodes suggested that "women rarely surface as the central issue on aging. They are a side issue. Problems of the old are cast as either generic or categorical" (205). Yet the important demographic fact for women is that aging is populated by women. In 1982, Emily M. Nett recognised that "no one has much knowledge about women over the age of 65," including feminists, in spite of the fact that women are the majority of elderly people (201, 203). Greater numbers have not translated into women being the focus of major research efforts in gerontology, says Nett. In 1982, no sessions at the Canadian Research Institute for the Advancement of Women conference addressed older women (Nett). Since then, some research has been done on women and aging from a feminist perspective, but little. Much remains to be done.

> The old woman finds herself captured by stereotypes which drain her initiative and shatter her self-respect. The mythical prototypes of the Wicked Old Witch with unnatural powers, the Old Bad Mother with neurotic power needs, and the Little Old Lady, ludicrously powerless, cloud the individuality of every woman past sixty. Since childhood all of us have been bombarded by systematic distortions of female aging in fairy tales, legends, books, movies, plays and TV. Age prejudice en-

courages substitution of these manufactured realities for the real human being with real personal powers whom we encounter. Ageism rationalizes the discarding of old women.[10]

In our society of images and print, the elderly are often misrepresented or invisible. "Our culture gives us many images from grandmothers in Norman Rockwell magazine covers to bag ladies on street corners to adolescent mentalities in aged bodies on TV sitcoms" (Bell, 1986: 1), all stereotypes of rigid roles, poverty, or social conventions. Recognising that what we see and what we do not see affect our perceptions, Kelchner suggests that the absence or misrepresentation of elderly people lead us to believe that "their existence is insignificant and inconsequential to our lives" (93). She reports the findings of her literature review on the portrayal of elderly people in the media:

Vasil and Wass (1993) found that in print as well as electronic media '28 studies…suggest that the elderly are widely misrepresented' (80) both in terms of the true size of the population and in supporting and strengthening negative stereotypes of older persons. Other studies [found] older persons underrepresented or misrepresented in television commercials (Francher 1973, Harris & Feinberg 1977; Swayne & Greco 1987), on daytime serials (Elliott 1984), in drama productions (Bell 1992; Harris & Feinberg, 1977) and in children's (McGuire 1993) and adolescent's (Peterson & Eden 1977) literature. In a review of commercial films spanning fifty years, from the 1940s through the 1980s, Bazzini, McIntosh, Smith, Cook and Harris (1997) found that 'few older women appear in film,' and when they do appear they are portrayed as 'less friendly, having less romantic activity, and as enjoying fewer positive outcomes than younger characters.'[11]

As we enter the 21st century, some media coverage is moving from a historical portrayal of older people "as a deserving group in need of income assistance, health care protection, and advocacy to a modern picture of older adults as 'greedy geezers,' affluent, selfish, and influential" (Jirovec and Erich 85-86). While some elderly men and women are wealthy, the majority of old women are not. Portraying them as greedy and affluent is to misrepresent them and can make their already difficult situation more precarious. The media are not the only culprits lacking inclusivity; more serious than their, and the professional gerontologists' blindness to ageism, has been the failure of feminists to recognise the theoretical and experiential importance of old age and its impact on all women. The women's movement "has resonated with its silence on…the status of old women" (Ford and Sinclair 160). The concerns of second-wave feminists "reflected…young women's concerns: reproductive issues; female sexuality; child care; violence against women; equal opportunity in education and jobs; balancing careers and intimate relationships" (Rosenthal 1). In the early 1980s, Nett claimed that the collective feminist voice was not very loud on behalf of older women and commented that gerontological research took place within the male paradigms of academic sociology and psychology. That same year, Arlene T. McLaren called for more research on the contributions of elderly women to society, suggesting that many

…elderly women in Canada…tend to subsist below the poverty line set by the Economic Council of Canada (National Council on Welfare, 1979) and are 'underemployed, underpaid, underfinanced, underhoused, undervalued, and underloved' (Jacobs 1976). These portrayals greatly underestimate the contributions elderly women make to society.[12]

In 1987, Janet Ford and Ruth Sinclair, two feminist authors visiting a bookstore in Cambridge (U.S.), observed that only half of their lives had been written about—childhood, youth, the forties—but the last half of women's lives was unknown. In 1990, Jo Searles found a lack of material on older women in women's studies: "We have been so slow to speak, slow to insist on being heard" (154):

> In the academic realm, few writers of textbooks address elder women at all. A quick review of text materials in women's studies…will immediately show the reader that little is included regarding elder women; a few paragraphs on the empty nest syndrome, menopause, depression in middle age, or the lack of older women in the movement seems to suffice. A similar situation can be found in gerontology texts…A few paragraphs on widowhood appear, perhaps mention of menopause or depression. The research underlying the theories of aging has often not even included women.[13]

Also in 1990, Denise Belisle Gonault published an annotated bibliography on women and aging in Canada and remarked that "the striking conclusion of this research is how very few clearly feminist works on older women there are, those that take the standpoint of women" (v). She suggested that the overall majority of works listed focussed on medical and social problems older women encountered and individual coping mechanisms to deal with ageing. Little was said about older women's contributions or collective political potential. By 1992, Margaret Ann MacQuarrie and Barbara Keddy felt that much of gerontological literature still did not address gender in relation to aging. In 1996, fourteen years after McLaren's call for older women's contributions to be recognized, Meredith Minkler echoed it once again, demanding that we look at older women's strengths as well as their problems. According to Evelyn R Rosenthal, feminists still had not confronted ageism or challenged the ageist constructions of women's experiences beyond mid-life. As recently as 1999, older adults, especially women, were still characterised by "dependency, disease, disability, and depression" (Scheidt, Humpherys, and Yorgason, 1999: 278). My own recent literature search revealed that research and writings about older women still relate almost exclusively to their needs and deficiencies, medical and social. I found very few articles pertaining to the elderly's political participation, even less so to older women's collective and positive contributions, let alone political activism. The few that discussed older women's activism focussed on medical issues, especially breast cancer. Recently, the books about older women at the Toronto Women's Bookstore fit on two small shelves in a store dedicated to works about or by women; of those two small shelves, all except two were about menopause, medical issues, or advice for "successful ageing." The two exceptions addressed feminist theories of gerontology, but none addressed older women's collective contributions or political involvement. The medicalization of older women is remarkable: other than their needs for medical treatment or advice, older women are almost invisible. Women's invisibility, it seems, increases with age: patriarchal societies lose interest in women beyond reproductive age and, so far, that also seems to be the case with feminists.

Why is so little written about older women, their lives and their contributions? Do they not merit greater consideration? Janet Ford and Ruth Sinclair ask if stereotypes get in the way and wonder if "our old women" are "too depressing" or "an embarrassment to us, or beyond the reach of our feminist analysis" (160). Searles suggests that "witches' words lack respectability; old women's opinions [are] discounted" and adds, "not only does society impose silence on us; we impose it on ourselves" and suggests that a Black woman's muteness described by Ntozake Shange could stand for a diffidence that has muffled our own utterances.

> she's been dead so long
> closed in silence so long
> she doesn't know the sound of her voice             (Shange in Searles 154)

Like J. Dianne Garner, others suggest the invisibility of older women protects us from the need to confront "patriarchal myths about what makes life valuable or dying painful" (3). The social and economic conditions in which older women live reflect the fact that old age is a gendered experience. Western society assigns worth to women according to their physical attractiveness to men: youth is equated with beauty, and beauty is women's social value. In Western society, growing old, for women, means a loss of value, but not so for men who are evaluated and rewarded for what they do. While men gain maturity as they age, "women lose the freshness of youth" (Rice in Hurd 421-422). Wilkinson suggests that the wrinkles, the lines, the heavy paunch, signal character, maturity, and fortitude in men, but obsolescence in women as they no longer fit the perfection that society expects. The ageism older women face is embedded in sexism, "an extension of the male power to define, control values, erase, disempower and divide" (Copper 73): "male contempt for the old woman as unfit for the reproductive/sex object roles filled by younger women (still the primary source of female power in the patriarchy) is the foundation of the old woman's powerless position" (16, 17). Copper adds that aesthetic rules and erotic choices are still set according to patriarchal standards, which help maintain male structures of power and female powerlessness; feminists have yet to resist male aesthetics. For women, to deny one's age becomes a way to cope and deny the harsh reality:

> Age passing…is part of all female experience. The foundation of lies built into passing and the fear and loathing of female aging keep the generations of women—decade after decade—divided from each other. Age passing is one of the primary learning arenas of female competition, as well as an apprenticeship in hatred of old women.[14]

As an old woman, Copper feels the pressure to adopt a meeker, more docile, and more submissive personality than she was expected to have in her youth. Such a personality runs counter to who she is now, an "independent assertive dike," an independence she gained by "smashing her traditional world into bits" (23). Old women's substantial experience has always been a part of what Adrienne Rich called "the enormous potential counterforce of patriarchy that is having to be restrained" (in Copper 15). Old women, says Copper, "are the throw-aways of our society, marginal to both the work and marriage marketplace" (39).

> There are grim statistics, which reveal the economic plight of old women—a demographic category with lower income than any other. There is a profession exclusively devoted to the study of age, gerontology. There are political organizations that promote the legislative and regulatory defense of the aged. Yet despite all this, we know next to nothing about what it is to be an old woman in this society.[15]

Linda M. Rhodes astutely asks:

> Is it so far-fetched to speculate that government officials who have a keen eye for sizing up the powers that keep them in office have assessed the elderly precisely as a constituency of 'dependent, harmless old ladies?'…Policy-makers have not been in the practice of perceiving the aged in their society as 'power-brokers.' Old age for females accelerates the discriminating imbalance experienced by women during the life span. It does not reverse it.[16]

Sheila Ritcey suggests that it is not biology but a social construct that perpetuates the experience of old age for women. In 1982, the situation of many Canadian or American older women was less than glamorous. "They were poor, widowed, lonely, over-medicated by physicians who often ascribed their complaints to hypocondriasis" (Burwell 208). According to the Older Women's League (OWL), "the greatest number of bank foreclosures on homes are among older women living alone" and they constituted "75 % of the population of institutions for the aged" (Breeze 7).

♪♪♪♪

**Home, Home on the Streets**

Oh, give me a home,

Just a mattress of foam,

In a most aromatic doorway,

Who needs room an dboard,

Where a bed is ensured,

And their own stuff could stay there all day

Chorus: Home, Home on the streets

Where the mutts and the alley-cats meet,

I recline for an hou-our,

I get my dog show-wer,

I'm Downtown Vancouver Elite!!!

There are poor little kids,

Down there on the skids,

'Cause their mothers have no place to go,

With a job at six bucks,

And a life-style that sucks,

Why don't they just move to

(Shaunnessy? Kerrisdale? Kilimanjaro?)

*Tune: Home On the Range. Downtown Vancouver Raging Grannies.*

In 1996, the situation had not greatly changed, according to Minkler: "Older women in Britain and the U.S. [were] twice as likely to live in poverty as men, and…in the U.S., fully three-fourths of the elderly poor are women" (1996: 469). In spite of this dire picture, two well-known male gerontologists, Borgatta and Loeb, made the following suggestion: "One might suggest…that an equally appropriate action might be to examine why women live so long, and to remove the factors that lead to this persistence" (in Burwell 209). They added:

> The equitable thing would appear to be, on the face of it, to institute policies that will equalize the average length of life of men and women…From the point of view of policy, the growing number of women living to older ages does not suggest emphasizing female studies in the expectation that they may need special care. Rather, even a casual examination of the value system and society as it operates suggests that the emphasis should be on men, to seek knowledge on how to improve their lot so that they may live as long as women.[17]

Burwell was indignant. She could not object to the idea of improving men's life expectancy, but found astonishing and frightening their suggestion, "that *priority* should be given to the study of men's lives" in spite of the fact that "much of the research in the past has focussed on older men and has slighted the study of the process of aging in women" (209). How could "two well-known gerontologists blithely ignore, even for the sake of making a point, the desperate position of many older women in our society?" asked Burwell (209).

Meredith Minkler suggests that we must understand "old age as a 'problem' for societies characterized by major inequalities in the distribution of power, income and property" (1996: 470). In fact, the resources directed to the elderly reflect "inequities [that] exist in our society," and "are exacerbated in old age and increase the disparities that exist between different groups of elderly," says Nancy Breeze (7): " 'Politics, not demography,' determine how old age is defined and approached in a society" says John Myles (in Minkler, 1996: 470). The situation has not improved much since the 1980s when Emily M. Nett and other feminists issued their call that older women deserved attention. Women's fear of ageing may be quite justified given the stark reality.

> There has been much written about the almost desperate attempt by millions of women to continue to look young through use of 'age defying' products and surgical procedures. Yet men spend very little on products designed to hide the signs of aging. Women's earnings do not increase with age in the same way that men's earnings increase. In fact the disparity in earnings becomes more pronounced with age. Women, therefore, enter old age with significantly fewer resources than do men. In fact, women constitute more than 75% of the elderly poor. While women outlive men, women encounter more health problems that interfere with activities of daily living than do men. It is not surprising, then, that many women approach old age with a sense of foreboding.[18]

But gerontologists focus "on the ever more technical and instrumental" orientation of academic gerontology, within which "the problems of later life are treated with scientific and managerial efficiency, but with no grasp of their larger political or existential significance" (Moody in Minkler 1999: 2). Approaching problems of old women as individual problems rather than systemic problems re-victimises women. Moody suggests that "the last stage of life is progressively drained of meaning" (in Minkler 1999: 2).

Yet, others find the "conspiracy of silence about ageism both in the women's movement and among those professionals who provide services for the old" very surprising given it is "a multi-billion dollar industry [that] focuses on the special needs of people over sixty who are perceived as…government-subsidized consumers of age-specific products and services" (Copper 1988: 3). The growing number of elderly has been called the "aging enterprise" (Nett 203); their increase in numbers is seen as a new expanding market for those in search of markets to exploit and "expanded" profits. Although little research has been done on older women, the market seems to be among the first to engage in further research:

> The Institute for Standards Research of the American Society for Testing and Materials did a study of 7,000 women aged 55 and older to reveal the customary women's dress sizes are geared to the young and inadequate for older women. Since older women are a fast growing market segment, business is likely to pay attention.[19]

Haug also suggests that the source of power for older people in the first few decades of the 21st century will be their greater numbers and their consequent influence on the market (Haug, 1995: 4), but power here means mostly as consumers. Manheimer sees "a vast army of helpers" surrounding the aging population, "a veritable growth industry" (5). Copper suggests that "a multi-billion dollar industry focuses on the special needs of people over sixty who are perceived as retired, government-subsidized consumers of age-specific products and services" (Copper 3). Yet, she sees that numbers or market interest do not translate into awareness, but rather perceives a

> …conspiracy of silence about ageism both in the women's movement and among those professionals who provide services for the old. In the two hundred subheadings for possible presentations to

the 34th Annual Meeting of the American Society on Aging in 1988, ranging from Contracts and Grant Management to Suicide, the word ageism never appeared.[20]

The elderly have been described as economically "non-productive," as "overburdening" the health system, and as "capitalizing resources and leaving the young without sufficient assets" (Schindler 171). Yet "all over the world old women do much of the undesirable or unpaid labor designated in the culture as female work—agricultural work, child care, household maintenance, cooking" (Copper 79). She read about a Nicaraguan revolutionary heroine who became the Foreign Minister and had no time for her children so she got her old mother to take care of them. This pattern is not new: while opportunities take younger women out of the home, grandmothers are recruited to care for children and home. This is not unique to Nicaragua: in China, in the Soviet Union, and even in our own society, younger women escape the home and older women re-appear to take the slack left by the careers of younger women: "If women are the mules of the world, the grandmother is the mule's mule" (Copper 79). As feminists, we must understand the pattern of men unloading responsibility for their children upon women, who become "liberated" and then in turn "unload their children on their old mothers" (Copper 9) displacing the care of children to women less privileged than they are. Without an analysis of age as an important factor of women's life, we risk re-victimising some women while some claim a very narrow "liberation." The Raging Grannies, by their name and their active participation, offer us the opportunity to question taken-for-granted notions associated with age. They boldly defy the pervasive invisibility of older women.

## Ageism: Distortion in the Web of Life

In some societies age gives status, so that only those towards the end of their lives are regarded as having enough experience and wisdom to deal with the most important issues and crises in their societies. We, however, have successfully deprived age of authority and of interest…In Britain, as elsewhere, older women are regarded at best as amiable old ladies, at worst as a group of weak and defenceless pensioners. The label is unjust, unkind and unsuitable.[21]

Aging appears as a biological phenomenon, but some feminists and gerontologists suggest it is also the product of a social construct. Age is both a social category and an experience, says Tracy X. Karner, and like the recognised iron triangle of class, gender, and race, age also serves as a significant organising principle for individual identities as well as social life in general. Hepworth agrees: there is an illusion that age and aging are ahistorical, prediscursive-natural. Margaret Morganroth Gullette argues that contemporary age ideology is a narrative of natural decline, something that can happen only because "age is still at the stage where gender and race used to be: hidden by its supposed foundation in the 'body': that master narrative, like those of race and gender, deeply affects our own personal experience" (202). But unlike class, gender, or race, oppression by age gradually invades

…defences carefully constructed against it. Passing begins long before the ritually endowed age of thirty. It starts when women (lesbians included) start equating youth and well-being. Age passing becomes a state of mind, a measure of self-worth, a guide to choice.[22]

Culture in a broad sense—discourses, feelings, practices, institutions, material conditions—is saturated with concepts of age and aging, says Gullette. In North America, there is a cult of youth and youthfulness, which is assumed to be the "normal" human condition; as long as "old age is equated with illness and dependency…it defies the cultural ideals of youth, activity and independence…of the "normal" human condition," suggests Hennessy (in Hurd 420). Age, says Tracy X. Karner, becomes something to be "defied," "an example of which is a makeup campaign telling women that age can be separated from one's inner identity" (7). To grow old in a society whose dominant values are speed, productivity, efficiency, increase of material wealth through work and competition means to be devalued. An ambivalent attitude toward non-work means that we do not have ways of thinking that give it status and legitimacy say Janet Ford and Ruth Sinclair.

> We lack a concept like 'gender' or 'race' to identify the system that keeps a regime of age knowledge circulating. We have no word like 'patriarchy' that permits us to conceive of age as another field of power and hierarchy, politics and narrative, demystification and resistance. I use 'age ideology.'[23]

In spite of the diversity of circumstances, personalities, and experiences of older people, "old age is frequently assumed to be a homogeneous and uniformly negative life stage" (Hurd 420). While aging is real, a process that happens differently depending on many factors, including class, gender, race, sexual orientation, ageism "rearranges power relationships, just like any other kind of discrimination or prejudice. When one ages, one may gain or lose. With ageism, one is shaped into something that is *always* less than what one really is," writes Copper (3) who has much to say on the subject: "Ageism is the negative social response to different stages in the process of aging and is a political issue": it is not aging but ageism that is oppressive (73). "Those who 'service the elderly' are trained not to identify with them, but to make decisions for them, to 'expedite' filling their needs. Old people, like most involuntary consumers, are easier to manage if they see themselves as powerless" (4).

> How can old women [re]define age and ageism so that false understanding of these subjects does not dominate?…Aging begins the day we are born…a process of challenge—not necessarily growth and development when we are young as opposed to loss and deterioration when we are old—but learning through change.[24]

We need a new alternative framework to interpret old age. Gullette suggests that an alternative is to construct "life as a process of losing our false fears, our overly pessimistic anticipation" (xix): "It is not by facing the past but by facing the future and not losing one's nerve…In terms of potential to handle whatever [the future] is likely to bring" (Gullette in Hepworth 146). Ronald J. Manheimer suggests old age is in a

> …crisis of meaning and its resolution lies in the field of aging. But it is not a field, it is a battleground…The battle is over the gifts of age, the bounty of a lengthened life course. Boon or burden for the individual and for society? Maybe some of both…Yet the awareness of growing old defines in part our humanity.[25]

## Historical Backdrop

Old age has a history. Demographically, there have been changes. Cheryl Elman wrote that in 1930, "the proportion of the U.S. population aged 65 and over…was about five percent. While this proportion is small compared to the proportion of elderly in the U.S. today (about 12%), it was twice that of 1870 and growing" (308-309). "As we enter the next millennium, the percentage of Americans over the age of 65 is expected to be close to 14%, almost triple the number at the beginning of this century" (Barrow cited in Kelchner 87). In Canada, the situation is similar: "In 1990, the number of elderly persons in Canada exceeded 3 million (Statistics Canada, personal communication, August 1991) and represented approximately 11 percent of the total population. By 2011, this proportion is projected to reach almost 5 million, and will claim almost 16 percent of the total population" (MacQuarrie 21). That life expectancy has doubled, and more, leaves the developed societies "without a relevant intellectual, cultural and religious tradition as to our own aging" (Laslett 150).

Through the development of language we can also gain some information on the evolution of thinking about old age. The vocabulary has changed as greater numbers of people reach old age. Peter Laslett wrote that up to a century ago, "death took place throughout the lifecourse and was not concentrated in the period ignominiously labelled 'old age,' and when, above all, what we now call 'the third Age' had not yet arrived" (150). The word ageism was only "coined a mere 25 years ago (by Robert Butler)" but is now part of popular discourse. Some think ageism protects younger individuals from thinking about aging, illness, death, which they may fear. The gendered nature of the language of old age is also historical:

> Whereas a more pejorative vocabulary for old men developed recently (1800s) in North American society, virtually every term of abuse used for old women (hag, crone, old maid, etc.) appears to be as old as the English language itself.[26]

A contemporary author wrestled with how to name herself:

> The decision to abandon the tag 'older woman' was easier than claiming the identity of *old*. *Old* was without hope, ignored, invisible, trivialised, patronised, limited, powerless. If I didn't want to accept this definition, how *was* I to speak of myself? [27]

Maggie Khun, founder of the Gray Panthers at age 65, rejected the term "senior citizen" as "euphemism…part of the denial…I just call myself an old woman, and I say it with trumpets. I have survived" (in Searles 155). Lou Cottin thinks we need to reclaim the meaning of "old" as "sagacity, kindliness, wisdom, generosity, even graciousness and beauty" (1). Some have started calling themselves Crones, at times Hags, reclaiming the devalued

> …archetype of female age…The Crone, under one name or another, was part of the mythology of people from eastern Asia to Ireland, from Scandinavian to Northern Africa. In Christian Europe, she suffered the most complete obliteration; the persecution of her earthly representatives was carried to the greatest extremes in the burning times. Walker builds a strong case that the ageism and social rejection which limits old women today is one of the most persistent legacies of that erasure.[28]

Copper continues:

> [The] archetypes of the Virgin and the Mother were consolidated into the Christian figure of Mary, but the feared archetype of female age, the Crone, was eradicated…Thus the 'wise, wilful, wolfish Crone' was female power and danger in its most potent form. In patriarchy, she had to be erased.[29]

That stage of life for women was a time of freedom from conventions: "It is only the hag that rides free," wrote Shelagh Wilkinson and "that is why she is feared, ostracised, tortured and murdered. Or worse, she is deformed into a stereotype—the easier to recognise and discount her. But the old woman, the Crone, is that aspect of womanhood that is no longer controlled; she is the self that flies free" (103):

> Here I go, flying
> high, disguised as
> a fairy grandmother
> whirling and twirling
> my old-age wand;
> just watch me—
> I'm about to turn
> a million glittering
> cartwheels in milky
> outer skies…[30]

The Crone survived limitations and lack of freedom, but now refuses to be confined: she crosses freely over lines drawn by a patriarchal system intent on labels and divisions (Beadle xiii). The historical record holds information that can change our perception of aging. Feminists are reclaiming "the long line of history that stretches across cultures…that has been neglected until recently. Only now because of feminist scholarship are women retrieving their cultural memory" (Wilkinson 106). What would it mean to know of the past? Adrienne Rich asked this question so poignantly (1990). Copper expresses that longing for historical memory:

> As I burned my bridges behind me I believed that in my own way I was a pioneer like my foremothers. I was inventing my life as well as reflecting the movement of women in the 1960s. I knew nothing of the repeated herstory, the waves of ingenuity women have shown to develop life styles which evaded male exploitation. Feminist scholarship had not yet unveiled the communities of women such as the Beguines, or the lively, independent nuns of the walled cities of the Visroyalty of Peru. Patriarchal erasure had successfully withheld from me the choices that other women had made before me which might have provided models for my own rebellion.[31]

Some remnants of this historical recognition of old women's wisdom have survived in literature.

Euripides in his drama about the Trojan women gave the greatest perception to the old Queen Hecuba. Hecuba is the wise old woman who knows that 'malestream' history is

> All a web of lies
> Where all the gore becomes glory
> In the telling and re-telling
> Of the lies.

Through the rage and despair of Hecuba's poetry we make discoveries about the roles of men and women—about the false code of honour that betrays men into death and about the illusionary role of beauty that betrays women even into old age.[32]

In more recent times, Wilkinson reports that in *Trojan Women*, Gwendolyn MacEwan

…shows that an unquestioning loyalty to a bankrupt culture, especially one that is built around the paradigm of stereotypic gender roles, is deadly. But MacEwan also shows that it is the figure of the Crone who is the freeing agent; the old woman (who knows all the past and who is willing to call the present into account) is able to accomplish this because she moves beyond patriarch rules. And because she is more free than most of us it is old woman who is righting our stories.[33]

To reclaim the Crone, then, is to enter a process of liberation: the Crone is about strength, vision, vulnerability, and insights. To reclaim the Crone is our last chance to pull the veil of lies and look at the reality in stark honesty. Strength and insight gathered from surviving the long journey become necessary resources to confront the difficulties of old age for women living under a patriarchal system. Gatherings of hags "have embarrassed and harassed the powerful into responding to their demands…have refused to be silenced by a thrown bone, or discouraged by the lack of female support or impressed by belated congratulations," wrote Shelagh Wilkinson (xiv). The gaggles of Raging Grannies also create embarrassment and disturbances for authorities. They play with stereotypes and challenge them while using their voices to speak out. The irreverence and subversivity of the Grannies is in part due to the fact that they identify themselves as older women with an "un-motherly" public rage. Calgary Raging Grannies have "passion and pizazz" and like to introduce themselves with a jazzy song:

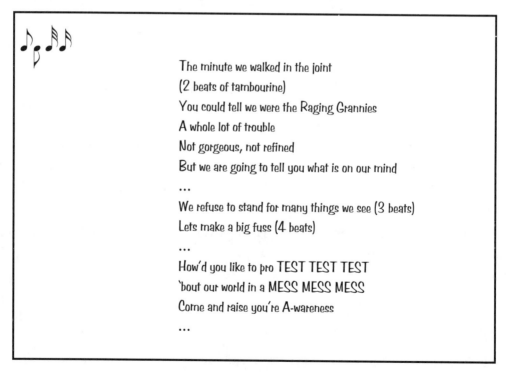

*Tune: Big Spender. Calgary Raging Grannies, Granny Grapevine, Spring 2001: 30.*

## Never Grow Too Old to Dream: Political Potential of Aged Agitators

Millions of long-living women scheme to change the world.     —Ruth Harriet Jacobs

Haug acknowledged in 1995 that little information is available on older people's political participation. What is written, she says, boils down to their power in the market as consumers (4, 9-10).

> Forecast in other types of political action, like mass demonstrations, lobbying of elected officials, or other methods of applying pressure for achieving political ends, seems virtually impossible. There are no published data known to this gerontologist on the cohort characteristics of people on picket lines or political parades. [34]

In an article published in 1995, Ronald L. Jirovec and John A Erich mentioned previous research on the political participation of the elderly and "the much smaller branch of the research" which "investigated political participation among older women" but report inconsistent findings (87-88), in spite of the fact that their definition of political participation was limited to the very "radical" act of voting! Yet, there are precedents of age-based political movements.

Cheryl Elman reports that the demographic doubling of elderly people in the U.S. between 1870 and 1930 gave rise to a little talked about, but influential, old age political movement called the Townsend movement. In spite of its influence at the time, Elman claims the fact that such

> ...age-based mobilisation poses a problem for contemporary theory is evident in the scholarly silence about the Townsend organisation, a social movement organisation of old people that emerged in the 1930s. It is well known that the U.S. elderly were a highly visible and vocal force well before the mass actions of youth in the 1960s. The Townsend organisation mobilised an enormous old-age constituency before their direct representation as an interest group in the polity, during the critical time of the political restructuring of the U.S. into a social welfare state...But even when social movement and political theorists note the importance of this movement they do not attach special significance to a mobilisation of the old.[35]

That movement grew faster in the sunny paradise that was Southern California then, where hundreds of thousands of elderly Americans retired, reports Elman. Apparently, states with the greatest number of old people or with the sharpest increases in their proportion saw their activity increased, making them easy to identify; it seems that many people got involved politically where numbers gave them visibility. Some interesting parallels, although on a smaller scale, exist with the Raging Grannies and the fact that they originated in Victoria, BC, a well-known retirement center in Canada. Vancouver Island, having the mildest climate in the country, attracts retired people, therefore providing greater possibility for interactions between the large number of elderly and creating possibilities for the growth of activism amongst them. Another similarity exists in their social and economic contexts.

> [The Townsendites] fashioned their social, economic, moral, and political belief systems, core aspects of their social identities, in the decades following the Civil War. While they comprised a large cohort, the promise of American abundance after the Civil War was equally powerful.[36]

The Raging Grannies also fashioned their identities during the decades after WW II and the post-war prosperity. Yet, like those elderly of the 1930s, they faced a deep recession in the 1980s.

[The Townsendites] sought to redefine old age [and] contested the negative social depictions and definitions of the elderly that prevailed in this time period. Their speeches stressed recognition and dignity while activities were often group-oriented, non-strategic and informal.[37]

The Gray Panthers is another age-based movement that met with success. Founded in 1970 by Maggie Kuhn and six other women over the age of 65 to oppose the Vietnam War, it is now a network that works for the rights of people of all ages and has been effective in bringing societal changes. Referring to the effectiveness of the Gray Panthers, J. Dianne Garner states:

Not only is there a responsibility for feminist gerontologists to advocate for old women, but there is a responsibility to facilitate advocacy efforts by older women themselves. One need only consider the advocacy and social change efforts of the Gray Panthers to recognize that old women need not be excluded from advocating for themselves and others.[38]

Cheryl Elman suggests that the elderly, as a group, have experienced a loss of roles in the last century and gain large amounts of unstructured time. The loss of a recognized role has led to what Manheimer calls a "diminished sense of identity and personal worth" (5). But participation in the Townsend movement compensated for this loss of role (Elman). The lack of attention to the Townsend movement and other age-based movements robs elderly people of a sense of their past political achievements as a group and their potential power for change toward social justice. A well-known quote suggests that:

Human history has been written by a white hand, a male hand, from the dominating social class… Attempts have been made to wipe from their [non-white, female, dominated class] minds the memories of their struggles. This is to deprive them of a source of energy, of an historical will to rebellion.[39]

To this list we might add a "not old" hand.

## Feminism and the Challenge of Age

As of late, feminists and feminist gerontologists are raising their voices to

…prod us to look at 'the multiple roots of oppression'…in marginalised groups of older people, but…also at their strengths, including…how they construct maps of meaning on a journey through age that is often fraught with hardships.[40]

Feminists must "search for the images of women as elders" in a diversity of fields, "investigate the multitudes of meanings for this stage in our human life…To discover more about strengths, our creativity, and the continuity of our Selves over our lifetimes," says Emily Nett (226). Reclaiming women's, and older women's, positive images and contributions is necessary in order to gain a sense of continuity:

Women are and always have been marvellous pioneers, although the history of our accomplishments has been deemed insignificant by men. We've been the best damned community developers for centuries, albeit unpaid and unrecognized. We need to do much more organizing with women as Elders, so as to unlock all the marvellous energy, imagination, drive and wisdom that older women have to offer one another and to the world.[41]

The framework we adopt to examine old age for women must emphasise "both social hierarchy and human agency," says Sheila Neysmith (392). There is a need "to uncover and report upon the lives of older women, concentrating upon a more complete account of their thoughts, feelings and activities," as Janet Ford and Ruth

Sinclair wrote (5). As Bond and Coleman put it, we should be "less concerned with charting decline and predicting outcomes, and more with outlining possibilities" (in Minkler 1996: 481). Although not acknowledged much in the literature, experience shows that female old age "provides excellent potential for radical change and self-expression" (Copper 60). It has been many centuries "since there were old matriarchs who could have threatened the power of the patriarchs. Yet the conditioning against the possibility of powerful, respected, or influential old women continues," says Copper (61). Barbara Walker believes:

> The real threat posed by older women in a patriarchal society may be the 'evil eye' of sharp judgement honed by disillusioning experience, which pierces male myths and scrutinizes male motives in the hard, unflattering light of critical appraisal. It may be that the witch's evil eye was only an eye from which the scales had fallen.[42]

Baba Copper wants the Crone "to be integrated into the feminist model of female identity. We need to reinvent the image of powerful, rebellious old women" (59).

Just as our challenge "to patriarchal constructions of women's nature" has made a difference in young women lives, it is time for feminists "to accept the challenge aimed at transforming older women's lives," says Evelyn R Rosenthal (2). Feminist activist researchers must work to "provoke a deep curiosity about, indeed an intolerance for, that which is described as inevitable, immutable, and natural" (Fine cited in Ray 171). For Sondra Farganis, empowering feminist research seeks to raise consciousness about "social arrangements as a prelude to action," allowing questions to be raised about how we come to think of ourselves as individual, and how we come to know power and the capacity to change or resist it: we must understand who we are and "refuse to be what [we] have been socialized to be" (in Ray 174), especially "when that culturalization has negated [our] potential" (Ray 174).

> Patriarchal reversal teaches us to do things against our own best interests—nationalizing them, psychologizing them, minimizing them—while at the same time taking the blame for them upon ourselves and socializing our daughters to do the same. We are taught to expect certain things when we get older—all negative—all diminishing.[43]

But "the mind of post-menopausal woman is virtually uncharted territory" (Walker cited in Copper 60).

> Feminists whose analysis of sexism brilliantly and devastatingly changed ideas about the nature of women must recognize how a parallel analysis of ageism uncovers similar mechanisms at work constructing the nature of old age. By investigating the lives of old women we can challenge stereotypes, critique old age as a social construction, and discover that much of what we as women fear about our own aging is not natural to old age.[44]

In literature "old women have rarely been portrayed as the resourceful, productive, vital, angry and joyful women many of us are" (Wilkinson 103). In fact, feminist research has recently shown that post-menopausal women "are often endowed with new energy and vitality" in spite of a society that "perceives them as declining and almost obsolete" (Cohen in Wilkinson 103). Already, the "seemingly fixed pattern of largely negative associations" with old age is being disrupted as scholarship shows it is "not really the result of 'nature' but of cultural attitudes, the economic organization of society, and other factors"; we must seek "patterns that contain hopefulness...meanings that bring new initiatives, that encourage deeper understanding, that inspire without looking at old age through rose-colored glasses" (Manheimer 7). Confronting "the narrow range of negative images of aging pervasive in our culture" and seeking to "challenge and disrupt conventional story lines of women and aging" becomes a necessity (Kamler and Felman in Ray 178).

One of the key issues is inter-generational communication. "Youth provides women with a temporary illusion of opportunity in the work world" (Copper 29). "In a society dominated by youthful and middle-aged males, only women who are useful to such men are sponsored and protected" (Nett 225). Since youthfulness is a primary requirement for sexual attractiveness to males, many jobs are open only to young women," says Copper. "Only women who are sexually stimulating and accessible and those who are capable of reproducing them and their male world, and who thereby become dependent upon them, are even seen" (Nett 225). The chasm of identity between older and younger women provides a comfortable separation from women who youth perceive as "not passing" (Copper 29). "The older woman is who the younger woman are better than—who they are more powerful than and who is compelled to serve them" (Macdonald and Rich cited in Copper 25). "The patriarchs have taught us to contain and defang the potential revolt which the experienced woman might ferment against him" (Copper 34).

> But feminist scholarship has uncovered the repetitive quality of women's resistance down through the years. We are beginning to recognize that rejection of knowledge about the lives of the preceding generation of women is part of the problem. Feminists, like anyone else, act from a socially conditioned view of aging. That view reflects values contradictory to women's interests. The irrational loathing and terror of female aging casts a long shadow, influencing the choices of women of all ages. By dividing the generations, ageism robs women of the continuity of identity necessary for successful feminist resistance. Analysis of the historical sources of woman-directed ageism, as well as documentation of how it impacts women's self image and life experience, is now beginning to emerge.[45]

Old age must be politicised and become an issue to those not yet old (Ford and Sinclair). Rebellious youth do not perceive the possibility of a rebellious old woman (Copper). Younger women must understand old women "are not a special interest group" but our roots, and we, their continuity (Pauli in Copper 73). But old age holds little interest until one gets there, "a foreign country with an unknown language to the young and even the middle-aged" (Ford and Sinclair 14). Without dialogue between generations, feminist theory cannot develop a model of the female life cycle and without that old women are "stereotyped as Other—old fashioned, ugly, apolitical, powerless among women, invisible—just as the patriarchs hoped when they eradicated the Crone" (Copper 60).

Women must hear of past examples of resistance to oppression by women of all ages. Older feminists are discovering a new potential (Copper). While we must guard against creating positive portrayals of aging that are "potentially as pernicious as negative ones in that they deny the reality of aging" and show "no more tolerance or respect for the intractable vicissitudes of aging than the old negative mythology" (Cole in Baltes and Carstensen 398), broadening the range of roles available for old women is necessary (Garner). More research needs to focus on elderly women's contributions to society (A. McLaren). Otherwise it makes it easier

> …to think of the elderly in this one-dimensional way, and to accept the picture of them as problematic, demanding and unreasonable…What is necessary is a counter-balance to the problem-centered stance, an approach that draws out a more holistic picture of their lives.[46]

Knowledge about the Raging Grannies contributes to this more holistic picture. Aging is simultaneously "an academic problem, a pressing social issue and an urgent personal concern" (Hepworth 139).

> It's time we gave witness,
> attention, attention must be paid,
> or we'll march hand in hand,
> together strong as a battering ram,
> create situations until others
> understand we're not designed
> to rust. Some day they'll be us.[47]

## Notes

1. Vermont women against the nuclear power plant (March 1980), cited in Catherine Reid, "Reweaving the web of life," in Pam McAllister, ed., *Reweaving the Web of Life: Feminism and Nonviolence,* 289-294, Philadelphia: New Society Publishers, 1982: 289.

2. Pam McAllister, ed., "Introduction," *Reweaving the Web of Life: Feminism and Nonviolence* (i-viii), Philadelphia: New Society Publishers, 1982: iv.

3. Marjorie Johnson Williams and Colleen Nadjiwon Johnson, "Minobimaatisiiwin—We are to care for her," in Miriam Wyman, ed., *Sweeping the Earth: Women Taking Action for A Healthy Planet* (251-257), Charlottetown, PEI: Gynergy Books, 1999: 254.

4. Comfort cited in D. L. Boggs, D. L., "Civic education: An adult education imperative," *Adult Education Quarterly,* 42(1), 1991: 51.

5. Marilyn Waring cited in Miriam Wyman, ed., "Introduction," *Sweeping the Earth: Women Taking Action for A Healthy Planet* (13-25), Charlottetown, PEI: Gynergy Books, 1999: 201.

6. Anna Golubovvsska Onisimova, "Health and environmental issues in Ukraine," in Miriam Wyman, ed., *Sweeping the Earth: Women Taking Action for A Healthy Planet* (192-199), Charlottetown, PEI: Gynergy Books, 1999: 193-195.

7. Judy Brady, "Looking back to go forward," in Miriam Wyman, Ed., *Sweeping the Earth: Women Taking Action for A Healthy Planet* (121-128), Charlottetown, PEI: Gynergy Books, 1999: 127.

8. Cited in Miriam Wyman, ed., *Sweeping the Earth: Women Taking Action for A Healthy Planet,* Charlottetown, PEI: Gynergy Books, 1999: 85.

9. Baba Copper, *Over the Hill: Reflections on Ageism Between Women.* Freedom, California, The Crossing Press, 1988: 11.

10. *Ibid.,* 14-15.

11. Elizabeth S. Kelchner, "Ageism's impact and effect on society: Not just a concern for the old," *Journal of Gerontological Social Word,* 32(4) 1999: 93.

12. Arlene T. McLaren, "The myth of dependency." *Resources for Feminist Research/Documentation pour la Recherche Féministe,* 11(2) 1982: 213.

13. Marilyn J. Bell, ed., "Introduction," *Women As Elders: The Feminist Politics of Ageing,* New York: Harrington Park Press, 1986: 1.

14. Copper, 1988: 73-74.

15. *Ibid.,* 85.

16. Linda M. Rhodes, "Women aging: Address before the United Nations NGO Committee on Aging at the Secretariat, New York, January 17, 1982," *Resources for Feminist Research/Documentation pour la Recherche Feministe,* 11(2), 1982: 205.

17. Borgatta and Loeb cited in Elinor J. Burwell, "The handwriting is on the wall: Older women in the future," *Resources for Feminist Research/Documentation pour la Recherche Féministe,* 11(2), 1982: 209.

18. J. Dianne Garner, ed., "Feminism and feminist gerontology," *Fundamentals of Feminist Gerontology,* New York, The Haworth Press, 1999: 4.

19. Marie R. Haug, "Elderly power in the 21st century," *Journal of Women and Ageing,* 7(4), 1995: 3-4.

20. Copper, 1988: 3.

21. Janet Ford and Ruth Sinclair, *Sixty Years On: Women Talk About Old Age,* London, The Women's Press, 1987: 1.

22. Copper, 1988: 18-19.

23. Margaret Morganroth Gullette, *Declining to Decline: Cultural Combat and the Politics of the Midlife,* Charlottesville and London, University of Virginia Press, 1997: 212.

24. Copper, 1988: 73.

25. Ronald J Manheimer, "Introduction: Is it practical to search for meaning?" *Generations* XXIII(4), 1999-2000: 6.

26. Nett, 1982: 225.

27. Copper, 1988: 75.

28. *Ibid.,* 58.

29. Copper, 1988: 58.

30. Miriam Waddington, "Old age blues," *Collected Poems,* Toronto, Oxford University Press, 1996: 326. By permission of Oxford University Press.

31. Copper, 1988: 5.

32. Shelagh Wilkinson, "Old woman, 'Bearer of keys to unknown doorways'," *Canadian Woman Studies,* 12(2), 1992: 107.

33. *Ibid.*

34. Marie R. Haug, "Elderly power in the 21st century," *Journal of Women and Ageing,* 7(4), 1995: 9.

35. Cheryl Elman, "An age-based mobilisation: The emergence of old age in American politics," *Ageing and Society,* 15(3), 1995: 300.

36. *Ibid.,* 310.

37. *Ibid.,* 319.

38. J. Dianne Garner, ed., "Feminism and feminist gerontology," *Fundamentals of Feminist Gerontology,* New York: The Haworth Press, 1999: 9.

39. Gustavo Gutierrez cited in Elizabeth Schussler Fiorenza, "In search of women's heritage,"in Judith Plaskow and Carol P. Christ, eds., *Weaving the Visions: New Patterns in Feminist Spirituality,* New York: HarperSanFransisco, 1989: 34.

40. Ovrebo and Minkler cited in Meredith Minkler, "Critical perspectives on ageing: New challenges for gerontology,"*Ageing and Society,* 16(4), 1996: 472.

41. Helen Levine, "The Crones of Ottawa," *Resources for Feminist Research/Documentation pour la Recherche Féministe,* 11(2), 1982: 223.

42. Walker cited in Copper, 1988: 62.

43. Copper, 1988: 1.

44. Evelyn R. Rosenthal, "Women and varieties of ageism," *Journal of Women and Ageing,* 2(1), 1990:6.

45. Copper, 1988: 55.

46. Ford and Sinclair, 1987: 4-5.

47. Elsen Lubetsky in Jo C. Searles, "Inventing freedom: The positive poetic 'mutterings' of older women," *Journal of Women and Ageing,* 2(2), 1990: 157.

Chapter Nine

# IS THERE A LAST WORD?

And for ourselves, the intrinsic "Purpose" is to reach, and to remember, and to declare our commitment to all the living, without deceit, and without fear, and without reservation. We do what we can. And by doing it, we keep ourselves trusting, which is to say, vulnerable, and more than that, what can anyone ask?                                        —June Jordan[1]

# A PASSION FOR PROTEST

*Figure 85. Halifax Raging Grannies celebrate the ban on landmines.*
*Source: Southender, March 2001: 12. Photo courtesy of Southender Magazine.*

## Canadian Grannies and Activism
## From the 1960s Voice of Women to the 1990s Rage of Grandmothers

The Raging Grannies are an example of a small group that uses creativity to get much greater visibility than their relatively small numbers would suggest. Creativity becomes political as it offers alternative views and, according to Gregory Bateson, "is the only way to resolve systemic contradictions" (cited in Berman 230). They have boldly moved towards Göran Brulin's "artistry of pedagogy" (445) and combine visual (costume and props), auditory (songs), and cognitive (humour and information in the lyrics) aspects. They understand what Jane Vella suggests about other groups, that systems of domination cannot be overcome without humour and wit. They successfully integrate three factors important in what Budd Hall (1981) sees as effective education: social investigation, education, and action. By doing so, they take for themselves the right to speak, or what Diane Margolis calls the political power of naming (in Moore 92), something essential in a democratic society and for a population often marginalized. Budd Hall also suggests that "the natural processes of knowledge creation being undertaken within social, environmental and political action settings can also be understood within what we call 'research,' " (2001: 174). I suggest the Raging Grannies' activism is such an example of knowledge creation.

Although the Voice of Women is still very active in Canada, it is interesting in a symbolic way that between the 1960s and 1990s the voice of Canadian women has become the rage of grandmothers at the still-present nuclear threat and at the increasing environmental destruction. The multi-generational aspect reflects the social changes due to the impact of feminism; while being able to voice opinions was a challenge for women in the 1960s, now women feel empowered to express rage and anger, emotions considered un-feminine, although they do it in a witty and humorous way. Voice of Women and Raging Grannies share common concerns but use different ways to communicate their message.

The Grannies are cultural activists who use humour to highlight issues rather than to deny, dismiss, or pacify situations. Cultural activists challenge assumptions, says Richard Hofrichter, and Grannies' forms of activism, stereotypes of older women, and fragmentation of issues. Cultural activism is not entertainment; it is provocative and confronts the status quo while providing an example of resistance and giving voice to communities often without one (Hofrichter). Their ability to use humour in protest is unique; unfortunately humour is rarely considered a worthy subject of inquiry and has only recently become a legitimate topic of research. Humour is "still not well represented in the psychological literature" (Lefcourt 11).

Through satirical songs the Grannies display an ability to use ambiguity and paradox that encourage the audience towards critical thinking (Barrios). Satirists "tend to bloom in seasons of drought" and throughout history satire has been used to counteract the excesses of the Roman empire, the Church, or European bourgeoisie, says Melvin Maddocks, who sees satire as "literature's alternative to revolution" (1987). Yet the Grannies also discovered that with their satirical street theatre approach they walk a thin line: too far off, they talk only to the converted, but too sweet and tolerable, they become entertainment and stop people from thinking, as Tony Coult and Baz Kershaw suggest. John Burns also makes the point that for political theatre, success is often "as dangerous as failure to the purity of their politics" (24). Because the Grannies managed to transform the stereotype into something positive they are in demand by seniors' clubs and others. Singing in old-age homes may satisfy some Grannies, but does not satisfy those who seek to intervene on the socio-political scene. John Burns makes the point that for political theatre, success is often "as dangerous as failure to the purity of their politics" (24). To be identified only as entertainment is to lose the capacity to inter-vene on the socio-political scene. This issue of entertainment versus intervention is still alive, a question that groups of Grannies need to revisit periodically.

All the Grannies interviewed saw the spread of Raging Grannies groups as a sign of success. At the start of this research I tended to agree with Burns' suggestion in 1992 that some of the groups who copied the orig-inal Grannies found it hard to decide if they were entertainers or activists, but after meeting thirty-seven Raging Grannies in twelve groups across the country, I have come to the conclusion that although not each "performance" of the Raging Grannies is an intervention on the political scene, the intent of the original Raging Grannies to be disruptive of the status quo holds true for present-day Grannies. All the Grannies I met saw themselves as activists and vow not to be entertainment but intervenors on the socio-political scene. Their creative, daring, or humorous actions are Jonny Ebstein and Philippe Ivernel "grains of sand" which disrupt social life, complacency, and habits of thought (9), grains of sand often newsworthy. Not only have they de-veloped a new form of activism that uses humour, but they have broadened what Catriona Sandilands calls an "horizon of possibilities" for older women activists (85).

## Power of Vulnerability

Phyllis Cunningham suggests that "the struggle begins on the margin" (157). The confines of gender and age stereotypes for older women qualify as margins in a patriarchal society with an active idolization of youth. Their use of humour is possible because they are willing to make themselves vulnerable. Lorna Drew brought up vulnerability as a factor involved in humour:

> You can't make people [laugh] without exposing yourself. I don't think so. I think a stand-up comic is probably a good example of being terrified but you go and you do it anyway, and you say, 'look, this is me making a fool of myself. I can do this, and if I can do it then you can do it. It's okay to act a fool.' But it's scary to act a fool. It's not okay to act a fool in this culture; the other people don't like fools and lock them up. Now they're doing worse than that. So the old comeric notion of the clown is part of the Grannies' agenda, the wise fool. To act a fool you run the risk of being as vulnerable as fools are. But then you invite people to put down their defences as well when you're doing that, and to laugh at you and then it turns out that they're laughing with you.

Regina Barreca, a feminist who writes about humour, agrees:

> Humor is a show both of strength and of vulnerability: you are willing to make the first move but you are trusting in the response of your listener…Making a generously funny comment, pointing to the absurdity of a situation, turning embarrassment or unease into something to be shared instead of repressed is risky, but it is also often exactly what is needed.[2]

Although it takes courage to stand out there, the unrecognized ferment in most resistance is a willingness to be vulnerable, to allow oneself to be reached by the world and its pain. A nurse who cared for many elderly people was asked if Muriel Duckworth was unusually vibrant. After reflection she replied to Marion Douglas Kerans that elderly people full of vitality have one thing in common, their vulnerability: "It's because they keep themselves so open to others, to pain and to joy, that's why Muriel and people like her remain so vital" (in Kerans 231). While militaristic thinking searches for invulnerability, non-iolent thinking honours vulnera-bility as a condition of growth, relationality, and connection. The theologan Dorothy Soelle writes:

> The window of vulnerability
> must be closed—
> so the military say
> …
> My skin
> is a window of vulnerability
> without moisture, without touching
> I must die[3]

And,

> It doesn't happen without risk. Life that excludes and protects itself against death protects itself to death…Only life that opens itself to the other, life that risks being wounded or killed, contains promise.[4]

From the vulnerability of sexism, ageism, and feeling threatened by environmental destruction the Raging Grannies have invented a form that allows them to break stereotypes and voice their views. Humour and solidarity make vulnerability tolerable. Without a willingness to be vulnerable to the world there is no resistance.

The Grannies acknowledge the role of emotions and intuition as worthy and valuable sources of information while also pursuing information in a more analytical fashion. Bonnie Burstow has suggested that recognition of the role of emotions is often lacking in our understanding of adult learning, while Darlene Clover has pointed out the lack of recognition for the role of creativity. The Raging Grannies' approach to activism acknowledges both of these, making their contribution an important one to adult education. The Grannies' love for their families and the world is not separated from their activism but intrinsic to it. In fact, studies

> …reveal that affective learning has to take place before critical reflection can begin…Some insight into these questions has already been revealed in the field of neurobiology, where emotions are seen as essential to the process of reason and decision-making…In essence, critical reflection and feelings should no longer be viewed as separate, but instead as operating in an interdependent relationship, with each relying upon the other in the search for clarity and understanding.[5]

Along with emotions and creativity, the Grannies demonstrate that relationships are central to transformative learning and to activism and exemplify the role of collaboration, support, trust, and friendship in learning:

> It is through relationships that learners develop the necessary openness and confidence to deal with learning on an affective level, which is essential for managing the threatening and emotionally charged nature of a transformative learning experience. Without the medium of relationships, critical reflection is impotent and hollow, lacking the genuine discourse necessary for thoughtful and in-depth reflection…Transformative learning is not about promoting and striving for individual autonomy, but about building connections and community.[6]

## "Dangerous" Motherhood

> Sometimes we lose. Our love of life can be destroyed, yet our love of life can also be nourished by the healing waters of rage, compassion, and respect. Justice, compassion, decency, all well up from deep reservoirs of respect…for the rhythms of life…respect even of death and decay…even of pain. The wellspring of insight and persistence is also rage: rage at that which violates unnecessarily the rhythms of life.[7]

One element that has not been mentioned much yet is motherhood. The Grannies repeatedly affirm they want to protect this world for the next generations. Motherhood also provides motivation for liberatory political action. As Temma Kaplan said about the Love Canal protesters, "citizenship can grow out of conscious motherhood" (40). She mentions the Mothers of the Plaza de Mayo who started from their individual motherhood but quickly expanded their commitment to human rights and who chose to represent themselves as mothers because it made it harder for soldiers and police to attack them than if they had claimed citizen's rights. Feminists have often focussed on the limits of motherhood, but we must also see its empowering capacity. The irreverence and subversivity of the Grannies are in part due to their identification with an "un-motherly" public rage. The recognition of the importance of passion in women's (and mothers') activism comes from unlikely sources. Marjorie Agosin reports the comments of a Brazilian military officer, "[that] women constitute the most effective political weapon; they have time, they are capable of great emotion, they can mobilize quickly" (30). A similar comment was made by some police spies of the Russian Interior Ministry at the turn of the century:

> Mothers of families, exhausted by endless standing in line at stores, distraught over their half-starving and sick children, are today perhaps closer to revolution than Mssrs. Liliutov and Rodichev [the liberal opposition] and of course they are a great deal more dangerous because they are the combustible material for which only a single spark is needed to burst into flames.[8]

And the fire happened: women took to the streets and, according to Trotsky, it became "the first day of the [Russian] revolution" (in Rowbotham 134). Time, passion, and a threat to survival combine in an explosive mixture for women.

The Raging Grannies came to be because of an ethic of care connected to their caretaking work with their families. Ardra Cole and Gary Knowles suggest that "meaningful and relevant learning begins with experience" (xii). Mechthild Hart, that the mothering work of caring for the body cannot be easily separated from the work of caring for the mind and that theory cannot be separated from practical application as it must apply to particular individuals, a process which challenges masculinist epistemologies where reason and emotion are divided (183, 186). Such work, says Hart, requires close contact and involvement, as the knowledge of one child is never absolute and does not lend itself to general propositions, so the mother must remain open to future discoveries (187, 188). The skills required for such work is an ability to move between "critical distance" and "mimetic nearness" where "both mutually influence and enhance rather than exclude each other, which is at the heart of an epistemology," an experience which reflects relations based on equality and reciprocity rather than dominance: "Only such dialectical unity…can keep the bond between work, knowledge and experience intact" (Hart 183). The Raging Grannies demonstrate their grasp of this dialectical unity when they use ambiguity and paradoxes so effectively in humour, criticizing the powers-that-be yet at the same time making a bond with the audience, or emphasizing caring and anger at the same time as in their name, or the use of humour with highly serious factual information. It is also shown when they push a point to the absurd and volunteer for the Gulf War wearing uniforms that are instantly seen as uniforms but also as not-uniforms. They can evaluate, judge, confront, protest, and support. This requires a cognitive process that is both comprehensive as well as differentiating, a process that allows for the more complex reality of similarities and differences (von Werlhof cited in Hart 5). They equally value what Hart describes as thought and emotion, analysis and creativity, process and content or task, caring and judgement, listening and speaking (192, 193). Prétat, a Jungian analyst, suggests that later years are a time of metanoia when one challenge for the Crone is to integrate opposites (14, 106). Jung even suggested that an atomic war

> ...depends on how many people can stand the tension of the opposites in themselves. If enough can, I think we shall escape the worst. But if not, and there is an atomic war, our civilization will perish, as so many civilizations have perished before, but on a much larger scale.[9]

The invasion of Iraq by the United States and the United Kingdom gives this comment added significance. Hopefully, the Grannies' ability to handle contradictions and paradoxes with humour and daring can find resonance in those who are 'world' leaders. The Grannies demonstrate their willingness to honour various dimensions by refusing hierarchies, knowing full well that a child needs to be fed and washed and loved and taught. Their values are reflected in their organization. The Grannies resisted creating a hierarchical organization requiring conformity; instead they elected to promote non-hierarchical relations which emphasizes respect for differences and diversity. In spite of a lack of centralized structure and organization, great distances, and regional differences, they are surprisingly consistent across the country on the positions they take. They have found a format that allows both a common outlook across widely different regions and the expression of differences. The fluidity of such a non-hierarchical organization can be scary for those who fear spontaneity and its necessary chaos. Yet that very ability to embrace the uncertainty of the creative process is one of the things that make the Raging Grannies noteworthy.

## A Middle Not So Neutral: The Call to Solidarity

As active citizens, the Raging Grannies enjoy a measure of respect in their communities and are willing and able to devote the necessary time to their activities. Although many claim a measure of social (race, class) privilege, their activism proves that critically thinking women, creatively acting together, can express solidarity and play a positive role in promoting awareness and social change. While a small number hold jobs, most Grannies are not employed in the paid workforce. In an article on housewife activists, Harriet G. Rosenberg uses Eric R. Wolf's disagreement with "the notion that it is the most oppressed who mobilize": the under-resourced poor or the ideologically constrained rich are not as well positioned or willing to challenge cultural assumptions or social structures because they have too much to lose (191). But those in between are strategically positioned for doing so. Rosenberg suggests that corporations especially dislike housewife activists because they know they are unwilling to compromise with the health of their families (198). The Grannies may not see concrete results on all the issues they tackle, but they have succeeded in being a meaningful part of a chorus of dissent: "It is not the size of the voice that is important: it is the power, the truth and the beauty of the dream" (Okri cited in Gordon 314). Yet we should make no mistake about the power of such grassroots examples. Even today unlikely sources fear grassroots' activism, as a memo sent by an executive of Union Carbide to other executives reveals:

CCHW [Citizen's Clearinghouse for Hazardous Waste] is one of the most radical coalitions operating under the environmentalist banner. They have ties into labor, the communist party and all manner of folk…In October, at their grassroots convention, they developed the attached agenda which if accomplished, in total, would restructure U.S. society into something unrecognizable and probably unworkable. It's a tour de force of public policy issues to be affecting business in years to come.[10]

More recently, the Grannies' and others' participation at the WTO in Seattle garnered this analysis from Richard Gwyn of the *Toronto Star*:

In advance of the World Trade Organization meeting in Seattle—Oxfam, the Sierra Club, the Raging Grannies, among hundreds of others—were regarded as a tiresome nuisance. *New York Times'* foreign affairs columnist Thomas Friedman dismissed them as 'Noah's Ark of flat Earth advocates, protectionist trade unionists and yuppies looking for a 60s fix.' By the session's end…these groups had pulled off a series of stunning successes. Those on the inside were reaching out to the protesters—albeit with gritted teeth…More amazing, the protesters, while standing in the streets amid clouds of teargas, succeeded in rewriting the agenda painstakingly cobbled together by the WTO's bureaucrats on the advice of all those business lobbyists. The organization's secrecy was attacked by none other than President Bill Clinton…The truly amazing—nearly unbelievable—thing that happened there was that for three days, groups of private citizens, armed with nothing much more than the Internet and a certain flair for political theatrics, compelled a major international institution, staffed by highly experienced officials and backed by national governments and by all multinational corporations and business lobbyists, to talk about something other than their favourite subject of conversation, and in normal circumstances, their sole one…This time, these raggle-taggle protesters managed to change the subject from money and profits to the survival of sea turtles or cultural identity or hormone-injected beef or child labour. This change in perspective may not last long…[But] in Seattle…what happened was a wake-up call.[11]

The Raging Grannies were part of the wave experienced at the WTO in Seattle in 1999, and since then in other major protests. They reveal, even to feminists, that older women's passion and playfulness had been left out: it is not anymore. We now hear the George Eliot raging "roar on the other side of silence" (in Belenky et al. 4). The Grannies' activism contributes to the democratic process of our society. Temma Kaplan reminds us that without citizen's continued activism and willingness and commitment to demonstrate, democracy does not exist in a representative democratic system. Those who dare to stand on the edge open up greater space in the middle for moderates: without what is seen as the extreme, the middle would be closer to the status quo. Those standing on such an edge rarely see their hopes realised right away but help moderates get a hearing, a procss which can result in the mainstream moving toward a less conservative position and towards change. The more radical elements broaden the range of possibilities: in that sense the Grannies open a wider range of behaviour for many, including older women. By their challenge to various authorities and by acting against the grain, they keep alive the possibility of alternative visions. What Vandana Shiva, an Indian physicist, wrote about agriculture can be transposed to social life: "Monocultures of fields start in the minds: they spread because control makes the conditions of alternatives impossible, and lack of alternatives results in total control by the dominant power" (1993: 7). Adding their voices to dissenters, the Raging Grannies help keep the dominant power from such total control.

## Hope, Interconnectedness, and Authenticity

The Grannies use Nieburg's "combined power of hope, impatience, and impulsiveness" to express power not in terms of individual power but as collective power (341). Marjorie Agosin calls it a feminine form of political action. "The individual woman, the woman of true individuality, with the power and freedom to be herself, can only be born in large numbers" because individuality was historically rooted in privilege, which meant that for a few to have a face others had to remain faceless, says Susan Griffin (9). Solidarity can lead to the development of new cultural forms, and it has done so in the case of the Raging Grannies. A sense of connection is part of the Grannies' impetus to act. Muriel Duckworth, who was an activist for a long time before being a Raging Granny, acknowledges a sense of connection that is essentially tied to her motivation as an activist:

> If you feel your link to all people, that other people matter as much as you do yourself and you matter a lot, then that link with people makes you do what you can so that other people should have a chance too.[12]

Isabel Carter Heyward goes as far as suggesting that evil is "a break in relationship" (cited in Kerans 232). Martha Ackelsberg writes that a sense of connection makes it possible to overcome the feelings of powerlessness which inhibits social change and that "radicalization is [often] born of action" (1991: 163, 165). The Raging Grannies demonstrate what Vaclav Havel calls deep hope, an orientation of spirit which "is not the conviction that something will turn out well, but the certainty that something makes sense regardless of how it turns out" (cited in Cohen-Cruz 65).

One of the Grannies' gifts to activism is their demonstration that interconnectedness is a principle of life and a principle from which to act in society as well. The Grannies demonstrate in songs and actions what Peter Reason and Hilary Bradbury assert, that not separate things but relationships make our world. John Heron also suggests interconnectedness is intrinsic to the web of relations that makes human lives. They engage with a myriad of issues, an engagement that reveals the links between militarism and the environment and violence against women and health and education and good governance and consumerism. In fact, few protest groups address such a wide variety of issues as the Grannies do. The principle of interconnectedness is also active on a personal level where "threads that hold together the interwoven fabric of…past, present, and future" (Cole and Knowles 15) become visible, linking early personal histories to historical contexts and to present day activism, threads that sometimes extend back to other generations. Grannies bring their individual connections to various networks and the particular issues of these larger networks to their Granny group. By exchanging views and concerns they educate themselves and help weave the fabric of social justice and peace into an integrated tapestry rather than a disjointed patchwork of various concerns. Their consciousness of interconnectedness extends between generations, as they seek contact with the younger generation, knowing that nurturing the next generation is necessary to develop a population willing and able to participate in the civil society (Gouthro). Interconnectedness requires what Ardra Cole and Gary Knowles call an ethic of authenticity and the ability and willingness to endure the truth, as Jung put it (in Prétat) in all its dimensions, especially when difficult situations are encountered. With wit, irreverence, daring, and creativity, the Raging Grannies honour their experience, thoughts, and feelings, and find ways to stimulate new perspectives on a variety of issues. Not denying complexities in exchange for the ease of simplicity and false certainty leads to greater and more meaningful integration. The Raging Grannies' pedagogy of persistence weaves love, authenticity, vulnerability, interconnectedness, solidarity, an ethic of risk, humour, creativity, and fun. The Grannies, these long-livers, refuse to give up, refuse to shut up. And they make us laugh so that we will also find the insights and courage to honour life and work for peace. Interconnectedness requires vulnerability and an ethic of risk. An ethic of safety is for those with privilege; for others, safety is too costly:

> The ethic of risk is propelled by the…vital recognition that to stop resisting, even when success is unimaginable, is to die. The death that accompanies acquiescence to overwhelming problems…the death of the imagination, the death of our ability to care.[13]

> rage and compassion in the face of suffering and injustice,
> resilience in the face of opposition and set-backs,
> laughter in the face of failure and mistakes,
> and virtuosity
> audacious, breathtaking, disciplined, and heartfelt
> in the face of limits.[14]

*Figure 86. Victoria Raging Grannies paddling with others to greet Greenpeace's Rainbow Warrior in Victoria's waters, September 16, 1990. Source: Times-Colonist (Victoria).*

## Notes

1. Cited in Alice Walker, *Revolutionary Petunias and Other Poems,* New York: Harcourt Brace Javanovitch, 1973: 67.

2. Regina Barreca, ed., *The Penguin Book of Women's Humor,* New York: Penguin Books, 1996: 10.

3. Dorothy Soelle, *The Window of Vulnerability: A Political Spirituality,* Minneapolis: Fortress Press, 1990: vii.

4. *Ibid.,* xi.

5. Edward W. Taylor, "Building upon the theoretical debate: A critical review of the empirical studies of Mezirow's transformative learning theory," *Adult Education Quarterly: A Journal of Research and Theory in Adult Education,* 48(1), 1997: 52.

6. *Ibid.,* 53.

7. Sharon D. Welch, *Sweet Dreams In America: Making Ethics And Spirituality Work,* New York: Routledge, 1999: 135.

8. William M. Mandel, *Soviet Women,* Garden City, New York: Anchor Press, 1979: 43.

9. Carl Jung cited in Jane R. Prétat, *Coming to Age: The Croning Years and Late-life Transformation,* Toronto: Inner City Books, 1994: 106.

10. Internal memo from Clyde Greenert, 14 November 1989, to other Union Carbide executives reviewing CCHW Grassroots Convention, reported by Mueller in Harriet G. Rosenberg, "From trash to treasure: Housewife activists and the environmental justice movement," in Jane Schneider and Rayna Rapp, eds., *Articulating Hidden Histories: Exploring the Influence of Eric R. Wolf,* Berkeley: University of California Press, 1995: 198.

11. Richard Gwyn, "People send wake-up call in Seattle," *The Toronto Star,* December 5, 1999.

12. Cited in Marion Douglas Kerans, *Muriel Duckworth: A Very Active Pacifist,* Halifax: Fernwood Publishing, 1996: 232.

13. Sharon Welch, *A Feminist Ethic of Risk* (rev. ed.), Minneapolis: Fortress Press, 2000: 46.

14. Sharon D. Welch, *Sweet Dreams In America: Making Ethics And Spirituality Work,* New York: Routledge, 1999: 61.

*Figure 87. Montreal Raging Grannies. Photograph by Joshua Radu. Source: Angela Silver Collection.*

| Maritimes | Ontario | Prairies | BC | USA | Other Countries |
|---|---|---|---|---|---|
| **New Brunswick** | Brantford | **Saskatchewan** | Argenta | Bellingham, WA | **Australia** |
| Fredericton | Elmvale | Regina-Grenfell | Bowen Island | Binghamton, NY | Sydney |
| Saint John | Guelph | Saskatoon | Cowichan Valley | Boston, MA | |
| | Halton | | Gabriola Island | Buffalo, NY | |
| **Nova Scotia** | Hamilton | **Alberta** | Kamloops | Chapel Hill, NC | **Greece** |
| Halifax | Huron | Calgary | Kelowna | Dallas, TX | Athens |
| Wolfville | Ingersoll | Central Alberta | North Okanagan | Denver, CO | |
| | Kingston | Edmonton | Penticton | Detroit, MI | **UK** |
| **Newfoundland** | Kitchener-Waterloo | Lethbridge | Saltspring | Los Angeles, CA | Exmouth |
| St John's | Leamington | | Sunshine Coast | Louisville, KY | |
| | London | | Surrey | Minneapolis, MN | |
| **Quebec** | Niagara | | West Vancouver | New York, NY | |
| Montreal | Ottawa | | Vancouver | Palo Alto, CA | |
| (English) | Oxford/Woodstock | | (Downtown) | Phoenix, AZ | |
| Montreal | Peterborough | | Vancouver | Plainfield, VT | |
| (French) | Simcoe County | | (Raincoast) | Pittsburg, PA | |
| | Ste Catherines | | Victoria | Portland, OR | |
| | Thunder Bay | | White Rock | Reading, PA | |
| | Toronto | | | Rochester, NY | |
| | Windsor/Detroit | | | Seattle, WA | |
| | Woodstock | | | Traverse City, MI | |

*This is a list of Raging Grannies groups compiled from references.*

*Some groups may not exist anymore as membership fluctuates, and some groups probably are not yet known to the larger network.*

Anyone interested in joining, or starting a group, can find information at the Raging Grannies International website:

www.geocities.com/raginggrannies

# Bibliography

Ackelsberg, Martha A. Communities, resistance, and women's activism: Some implications for a democratic polity. In Ann Bookman and Sandra Morgen, eds. *Women And The Politics Of Empowerment.* Philadelphia: Temple University Press, 1988.

Ackelsberg, Martha A. *Free Women of Spain: Anarchism and the Struggle for the Emancipation of Women.* Indianapolis: Indiana University Press, 1991.

Agosin, Marjorie. *Scraps Of Life: Chilean Arpilleras, Chilean Women, And The Pinochet Dictatorship.* Trenton, NJ: The Red Sea Press, 1987.

Allen, Paula Gunn. Grandmother. In *Life Is A Fatal Disease.* Albuquerque and San Fransisco: West End Press, 1997.

Anderson, B. S. and J. P. Zinsser. *A History Of Their Own: Women In Europe From Prehistory To The Present, Volume 1.* New York: Harper & Row, 1988.

Apte, Mahadev L. *Humor And Laughter: An Anthropological Approach.* London: Cornell University Press, 1985.

Are the Raging Grannies 'anti-Canadian?' *The Canadian Unitarian,* 40(1), January 1999. Joyce Stewart Collection.

Arendt, Hannah. *Eichmann In Jerusalem: A Report On The Banality Of Evil.* Toronto: Penguin Books, 1963.

Baltes, Margaret M. and Laura L. Carstensen. The process of successful ageing. *Ageing and Society,* 16(4), 1996.

Barreca, Regina, ed. *The Penguin Book Of Women's Humor.* New York: Penguin Books, 1996.

Beadle, Gert. The nature of Crones. In Marilyn J. Bell, ed. *Women As Elders: The Feminist Politics Of Aging.* New York: Harrington Park Press, 1986.

Belenky, Mary Field, *et al. Women's Ways Of Knowing: The Development Of Self, Voice, And Mind.* New York: Basic Books, 1986.

Bell, Marilyn J., ed. Introduction. *Women As Elders: The Feminist Politics Of Aging.* New York: Harrington Park Press, 1986.

Benton, Gregor. The origins of the political joke. In Chris Powell and George E. C. Paton, eds. *Humour In Society: Resistance And Control.* New York: St. Martin's Press, 1988.

Bergson, Henri. Laughter: An essay on the meaning of the comic. Translated by Cloudesley Brereton and Fred Rothwell. In John Morreall, ed. *The Philosophy Of Laughter And Humor* (rev. ed.). Albany, NY: State University of New York, 1987.

Berlak, Ann. Teaching for outrage and empathy in the liberal arts. *Educational Foundations,* Summer 1989.

Berman, Morris. *The Reenchantment Of The World.* Ithaca: Cornell University Press, 1981.

Bilger, Audrey. *Laughing Feminism: Subversive Comedy In Frances Burney, Maria Edgeworth, And Jane Austen.* Detroit: Wayne State University Press, 1998.

Boggs, D. L. Civic education: An adult education imperative. *Adult Education Quarterly,* 42(1), 1991.

Boskin, Joseph. The complicity of humor: The life and death of Sambo. In John Morreall, ed. *The Philosophy Of Laughter And Humor.* Albany, NY: State University of New York, 1987.

Breeze, Nancy. Crones nest: The vision. In Marilyn J. Bell, ed. *Women As Elders: The Feminist Politics Of Aging.* New York: Harrington Park Press, 1986.

Brightwell, Betty. Defending the differences. *Times-Colonist,* Victoria, September 23, 1995.

Brulin, Göran. The third task of universities or how to get universities to serve their communities. In Peter Reason and Hilary Bradbury, eds. *Handbook Of Action Research: Participative Inquiry And Practice.* Thousand Oaks, California, 2001.

Burns, John. Raging Grannies. *Canadian Theatre Review,* Guelph, 72, 1992.

Burstow, Bonnie. Problematizing adult education: A feminist perspective. *The Canadian Journal for the Study of Adult Education,* 8(1), 1994.

Burwell, Elinor J. The handwriting is on the wall: Older women in the future. *Resources for Feminist Research/Documentation pour la Recherche Féministe,* 11(2), 1982.

Butterwick, S. Lest we forget: Uncovering women's leadership in adult education. In Sue M. Scott, Bruce Spencer and Allan M. Thomas, eds. *The Foundations of Adult Education in Canada, Second Edition.* Toronto: Thompson Educational Publishing, 1998.

Caldecott, Leonie. At the foot of the mountain: The Shibokusa women of Kita Fuji. In Lynne Jones, ed. *Keeping The Peace: A Women's Peace Handbook.* London: The Women's Press, 1983.

Cameron, Ardis. *Radicals Of The Worst Sort: Laboring Women In Lawrence, Mass, 1860-1912.* Chicago: University of Illinois Press, 1993.

Clover, Darlene. Community arts as environmental education and activism: A labour and environment case study. *Convergence* XXXIII(4), 2000.

Cohen-Cruz, Jan, ed. Part Two: Introduction. *Radical Street Performance: An International Anthology.* New York: Routledge, 1998.

Cole, Ardra L, and J. Gary Knowles. *Researching Teaching: Exploring Teacher Development Through Reflexive Inquiry.* Toronto: Allyn and Bacon, 2000.

Copper, Baba. *Over The Hill: Reflections On Ageism Between Women.* Freedom, California: The Crossing Press, 1988.

Cottin, Lou. *Elders In Rebellion: A Guide To Senior Activism.* Garden City, New York: Anchor Press/Doubleday, 1979.

Coult, Tony, and Baz Kershaw, eds. *Engineers Of The Imagination: The Welfare State Handbook* (rev. ed.). London: Methuen Drama, 1990.

Cunningham, Phyllis. Race, gender, and the practice of adult education in the United Sates. In Frank Youngman and Paul Waangoola, eds. *Towards A Transformative Political Economy Of Adult Education: Theoretical And Practical Challenges.* Dekalb, Illinois: LEPS Press, 1996.

DeShaw, Rose. Goofy-hated reconcilers in the land. *The Globe and Mail,* April 10, 1997.

DeShaw, Rose. Making a promise for life. *The Globe and Mail,* October 28, 1997.

Ebstein, Jonny, and Philippe Ivernel. *Le theatre d'intervention depuis 1968: Tome II.* Lausanne, Suisse: L'Age d'Homme, 1983.

Elman, Cheryl. An age-based mobilisation: The emergence of old age in American politics. *Ageing and Society,* 15(3), 1995.

Elston, Suzanne. Nuclear awareness in rural Ontario. In Miriam Wyman, ed. *Sweeping The Earth: Women Taking Action For A Healthy Planet.* Charlottetown, PEI: Gynergy Books, 1999.

Feinberg, Leonard. *Introduction To Satire.* Ames, Iowa: Iowa State University Press, 1967.

Fiorenza, Elizabeth Schussler. In search of women's heritage. In Judith Plaskow and Carol P. Christ, eds. *Weaving The Visions: New Patterns In Feminist Spirituality.* New York: HarperSanFransisco, 1989.

Ford, Janet and Ruth Sinclair. *Sixty Years On: Women Talk About Old Age.* London: The Women's Press, 1987.

Fotheringham, Allan. Silly spy files aren't limited to U.S. *The Kitchener-Waterloo Record,* October 17, 1998.

Freire, Paulo. *Education For Critical Consciousness* (rev. ed.). New York: Continuum, 2000.

Garland, A. W. *Women Activists: Challenging The Abuse Of Power.* New York: The Feminist Press and the City University of New York, 1988.

Garner, J. Dianne, ed. Feminism and feminist gerontology. *Fundamentals Of Feminist Gerontology.* New York: The Haworth Press, 1999.

Gonault, Denise Belisle. *Women And Ageing In Canada: Multidisciplinary Annotated Bibliography 1975-1989.* Université d'Ottawa/ Carleton University, 1990.

Gordon, Gloria Bravette. Transforming lives: Towards bicultural competence. In Peter Reason and Hilary Bradbury, eds. *Handbook Of Action Research: Participative Enquiry And Practice.* Thousand Oaks, California: SAGE, 2001.

Gouthro, Patricia. Globalization, civil society and the homeplace. *Convergence* XXXIII(1-2), 2000.

Greenberg, Jeremy. These Grannies are raging. *Excalibur,* October 1999.

Greig, J.Y.T. *The Psychology Of Laughter And Comedy.* New York: Cooper Square Publishers, 1969.

Griffin, Susan. *Voices: A Play.* New York: The Feminist Press, 1975.

Gullette, Margaret Morganroth. *Declining To Decline: Cultural Combat And The Politics Of The Midlife.* Charlottesville and London: University of Virginia Press, 1997.

Hall, Budd L. Participatory research, popular knowledge, and power: A personal reflection. *Convergence,* 14, 1981.

Hall, Budd L. Global civil society: Theorizing a changing world. *Convergence* XXXIII(1-2), 2000.

Hall, Budd L. I wish this were a poem of practices of participatory research. In Peter Reason and Hilary Bradbury, eds. *Handbook Of Action Research: Participating Inquiry And Practice.* Thousand Oaks, California: SAGE, 2001.

Hammond, Jenny. *Sweeter Than Honey: Ethiopian Women And Revolution: Testimonies Of Tigrayan Women.* Trenton, NJ: The Red Sea Press, 1990.

Hammond, Merryl. Organizing against pesticide use in suburbia. In Miriam Wyman, ed. *Sweeping The Earth: Women Taking Action For A Healthy Planet.* Charlottetown, PEI: Gynergy Books, 1999.

Harford, Barbara and Sarah Hopkins, eds.*Greenham Common: Women At The Wire.* London: The Women's Press, 1984.

Harris, Leon A. *The Fine Art Of Political Wit.* New York: E.P. Dutton & Co., 1966.

Hart, Mechthild. *Working And Educating For Life: Feminist And International Perspectives On Adult Education.* New York: Routledge, 1992.

Harvey, Linda C. *Humor For Healing: A Therapeutic Approach.* San Antonio, Texas: Therapy Skill Builders, 1998.

Hepworth, M. In defiance of an ageing culture. Review of Margaret Morganroth Gullette, *Declining To Decline: Cultural Combat And The Politics Of The Midlife. Ageing and Society,* 19(1), 1999.

Heron, John. Transpersonal co-operative inquiry. In Peter Reason and Hilary Bradbury, eds. *Handbook Of Action Research: Participative Inquiry And Practice.* Thousand Oaks, California: SAGE, 2001.

Heyward, Carter. *Staying Power: Reflections On Gender, Justice, And Compassion.* Cleveland, Ohio: The Pilgrim Press, 1995.

Hofrichter, Richard, ed. Cultural activism and environmental justice. *Toxic Struggles: The Theory And Practice Of Environment Justice.* Philadelphia, PA: New Society Publishers, 1993.

Howard, Keith. Those comic Raging Grannies. *The United Church Observer,* 53(3), 1989.

Hurd, Laura. "We're not old!": Older women's negotiation of ageing and oldness. *Journal of Ageing Studies,* 13(4), 1999.

Isaak, Jo Anna. *Feminism And Contemporary Art: The Revolutionary Power Of Women's Laughter.* London: Routledge, 1996.

Jacobs, Ruth Harriet. *Be An Outrageous Older Woman.* New York: Perennial, 1997.

Jayawardena, Kumari. *Feminism And Nationalism In Third World.* London: Zed Books, 1986.

Jirovec, Ronald L. and John A. Erich. Gray power or power outage? Political participation among very old women. *Journal of Women and Ageing,* 7(11/2), 1995.

Junor, Beth. *Greenham Common Women's Peace Camp: A History Of Non-Violent Resistance 1984-1995.* London: Working Press, 1995.

Kaplan, Temma. *Crazy For Democracy: Women In Grassroots Movements.* New York: Routledge, 1997.

Karner, Tracy X. Introduction: Identity issues in research on ageing. *Research on Ageing,* 20(1), 1998.

Kerans, Marion Douglas. *Muriel Duckworth: A Very Active Pacifist.* Halifax: Fernwood Publishing, 1996.

Kelchner, Elizabeth S. Ageism's impact and effect on society: Not just a concern for the old. *Journal of Gerontological Social Word,* 32(4), 1999.

Kettel, B. A gender-sensitive approach to environmental health. In Miriam Wyman, ed. *Sweeping The Earth: Women Taking Action For A Healthy Planet.* Charlottetown, PEI: Gynergy Books, 1999.

Laslett, Peter. Review of Thomas R. Cole, *The Journey Of Life: The Cultural History Of Ageing In America. Ageing And Society,* 19(1), 1999.

Laurence, Margaret. Old women's song. *Dance on the Earth: A Memoir.* Toronto: McClelland & Stewart, 1989.

Lefcourt, Herbert M. *Humor: The Psychology Of Living Buoyantly.* New York: Kluwer Academic/Plenum Publishers, 2001.

Lerner, Gerda. *The Creation Of Feminist Consciousness: From Middle-Ages To Eighteen-Seventy.* New York: Oxford University Press, 1993.

Lerner, Gerda. *Why History Matters: Life And Thought.* New York: Oxford University Press, 1997.

Lofland, John. *Polite Protesters: The American Peace Movement Of The 1980s.* Syracuse, NY: Syracuse University Press, 1993.

Lynn, Helen. Women's environmental network. In Miriam Wyman, ed. *Sweeping The Earth: Women Taking Action For A Healthy Planet.* Charlottetown, PEI: Gynergy Books, 1999.

MacQuarrie, Margaret Ann and Barbara Keddy. Women and ageing: Directions for research. *Journal of Women and Ageing,* 4(2), 1992.

Maddocks, Melvin. Time ripe for satire. *Christian Science Monitor,* 1987, November 23, 1987. Doran Doyle Collection.

Magnusson, Warren. Critical social movements: De-centering the state. In Alain-G. Gagnon and James P. Pickerton, eds. *Canadian Politics: An Introduction To The Discipline.* Peterborough, ON: Broadview Press, 1990.

Magnusson, Warren. *The Search For Political Space: Globalization, Social Movements, And The Urban Political Experience.* Toronto: University of Toronto Press, 1996.

Maguire, Patricia. Uneven ground: Feminisms and action research. In Peter Reason and Hilary Bradbury, eds. *Handbook Of Action Research: Participative Inquiry And Practice.* Thousand Oaks, California: SAGE, 2001.

Mandel, William M. *Soviet Women.* Garden City, New York: Anchor Press, 1975.

Manheimer, Ronald J. Introduction: Is it practical to search for meaning? *Generations* XXIII(4), 1999-2000.

McAllister, Pam, ed. Introduction. *Reweaving The Web Of Life: Feminism And Nonviolence.* Philadelphia: New Society Publishers, 1982.

McAllister, Pam. *You Can't Kill The Spirit: Stories Of Women And Non-Violent Action.* Philadelphia, PA: New Society Publishers, 1988.

McAllister, Pam. *This River Of Courage: Generations Of Women's Resistance And Action.* Philadelphia, PA: New Society Publishers, 1991.

McLaren, Jean and Darlene Maceharvey, eds. *The Raging Grannies Song-Cookbook: Volume 1.* Gabriola Island, BC: Hutzler Press.

McLaren, Jean and Heidi Brown, eds. *The Raging Grannies Songbook.* Gabriola Island, BC: New Society Publishers, 1993.

Minkler, Meredith. Critical perspectives on ageing: New challenges for gerontology. *Ageing and Society,* 16(4), July 1996.

Minkler, Meredith. Introduction. In Meredith Minkler and Carroll L. Estes, eds. *Critical Gerontology: Perspectives From Political And Moral Economy. Policy, Politics, Health and Medicine Series,* Vicente Navarro, Series Editor. Amityville, New York: Baywood Publishing, 1999.

Moore, Henrietta L. *A Passion For Difference: Essays In Anthropology And Gender.* Bloomington: Indiana University Press, 1994.

Morreall, John. *The Philosophy Of Laughter And Humor.* Albany, NY: State University of New York, 1987.

Mulkay, Michael. *On Humor: Its Nature And Its Place In Modern Society.* New York: Basil Blackwell, 1988.

Nader, Ralph. Press release. Louise Swift Collection, April 15, 1998.

Nader, Ralph. Raging Grannies: An instrument of protest. *Briarpatch,* July/August 1998.

Nett, Emily M. Introduction. *Resources for FeministResearch/Documentation pour la Recherche Feministe,* 11(2), 1982.

Nett, Emily M. A call for feminist correctives to research on elders. *Resources for Feminist Research/Documentation pour la Recherche Feministe,* 11(2), 1982.

Neysmith, Sheila M. Review of Sara Arber and Jay Ginn, eds. *Connecting Gender And Ageing: A Sociological Approach. Ageing and Society,* 16(3), 1996.

Nieburg, H.L. Politics of confrontation. In R. Serge Denisoff, ed. *The Sociology Of Dissent.* New York: Harcourt Brace Jovanovich, 1974.

Portelli, Alessandro. *The Death Of Luigi Trastulli And Others Stories: Form And Meaning In Oral History.* Albany: State University of New York Press, 1991.

Powell, Chris and George E. C. Paton, eds. Introduction. *Humour In Society: Resistance And Control.* New York: St. Martin's Press, 1988.

Prétat, Jane R. *Coming To Age: The Croning Years And Late-Life Transformation.* Toronto: Inner City Books, 1994.

Protesting may be good for your health. December 23, 2002., http://story.news. yahoo.com/news?tmpl=story2&u=/nm/20021223/ hl.nm /protest_demonstrations_dc.

*Raging Grannies "Carry On" Songbook.* Collected by South West Ontario Grannies, Spring 2000.

Ray, Ruth E. Researching to transgress: The need for critical feminism in gerontology. In Diane J. Garner, ed. *Fundamentals Of Feminist Gerontology.* New York: The Haworth Press, 1999.

Reason, Peter, and Hilary Bradbury, eds. Introduction: Inquiry and participation in search of a world worthy of human aspiration. *Handbook Of Action Research: Participative Inquiry.* London: Sage Publications, 2001.

Reason, Peter. and Marshall, Judi. Research as Personal Process. In V. Griffin & D. Boud, eds. *Appreciating Adults' Learning,* 1987.

Reid, Catherine. Reweaving the web of life. In Pam McAllister, ed. *Reweaving The Web Of Life: Feminism And Nonviolence.* Philadelphia: New Society Publishers, 1982.

Reinharz, S. *Feminist Methods In Social Research.* New York: Oxford University Press, 1992.

Rhodes, Linda M. Women aging: Address before the United Nations NGO Committee on Aging at the Secretariat, New York, January 17, 1982. *Resources for Feminist Research/Documentation pour la Recherche Feministe,* 11(2), 1982.

Rich, Adrienne. Natural resources. *The Dream Of A Common Language: Poems, 1974-77.* New York: Norton, 1978.

Rich, Adrienne. *On Lies, Secrets, And Silence: Selected Prose 1966-1978.* New York: W.W. Norton & Company, 1979.

Rich, Adrienne. What does a woman need to know? In Pat C. Hoy, Esther H. Schor, and Robert DiYanni, eds. *Women's Voices: Visions and Perspectives.* New York: McGraw-Hill, 1990.

Ritcey, Sheila. Substituting an interactionist for a normative model in gerontological research. *Resources for Feminist Research/Documentation pour la Recherche Féministe,* 11(2), 1982.

Romalis, Shelly. Carrying Greenham home: The London women's peace support network. *Atlantis: A Women's Studies Journal,* 12(2), 1987.

Romalis, Shelly. *Pistol Packin' Mama: Aunt Molly Jackson And The Politics Of Folklore.* Chicago: University of Illinois Press, 1999.

Rosenberg, Harriet G. From trash to treasure: Housewife activists and the environmental justice movement. In Jane Schneider and Rayna Rapp, eds. *Articulating Hidden Histories: Exploring The Influence Of Eric R.Wolf.* Berkeley: University of California Press, 1995.

Rosenthal, Evelyn R. Women and varieties of ageism. *Journal of Women and Aging,* 2(1), 1990.

Roy, Arundhati. *The Cost Of Living.* Toronto: Vintage Canada, 1999.

Rowbotham, Sheila. *Women, Resistance And Revolution: A History Of Women And Revolution In The Modern World.* New York: Pantheon Books, 1972.

Rudkin, Ian. *To Halve And To Whole.* Vancouver: BRIO Books, 2001.

Sandilands, Catriona. Is the personal always political? Environmentalism in Arendt's age of the social. In William K. Carroll, ed. *Organizing Dissent: Contemporary Social Movements In Theory And Practice: Studies In The Politics Of Counter-Hegemony.* Toronto: University of Victoria Garamond Press, 1997.

Scheidt, R. J., D. R. Humpherys, and J. B. Yorgason. Successful aging: What's not to like. *Journal of Applied Gerontology: The Official Journal of the Southern Gerontological Society,* 18(3), 1999.

Schindler, Ruben. Empowering the aged—A postmodern approach. *International Journal of Aging and Human Development,* 49(3), 1999.

Searles, Jo C. Inventing freedom: The positive poetic "mutterings" of older women. *Journal of Women and Ageing,* 2(2), 1990.

Semenak, Susan. Social activists in sensible shoes. *The Gazette*, Montreal, April 14, 1991.

Sharp, Gene. *The Methods Of Non-Violent Action Part Two: The Politics Of Non-Violent Action*. Boston, MA: Porter Sargent Publishers, 1973.

Shiva, Vandana. *Staying alive*. London: Zed Books, 1988.

Shiva, Vandana. *Monocultures Of The Mind: Perspectives On Biodiversity And Biotechnology*. New York: Zed Books, 1993.

Sievers, Sharon. L. *Flowers In Salt: The Beginning Of Feminist Consciousness In Modern Japan*. Stanford, CA: Stanford University Press, 1983.

Silko, Leslie Marmon. *Ceremony*. New York: Penguin Books, 1977.

Soelle, Dorothy. *The Window Of Vulnerability: A Political Spirituality*. Minneapolis: Fortress Press, 1990.

Spender, Dale. *Women Of Ideas, And What Men Have Done To Them: From Aphra Behn To Adrienne Rich*. London: Routledge, 1983.

Stalker, Joyce. Women and adult education: Rethinking androcentric research. *Adult Education Quarterly: A Journal of Research and Theory in Adult Education*, 46(2), 1996.

Swerdlow, Amy. *Women Strike For Peace: Traditional Motherhood And Radical Politics In The 1960s*. Chicago: The University of Chicago Press, 1993.

Taylor, Edward W. Building upon the theoretical debate: A critical review of the empirical studies of Mezirow's transformative learning theory. *Adult Education Quarterly: A Journal of Research and Theory in Adult Education*, 48(1), 1997.

Vella, Jane. A spirited epistemology: Honoring the adult learner as subject. *New Directions for Adult and Continuing Education*, 85, Spring 2000.

Waddington, Miriam. "Old age blues." *Collected Poems*. Toronto: Oxford University Press, 1986.

Walker, Alice. *Revolutionary Petunias And Other Poems*. New York: Harcourt Brace Javanovitch, 1973.

We will grow back. *Connexions: An International Women's Quarterly*, 6, 1982.

Welch, Sharon. D. Dreams of the good: From the analytics of oppression to the politics of transformation. In David Batstone, ed. *New Visions For The Americas Religious Engagement And Social Transformation*. Philadelphia: Fortress Press, 1993.

Welch, Sharon D. *Sweet Dreams In America: Making Ethics And Spirituality Work*. New York: Routledge, 1999.

Welch, Sharon. *A Feminist Ethic Of Risk* (rev. ed.). Minneapolis: Fortress Press, 2000.

Wilkinson, Shelagh. Old woman, 'Bearer of keys to unknown doorways.' *Canadian Woman Studies*, 12(2), 1992.

Williams, Marjorie Johnson, and Colleen Nadjiwon Johnson. Minobimaatisiiwin—We are to care for her. In Miriam Wyman, ed. *Sweeping The Earth: Women Taking Action For A Healthy Planet*. Charlottetown, PEI: Gynergy Books, 1999.

Wolf, Margery. *A Thrice Told Tale: Feminism, Postmodernism, And Ethnographic Responsibility*. Stanford, California: Stanford University Press, 1992.

Wyman, Miriam, ed. Introduction. *Sweeping The Earth: Women Taking Action For A Healthy Planet*. Charlottetown, PEI: Gynergy Books, 1999.

Zygmunt, Joseph F. Movements and motives: Some unresolved issues in the psychology of social movements. In R. Serge Denisoff, ed. *The Sociology of Dissent*. New York: Harcourt Brace Jovanovich, 1974.

# INDEX

## The Grannies

## The Songs

## List of Illustrations

*in recognition of those Grannies who have departed this earth*
*—including Joyce Lydiard, Lanie Melamed and Millie Ryerson—*
*one final song*

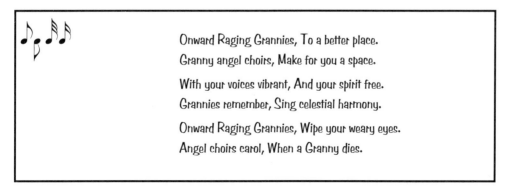

Onward Raging Grannies, To a better place.
Granny angel choirs, Make for you a space.

With your voices vibrant, And your spirit free.
Grannies remember, Sing celestial harmony.

Onward Raging Grannies, Wipe your weary eyes.
Angel choirs carol, When a Granny dies.

*Lorna Drew, Fredricton Raging Grannies. Sung at the Un-convention in Kingston in 2002.*

GRATEFUL ACKNOWLEDGMENT IS MADE FOR PERMISSION TO USE THE FOLLOWING COPYRIGHTED WORKS:

"Grandmother," from *LIFE IS A FATAL DISEASE* by Paula Gunn Allen (Albuquerque and San Francisco: West End Press, p. 69), copyright © 1997 by Paula Gunn Allen. By permission from Paula Gunn Allen.

"Ceremony," from *CEREMONY* by Leslie Marmon Silko, copyright © 1977 by Leslie Silko. Used by permission of Viking Penguin, a division of Penguin group (USA) Inc.

"Old Age Blues," from *COLLECTED POEMS* by Miriam Waddington (Toronto: Oxford University Press, p. 326), copyright © 1986. By permission of Oxford University Press Canada.

Figure 9. Photograph of Doran Doyle, © John Colville. Published in *The Province* March 10, 1989. By permission of John Colville.

Figure 22. Photograph Rose DeShaw, © Michael Lea of the *Kingston Whig-Standard*. Published on July 31, 2001. By permission of Michael Lea and the *Kingston Whig-Standard*.

Figure 26. Photograph Grannies Go Quietly, © *Times-Colonist*, published May 31, 2002, p. C1. By permission of *Times-Colonist* (Andrew Phillips).

Figure 29. Cartoon Singing badly for peace, © Trevor Bryden. By permission of Trevor Bryden.

Figure 36. Photograph Grey Activism by Shaughn Butts, © *The Edmonton Journal*. Published August 31, 2001. By permission of *The Edmonton Journal* (Roy Wood).

Figure 41. Photograph Raging Grannies support gays © CP/Fredericton Gleaner (Photographer Bob Wilson). By permission of Canadian Press.

Figure 45. Cartoon Esquimalt welcomes its new C.O., © Trevor Bryden. Published in the *Esquimalt News*, July 19, 1989. By permission of Trevor Bryden.

Figure 46. Cartoon Raging Grannies Tea Fest, © Trevor Bryden. Published in the *Esquimalt News*, November 20, 1990. By permission of Trevor Bryden

Figure 52. Photograph Grey power platoon ready and willing, © *Times-Colonist*, published November 3, 1990. By permission of *Times-Colonist* (Andrew Phillips).

Figure 53. Cartoon Got an environmental impact, © Trevor Bryden. Published in the *Esquimalt News,* January 30, 1991. By permission of Trevor Bryden

Figure 54. Cartoon In a surprisingly intelligent move, © Trevor Bryden. Published in the *Saanich News,* August 29, 1990. By permission of Trevor Bryden

Figure 56. Cartoon Raging Grannies take on porn, © Trevor Bryden. Published in the *Esquimalt News,* January 3, 1990. By permission of Trevor Bryden

Figure 62. Photograph Woman/riot police, © CP/ Tom Hanson. By permission of Canadian Press.

Figure 65. Cartoon Graphic of Raging Granny, © Antony Gamboli Harpes. Published in *The Gazette,* May 5, 1991. By permission of Antony Harpes.

Figure 74. Cartoon "I tell you Blanche," © Graham Harrop. Published in the *Vancouver Sun* October 9, 1998. By permission of Graham Harrop.

Figure 84. Photograph Rage against the machine, © Desmond Murray. Published in *Showcase Capital News,* November 2-8, 2000. By permission of Desmond Murray.

Figure 85. Photograph A passion for protest, © *Southender Magazine*. Published in the *Southender Magazine* in March 2001. Photo courtesy of *Southender Magazine*. Reprinted with permission.

Figure 86. Photograph Greenpeace protesters don colourful costumes, © *Times-Colonist*, published September 16, 1990. By permission of *Times-Colonist* (Andrew Phillips).

Figure 87. Montreal Raging Grannies. By permission of photographer Joshua Radu.

## REBEL MUSICS: Human Rights, Resistant Sounds, and the Politics of Music Making
*Daniel Fischlin, Ajay Heble, editors*

Original in concept and content, Rebel Musics examines how musical activism resonates in practical, political terms, how musical resistance brings together voices that might otherwise remain silent, and how political action through music increases the potential for people to determine their own fate.

> Casts a wide net with respect to musicians, span of years and nationalities.
> —*Small Press Review*

> Diverse and challenging, celebratory but refreshingly realistic...strongly recommended.
> —Chris Gibson, University of New South Wales

> A rich collection that inspires, delights, and educates.
> —Howard Zinn, *A People's History of the United States*

Apart from the editors, contributors include: cabaret artist, author and musician Norman Nawrocki; film makers Marie Boti and Malcolm Guy; musician Jesse Stewart; poet George Elliott Clarke; author Timothy Brennan; author Martha Nandorfy; radio host Ray Pratt; and editor, author, and music reviewer Ron Sakolsky.

DANIEL FISCHLIN is Professor of English at the University of Guelph. AJAY HEBLE is Professor of English at the University of Guelph and Artistic Director and Founder of The Guelph Jazz Festival.

> 264 pages, 6x9, photographs, bibliography, index
> Paperback ISBN: 1-55164-230-1      $24.99
> Hardcover ISBN: 1-55164-231-X      $53.99

## FATEFUL TRIANGLE: The United States, Israel and the Palestinians
*Noam Chomsky, Foreword by Edward Said*

Since its original publication in 1983, Chomsky's seminal tome on Mid-East politics has become a classic in the fields of political science and Mid-East affairs. For its tenth printing, Chomsky has written a new introduction, and added a foreword by Edward Said. This new, updated edition highlights the book's lasting relevance, and should be a treasure for fans of the first edition, and an eye-opener for those new to the work. It is invaluable to anyone seeking to understand the Middle East.

> Disturbing, provocative...expect controversy. —*Montreal Gazette*

> Raises difficult, painful questions for Israel. —*Globe and Mail*

> Chomsky's unrelenting tone paints a frightening picture. —*Maclean's*

> A devastating collection. —*Library Journal*

> A monumental work. —*Choice*

> Powerful and thoroughly documented. —*The Progressive*

> A must read for anyone following today's Middle East. —*The Financial Post*

NOAM CHOMSKY is a world-renowned linguist, scholar, and political analyst. He has written and lectured extensively on linguistics, philosophy, U.S. foreign policy, and other contemporary political issues.

> 485 pages, updated edition, 6x9, index
> Paperback ISBN: 1-55164-160-7      $28.99
> Hardcover ISBN: 1-55164-161-5      $57.99